CONFESSIONS OF A TV SEX JOURNALIST

D1462444

ROSS DALE

SOURCEBOOKS, INC.®
NAPERVILLE, ILLINOIS

This book is a memoir. It reflects the author's present recollections of his experiences over a period of years. Some names and characteristics have been changed. Some characters have been combined, events have been compressed, and certain episodes are re-created and not meant to portray actual events.

Published by Sourcebooks, Inc.
P.O. Box 4410, Naperville, Illinois 60567-4410
(630) 961-3900
Fax: (630) 961-2168
www.sourcebooks.com

Library of Congress Cataloging-in-Publication Data

Dale, Ross.
Embedded : confessions of a TV sex journalist / Ross Dale.
p. cm.
ISBN-13: 978-1-4022-1217-8 (pbk.)
ISBN-10: 1-4022-1217-8 (pbk.)
I. Title.

PS3604.A354E43 2008
813'.6—dc22
2007044256

Printed and bound in Canada.
TR 10 9 8 7 6 5 4 3 2 1

for my mother

Vice, Virtue. It's best not to be too moral. You cheat yourself out of too much life. Aim above morality. If you apply that to life, then you're bound to live life fully.

—Maude, *Harold & Maude*

CONTENTS

I

From Groton to the Grotto

*H*ave you seen the show?" That was the first question I was asked. Bruce Morgan, the Executive Producer of Playboy TV's *Sexcetera*, was doing the asking. He looked like an even shorter version of Michael Douglas—*Romancing the Stone* era—with wild, shaggy blond hair. Add his bare feet and a Hawaiian shirt and there he was—an eccentric Hollywood producer.

"No, I, uh… I don't get Playboy TV. But I've heard great things."

"Oh yeah? Who have you talked to?" Before coming in I'd found Bruce's credits on IMDb.com, so I knew that besides working for the Bunny he'd also won a Filmmakers Prize at Sundance in the early eighties for a documentary he'd directed on Howard Hawks. A respectable credit—not tickertape parade, fill the bathtub full of champagne respectable, but respectable nonetheless.

"A guy that used to work for you. Terry. He's at E! now, in another department, but I talked to him and he said only good things."

"Terry couldn't hack it. Couldn't handle the material. Poor guy didn't last a month." Bruce's office was scattered with various relics from his career, including a poster from the Howard Hawks project. There were also several framed photographs of younger, happier Bruces paired with big-name celebrities. Mike Wallace and

Walter Cronkite immediately caught my eye. And then Paul Newman. And Lauren Bacall. "So why should I believe *you'll* be able to handle it?"

"Well, I *think* I can handle it, you know... I mean, I don't see why not." Surely that coulda come out better.

"Look, buddy, your reel was good and your writing test was a home run. But I gotta know how you'll be in the field. What are you gonna do when you're standing over a three hundred pound woman, and she's buck naked and fucking herself like crazy with a big black rubber dildo, and you got to jump in and interview her? Will you be able to do it?" I bet he never spoke like that around Cronkite.

"I'd do whatever needed to be done." *Christ.* I practically tacked on a "sir" and a salute at the end. I hate the way job interviews and first dates make you trip yourself into being something you're not.

"Yeah, well, you haven't even seen the show yet. So listen, buddy, here's what I want you to do. Take a few tapes home with you. Watch 'em. Think it over. And we'll talk in a couple days."

So I left with three episodes of *Sexcetera* and I did my homework. I took a strip club tour of Atlanta, I attended San Francisco's Exotic Erotic Ball, I learned way more than I wanted to know about foot fetishists, I explored jealousy issues with several overweight members of a polyamorous sex commune, I met a vertically challenged porn star named Bridget the Midget, and I listened to a transsexual known as Vanity explain the difficulties he/she had maintaining a relationship given his/her surprising appendage. And all that was just one show.

Structurally, *Sexcetera* was basically *60 Minutes* but with a lot more blowjobs. Each one-hour episode was made up of six stand-alone segments featuring six different reporters covering the world of erotica in an extremely explicit manner. Evidently, on Playboy TV you could say or show just about anything. The result was a raw, pornographic barrage of images that were a tad harsh to the unaccustomed eye.

And my eye, without a doubt, was a long way from accustomed. Nobody ever believes me when I tell them this, but I swear it's true—before I started working for Playboy TV I'd never watched more than a few frames of porn in my entire life.

Growing up in the suburbs of Rochester, New York, I was an over-protected, over-sheltered, only child bouncing around in a bit of a bubble. There was never a single shred of porn to be found in our upper middle class home. And while I did have a few friends who were kind enough to show me the occasional girlie magazine in the privacy of *their* homes, I certainly never had access to hardcore films.

We never had them at Groton either. I went to one of those "elite" New England boarding schools and preppie paradise that it was, we weren't even allowed to have our own TV. And not only because watching the idiot box was decidedly un-prep, but because it was against the rules to have *any* appliances in our dorm rooms—no fridges, no toasters, no coffeemakers, no nothing. I guess it was a holdover from the muscular Christianity and cold shower days of the school's founder, Endicott Peabody— and, for sure, all us fancy lads needed some toughening up. Although I should say we weren't completely deprived. Every dormitory did have a television in the common area, but no one was gonna risk watching porn in public.

In fact, I don't even remember there being a lot of magazines around. The thing you have to realize about Groton is everyone had a roommate and no one had a lock on their door. We all lived so closely together, with so little privacy, that if you were gonna jerk off to a girlie mag you better be damn sure your roommate was in history class, and even then there was still a possibility someone else in your dorm might stumble in looking for some change for the soda machine. And getting caught woulda been a colossal bummer. I remember one poor bastard was known as "Emotion Lotion" for three full years. Not an easy thing to hear shouted across the dining room at a coed school. Much safer to use your imagination and masturbate in the shower.

By the time I got to Wesleyan University I had a single room and a lock on my door, and even a television. But I just wasn't interested in renting adult movies. In fact, I rarely rented any movies. There just wasn't time for it. There was too much drinking to do with too many attractive young girls. As far as I was concerned, watching porn in college was like bringing postcards of the *Mona Lisa* to the Louvre. And, besides, Wesleyan was Politically Correct University—literally. The guys that wrote the movie *PCU* were alums and the opening montage was shot on our campus. No joke, it took me almost fours years after graduating to get the balls to refer to girls as *girls* and not *womyn*. So naturally porn was *not* PC and *not* prevalent.

Also, my interview with Bruce was back in the summer of 2000. Porn wasn't on the public consciousness the way it is today. Jenna Jameson wasn't quite yet a household name, and the Internet was still more or less in its infancy. Me, I'd only had my dial-up connection for about a year and I was not what you'd call a savvy user. In fact, I'd only "misused" my computer on one occasion— the day I bought it I'd gone trolling for naked pictures of Stephanie Seymour, the greatest supermodel of all time. But that's as far as I went.

Not that I didn't believe in masturbation. Of course I did. I probably jerked off two or three, maybe four times a week. But to me a gentleman's inspiration was the latest Victoria's Secret catalog or the *Sports Illustrated* Swimsuit Issue, or, if I ever got up the nerve to actually buy one, a copy of *Playboy*. So yes, it's true, I was a twenty-seven year old porn virgin, and *Sexcetera* was about the last place you'd expect to find a politically correct, preppie fuck, mamma's boy like me.

And yet, despite being such an unlikely candidate, when an ex-girlfriend who happened to be freelancing at Playboy TV told me they were looking for another producer I decided to take the interview. Why not? After three years at E! Entertainment Television I was ready for a change. I wanted more money and more excitement. And like any other red-blooded American male with half a heartbeat I had visions of dry martinis, smoking jackets, pajama parties, and lots of glossy, airbrushed Bunnies spread out on pool tables and haystacks.

Seeing the show, however, had been a rude awakening. Because the world of *Sexcetera* turned out to be a helluva lot grittier than the world of Hef. So when Bruce called to see if I wanted the job I was gonna tell him, "Thanks, but no thanks." But then he mentioned the starting salary, which was considerably more than I was making at E!, and suddenly I heard myself saying, "Thanks, thanks a lot!"

After hanging up I couldn't believe what I'd just done. *What was I thinking?* Sure, more money was always good, but was that the real reason I took the job? Maybe. But maybe I wasn't quite as disgusted as I thought I was. Maybe I was a little curious. Even seduced. Well, whatever the reason, it didn't really matter because it wasn't forever. It was just a job. Another line on my résumé. And it *was* more money.

When I got up the nerve to tell my schoolteacher mother about my new job, she couldn't stop laughing. For some reason, she found it amusing that a product of Groton, Wesleyan, and L.L. Bean would now be hobnobbing with porn stars.

"Look Ma, the way I see it, staying at E! and doing red carpet interviews with people like Leonardo DiCaprio is just as obscene—and probably less useful to society. Remember what I told you about entertainment news? It's neither entertainment, nor news."

"Do you get to go to the mansion?"

"I don't know, Ma. Maybe."

"From Groton to the Grotto, eh?" And she was proud of her quip.

"Yeah, yeah." While the humor was not lost on me, I was glad neither of us pointed out that I had over a hundred thousand dollars worth of education behind me and not a whole helluva lot to show for it. Like Bob Dylan's Miss Lonely, I'd gone to all the finest schools but, you know, I only used to get juiced in them. And how did it feel? Well, writing for cable TV about the rise and fall of forgotten celebrities was a living, but it wasn't exactly the fast track. Meanwhile, most of my prep school friends were accelerating into the passing lanes of Wall Street and various prestigious law firms. They'd remained on the East Coast, secure within the warm shelter of the "Old Boy's Club." But not me, *noooooo*, I had to take the slow wagon train west as if making six figures in New York City was somehow a bad idea. I wound up in Hollywood—missing the seasons but loving the sun—and now I was about to abandon the borderline respectability of the basic cable package for the seedy luster of a premium adult channel. Definitely *not* the fast track.

And, as hard as I tried, I just couldn't imagine myself interviewing Bruce's buck naked three hundred pound woman. Of course, with any new job there is a degree of uneasiness. But this was something different. This was fear.

II

So, Are These Smoky
Blowjobs Dangerous?

*M*y first assignment was on a sexual predilection known
as the "smoking fetish," which even I could guess had
something to do with getting turned on by watching a woman
smoke a cigarette. Per my new boss's instructions, I was to build
my story around an ex-stripper turned web-girl named Taimie.

"What's a web-girl?"

"Well, buddy, web-girls are, ah… they're like Internet models."
Bruce explained they were girls with their own websites where
they got naked for their fans in exchange for a monthly membership fee. "They're not porn stars, they're not Playmates, they're
kinda their own special breed. Kira Reed, one of our reporters,
she's a web-girl. There're millions of 'em out there. It's one of the
great benefits of the World Wide Web." Bruce smiled and went on
to describe how, since the Internet boom of the late nineties, a lot
of strippers were turning to the web as an alternative to working
the sleazy clubs. With a pay site, these girls could make a living
from the safety of their home instead of in the lap of a stranger.

"So what's this smoking fetish thing all about?"

"Look buddy, I'm busy. Research is part of your job, so go
research. Get on Taimie's site and read up on it—go, go, go."

I went. Back down the hall to sit in my new office in front of my new computer. After typing in the username & password Bruce had given me, I was immediately met with a striking image—a totally nude Taimie reclining suggestively beneath the phrase *Thanks for Cumming*. She was obscenely beautiful. Huge breasts, long legs, tight stomach, manicured pussy, and easily the most devious smile I'd ever seen. And then I logged off. I had to. It just didn't feel right looking at porn in the workplace. I knew I was being ridiculous—after all, now porn *was* the workplace. Nevertheless, I waited until I got home to continue.

On Thursday, Bruce, Taimie, and I had a morning meeting at the office to discuss the shoot. When I walked into the conference room Taimie was already sitting in an overstuffed chair. She wore a super-tight, grey sweat-suit with a zippered top and a black racing stripe down the side, along with a pair of open toe, high heel shoes. But I didn't see her like this. Instead, as I stood before her, all I could see was the Taimie I now knew from so many naked photos on her site—the steamy seductress sprawled out & spread open, fingering her pussy, and, of course, smoking a cigarette.

I figured I should probably say something. "Uh, hi. I'm Ross."

"Ross is our new ace producer." Bruce was generous. "We stole him away from E! and we're lucky to have him." Extremely generous.

"Nice to meet you," she said.

As I leaned over to shake Taimie's hand, I tried not to focus on her breasts, which apparently were about to rip open her zipper and burst into the room. Although it hadn't crossed my mind while I was masturbating to her site, I found myself wondering if those breasts could possibly be real. Though not for long. By the time I had found a seat I decided that they were most definitely store-bought. But staring wasn't polite, so somehow I made eye contact. She wore heavy yet effective makeup, which served up saucer brown eyes below jet-black hair. I'd never met anyone like her—except maybe once at a bachelor party—and it seemed to me that her very existence was a slap in the face to the Talbot's feminism I'd been weaned on.

After some more small talk, we discussed the plan for the shoot, which was fairly simple. We would get a suite at the Argyle Hotel and Taimie would perform a private smoking fetish demonstration. As she described some of the things she had in mind I smiled dumbly, not registering a single word. Until I heard her say, "And then we'll do some smoky blowjobs." *Smoky what?* I had to be blushing.

"It's better for us if they're simulated," Bruce cautioned.

"Simulated?" I asked.

"I'll explain later, buddy." How was I ever gonna be able to direct this lusty, busty bombshell without Bruce there to translate? *Was it too late to get my old job back?*

Two days later I was once again sitting across from Taimie and her professionally sculpted breasts, only this time I was shooting her interview. My cameraman, an affable longhair named Ted, rolled tape over my shoulder as I began. "So Taimie, how would you explain the smoking fetish to someone who's never heard of it?"

The host of the segment, Ralph Garman, was watching quietly from a nearby couch. Sitting next to him was Taimie's red-headed "assistant" and fellow web-girl, Tiffany, who was on hand to help with the smoking demo. Having them as an audience was a little distracting, but it was nothing compared to watching Taimie fall out of her lingerie. If I looked at just the right angle and she turned slightly to the left, I could almost make out her left nipple.

"Well, it's all about smoking cigarettes and being sexy. The guys really get into the details, so, you know, the presentation really counts—lipstick, nail polish, it's all got to be just so. And then of course there's all the different tricks, like blowing smoke rings and the French inhale."

"What do your fans think of the, uh... of the, uh..." I wasn't gonna be able to look her in the eye and say it, so I glanced down at my list of questions instead. "Of the smoky blowjobs?"

"Oh, the smoky blowjobs are their favorite. I'm always getting emails from my fans saying, 'We want more smoky blowjobs, give us more smoky blowjobs.'"

"So, are these smoky blowjobs dangerous? I mean, I'm guessing you have to be careful with the cigarette, right?"

"Oh yeah. For all you girls out there, when you're giving your man a smoky blowjob, be sure to hold his cock in one hand and your cigarette in the other." And she held up her hands, miming the grips. "Never, ever, ever let your cigarette touch the guy's cock."

After that very important public safety message I moved the interview along, and soon we'd said everything that could possibly be said about the smoking fetish. Then Taimie and Tiffany needed a few minutes to get ready, so Ted, Ralph, and I went downstairs to shoot the intro on Sunset Boulevard.

By the time we made it back to the suite Taimie and Tiffany were still behind the closed door of the bedroom. So we waited. And waited. And nothing. Not a peep. *Were they still in there?*

"You wanna see if they're ready?" Ralph was looking at his watch.

"Sure." I got up and walked to the door. Deep breath. And a knock. Then it was open and Taimie was standing just as naked and just as stunning as she was on her website. I felt my heart suddenly shift gears and start pumping at a considerably faster rate. I tried to speak but my lips wouldn't move.

"You ready for us, honey?"

"Ye-yeah," I was barely able to manage. I could hear Tiffany giggling inside.

"Okay sweetie, we'll be out in a sec."

Somehow I made it back to my chair. And moments later, with my heart still racing, I heard the door open and from around the corner came Taimie and Tiffany. Both completely nude, both completely gorgeous as they padded softly across the carpet to the couch. In the past redheads hadn't done that much for me, but Tiffany was forcing me to reconsider. She was smaller than her brunette counterpart and carried herself with a little more spunk. And those rosy nipples and perky breasts were sexy as hell.

Once Ted was rolling, they began by seductively lighting each other's cigarettes. Then, in between gentle caresses, they started to slowly, sensuously exhale over one another's breasts. I was so close—at most, maybe five feet away—but I just couldn't look directly at them. However, as my eyes darted everywhere else desperately trying to avoid their sultry smoke laced tits, I realized that there was no way I could go the entire shoot without watching them. It was my job to know what my cameraman was shooting. I had to watch. So I did.

And after a few minutes I began to relax. Sort of. At least enough to admire the ease with which they touched each other. Both of them appeared completely comfortable and natural in what, to me, was an exceedingly *un*natural situation. At one point, when Tiffany went down to blow smoke over Taimie's pussy, she stopped and came back up to whisper something into her ear. Taimie laughed and removed a lingering piece of toilet paper from between her legs. Then I laughed too. And I realized that this wasn't so bad. There were certainly a lotta worse things I coulda been doing on a Saturday afternoon.

Once we were finished with the girl-girl part of the shoot, Tiffany went home. Up next was all the solo stuff Taimie had prepared. She brought me and Ralph into the bedroom where she had a suitcase overflowing with all kinds of lingerie. "Should I put on the leopard print corset or go for the purple garter?"

How could I possibly decide? "Let's shoot both. First the corset, then the garter."

"Look at you. *Both*," Taimie teased.

"Good idea, Ross." Ralph gave me an amused slap on the back.

So Taimie stepped in and out of various outfits, my favorite being a hot pink wig with a matching pair of sparkly, hot pink, thigh-high boots. To maximize the different looks within the suite we shot that set-up in the bathroom. She gamely got up on the toilet seat, somehow balancing in her high-heeled boots while looking incredibly sexy smoking what must have been her eightieth cigarette of the evening. But by far the most dynamic shot of all was when Taimie attached seven bright red balloons to her naked body and used a cigarette—her eighty-fifth?—to pop them one at a time.

For the final stage we needed a guy to help out with the smoky blowjobs. To play the role of "Man Getting Head" Taimie had cast a good friend of hers named Doug. He was a veteran of numerous softcore movies and had already performed in several scenes with Taimie, including some smoky BJs on her website. So Doug was the perfect man for the job. He also happened to be married to one of the other *Sexcetera* reporters, the web-girl Kira Reed. Evidently 'round here it was all one big happy family.

When Doug showed up, he was considerably older than I expected—at least late thirties, probably early forties. But immediately I was impressed with his calm, no-nonsense attitude. "You guys ready for me? Should I get naked?" I admit, it was strange hearing that from a man.

"Uh, sure, go ahead." Doug stripped down, and I saw that despite his age he was in incredible shape. After he stretched out on the bed, Taimie put an ashtray on his six-pack stomach and they went to work, giving us several minutes of simulated smoky blowjobs.

Bruce had cautioned that these BJs had to be simulated because one of the few things *Sexcetera* was not allowed to show was actual insertion—meaning a penis entering a mouth, a vagina, or an anus. "Listen buddy, whatever you do don't shoot any penetration. Playboy can't air it, so I can't use it." Because of this rare restriction, I was told all blowjobs on *Sexcetera* either had to be simulated or the cameraman had to "shoot around it." To simulate a BJ, I was supposed to direct the girl to bob her head up and down as if she was really blowing the guy, although in reality she'd be a few inches away. A commonly used technique was for the girl to toss her hair to the side to hide the fact that the guy was not actually inside her mouth. Lucky for me, Taimie and Doug were pros and didn't need to be told a damn thing.

Around 11:00 p.m., when we were finally wrapping up, I heard a knock at the door. Opening it, I saw a beautiful and familiar looking woman in a snug black dress. She was holding a large brown paper bag.

"Hi, I'm Kira." This was Doug's wife. "You must be Ross."

"Oh, yeah. Hi. I've seen you on the show."

"Yep, that was me." And as she walked past me in search of the nearest flat surface, her brown bag clinked—a sound I knew well.

Despite having seen her on TV, I was still surprised by how young she looked. Still in her twenties, she musta been at least ten years younger than her husband. "You're shorter than I expected," I blurted.

"Did Bruce tell you to say that?" She was irritated.

"No." And I wished I'd said something different, something complimentary, something like, *You do a great job on the show.*

"Everyone always says that. I guess I *am* on the short side." She pulled a bottle of Jack Daniels from the bag and put it on the table.

"Well, you do a great a job on the show." Better late than never.

"Oh really, you think so? Thanks." And then a stack of plastic cups and a bottle of Absolut joined the bourbon. "Is there ice?"

"No, but I'll get you some." I grabbed the bucket and went looking for the ice-machine. Bruce was letting Kira & Doug keep the room for the night—incidentals not included—so they could throw a small soiree. After I got back, there were more knocks and the living room filled up fast. Then, as I watched Ted pack the gear, it hit me—I'd successfully survived my first Playboy shoot! Hard to believe just last weekend I'd been in New York interviewing Allen Dershowitz about insulin injections for *The E! True Hollywood Story* on Claus von Bulow. But before I could smile at this, Kira was standing in front of me.

"What are you drinking?"

"Bourbon."

"How do you like it?"

"On the rocks."

Then she beelined for the makeshift bar. The following weekend Kira was gonna be hosting my next story in Orlando, so I assumed she was making a point to bond with me. It was the smart play. Moments later, she returned with my drink.

"This was your first shoot, right?"

"Uh, yeah. Yeah it was. Cheers." And we touched plastic cups.

"So how'd it go?"

"Alright, I think." The cool bourbon felt damn good.

"Doug said he had fun."

"That's good, I—"

"And he said you seemed to know what you were doing."

"Well, I wouldn't go that far. But that was nice of him to say."

"I'm excited for Florida."

"Yeah, should be fun." I smiled.

"I've never been."

"Really?" *I thought everyone had been to Florida.* "An old high school buddy of mine has a place in Palm Beach. We used go down for Spring Break." Immediately I wished I hadn't mentioned Palm Beach. Too lockjaw, too soon.

"Bruce emailed me the script yesterday. I thought it was really good."

"Oh, you liked it?"

"Yeah, it was funny and you did a good job telling the story."

"Thanks, I wasn't sure if—"

"Bruce tells me I might have to put on a little show."

"Oh?"

"Yeah, he said everyone's gonna be kinda old and flabby, so he wants me to get nakee butts."

"*Nakee* butts? Oh, right, yeah. He said he was hoping you could do something to spice things up. I don't really know what, uh. . . you know, whatever you're comfortable with, of course."

Although Bruce had told me Kira ran her own adult website, somehow she just didn't look the part. Or at least she didn't look like Taimie. With her fake breasts, big hair, and party-girl persona Taimie was a caricature of a stripper. Kira, on the other hand, was something different. Not that she wasn't sexy—she most definitely was. She just wasn't a vamped-out vixen. Instead, she was all natural—at least from where I was standing. She wore a simple black dress and was simply gorgeous. Youthful, energetic, accessible—there was almost a déjà-vu quality to her appearance. "Nakee butts" notwithstanding, she could have been any of the attractive girls I knew at Wesleyan— she just had that vibe. And watching her sip her Jack & Coke I was not wondering if, in fact, she had actually gone to college, or if she was jealous that another women's mouth had just been inches away from her husband's cock, or even if she ever lamented her bold decision to get nakee butts on the World Wide Web. Instead, all I was thinking about was how damn *nice* she was.

After getting my fill of conversation and bourbon I went down-stairs and got my battered black Chevy Blazer from the valet. And then I was heading east on Sunset Boulevard howling along with Bob Dylan's *Basement Tapes*, "Ooh, baby, ooh-ee... Ooh baby, ooh-ee... It's that million dollar bash...," until I was laughing out loud and marveling at how far a short week can take you.

III

Hide Your Wallet

*T*he following week I was on a plane to Florida. My final destination would be Orlando where I was producing a story on a masturbation club called Club Relate. But first I had to go to Pompano Beach. Bruce was giving a try-out to a potential new producer, and even though I'd been with the show for less than two weeks he wanted me to supervise the shoot. Really he just wanted me there to help out because the producer-on-trial was a young woman named Cindy with very little production experience. Ted was once again the cameraman, and the host of the segment was a young guy known as Mad Chad.

The story was on a BDSM club called Club Kink. I didn't know a damn thing about BDSM, and before leaving LA I had to ask Bruce what the acronym stood for. "Bondage, Dominance, Sadism, and Masochism, buddy." *Oh.* I gotta admit I was curious, but I didn't quite have the balls for the follow-up question, *And what might all that mean?* So I figured I'd just have to learn on the job.

Unfortunately I didn't get much of a chance. Because, as it turned out, supervising the new producer meant that I was stuck by the door all night getting our releases signed and photographing IDs. Releases and IDs were easily the most tedious part of the job, but as Bruce impressed upon me during my orientation they were also the most important. "Listen buddy, if you don't come back with all the releases and IDs, you might as well not come back at all." Everyone that appeared on *Sexcetera* had to sign a release. And anyone that appeared nude had to be over 18 and had to be able to prove it with two forms of ID—one with a picture (like a driver's license) and another with just a name (like a bank card or a library card or a Sam's Club card or just about anything short of a note from their mother).

Given Bruce's solemn warning I was worried about the possibility of someone slipping by without signing my paperwork. Luckily, a friend of the owner was kind enough to give me a hand. Her name was Jennifer. Beautiful gal—mid-thirties, but with a miraculously rockin' bod. She wore thigh-high black leather boots with scary long stiletto heels, a black & white pair of leather short-shorts, and the tiniest of black leather tops. I swear if you didn't count the boots you'd find more leather on a regulation Wilson football. Well tanned, wonderful legs, playful eyes—and helpful! At one point, when we were running out of releases, she even ran out to find a copy machine, and returned just in time with a fresh stack.

With Jennifer by my side, what could have been a boring evening suddenly became a lot of fun. She talked nonstop, but in a good way—or at least in a good-enough-for-right-now way. Among other things, I learned that she had two kids and, although she remained married to her husband, they'd been separated for over three years. I asked her what she did when she wasn't hanging out at bondage clubs and she said that she wasn't really into "the scene" and that she didn't go to places like this very often. But if I was asking what she did for a living, which I was, then she was a nurse.

"It's hard work, but the money's alright. I don't really mind being around sick people too much. They're always so appreciative. And the hospitals around here are pretty good, so, you know, it's a living." I bet Jennifer looked great in a nurse's uniform, although what she was wearing at the moment wasn't too bad either.

Right about then we were interrupted by a young woman wearing a skimpy leather excuse for an outfit that completely exposed her perfect champagne glass breasts. She put her arm around me and asked, "Are you the producer from Playboy?"

"Uh, yes."

"Can I show you my modeling portfolio?"

Wasn't I already looking at it? "Uh, sure, I guess you could send it to me."

"Actually, I brought it with me." She turned around and a man dressed in leather, presumably her husband or boyfriend, handed her a big black folder. "Let's find some light so you can really look at it."

I led her into a small side room where we'd stashed some of our gear. She closed the door behind us, then sidled up with those wonderfully perky breasts and helped me flip through page after page of gorgeous naked pictures. "Oh that's nice... Very nice... Excellent use of gauze... Wow, you must do yoga..."

"So," now she was touching my arm, "do you think you can put in a good word for me at the magazine?"

Suddenly I had the sneaking suspicion she was offering to do me a "favor" in exchange for a recommendation. And I couldn't believe it. "Ross from Playboy" actually meant something—at least in some circles. But I didn't have the balls—or the time—to find out for sure. Instead, all I said was, "I'll do whatever I can." Which, unfortunately, was nothing. Playboy TV didn't have a damn thing to do with the magazine.

By the end of the evening it looked like I'd pretty much reproduced the entire Pompano Beach phone book. And as the producer-on-trial wrapped things up inside, I was outside "supervising" Jennifer as we carried the fresh paperwork toward my rental car. "Have you seen the new Taurus?"

"No, I haven't."

"Oh, but you must... The bucket seats will change your life." That got us into the car for a few private minutes. Just enough time for a kiss. And it was a good kiss so we had another. Then I got a bit bold. "You should come up to Orlando so we can hang out after my next shoot." I knew it was a long shot. Who was gonna drive three hours to spend the night with someone they just met?

"Okay," she said. *What?* As she wrote down her number I tried to get over my shock. She hadn't even asked me to help her get into the magazine! What *was* it about this job?

The next morning Cindy and Mad Chad flew back to LA while Ted and I drove the Taurus up to Orlando. Around two hundred miles later we arrived at the Sheraton and went straight to the pool. We toasted rum drinks and reclined in the Florida sun until it was time to meet Kira at the airport. She was coming in from Montreal, where she'd just hosted a story about a group of amateur Canadian web-girls.

As I entered the baggage claim I realized I was kinda excited to see her—partly because I'd enjoyed chatting with her the previous weekend and partly because poor Ted had become quite verbose and was beginning to annoy me. And, I suppose, partly because I'd been drinking by the pool all afternoon.

Before leaving for Florida I'd asked around the office and learned that besides being a successful web-mistress, Kira Reed was a fairly big name in the adult world. Although she'd never made a hardcore porn film, she had starred in several softcore features—the kind without erections that aired late at night on Cinemax. Later, I'd IMDb'd her and found out "several" films was actually closer to fifty. While I was learning to expect the unexpected, I would never have guessed that this down-home girl-next-door was a major player on the Skin-a-max circuit.

When I spotted her waiting for her bag, once again she seemed familiar—and not because I recognized her from her film work. I just felt like I'd known her before. She was so natural—*sans* makeup, freckly and smiling, in her jeans and t-shirt with her hair pulled back in a ponytail. *Are you sure you're a late night cable queen?* is not what I asked her. Instead I opted for a friendly hug hello.

When we got back to the Sheraton, the three of us headed out on foot to find a place to eat. Kira wanted to go to Hooters, particularly when I said I'd never been, so that's where we went. It was exactly how I imagined it would be—a perfect advertisement of everything that was right and wrong with America.

Sitting across from Kira, sipping a Sam Adams, I found myself swelling with a hundred and one questions, most of which involved various facets of softcore movie making. However, I felt it might be a tad tacky to begin a conversation with, *Tell me, how does it feel to have a man you just met suck on your bare nipple while an entire film crew looks on?* So I kept it simple. "How'd you and Doug meet?"

"On a movie set."

"Oh yeah?"

"Yeah, it was on *Secret Places* back in '96. I was Holly, the stoner-nudist-receptionist, and Doug was the lead. He played my boss, the head of the advertising agency." She went on to give the short version of their off-camera love story. She was a struggling actor and so was he. They fell in love all at once and were married five months later.

"Five months?" I'd always thought five years sounded like the right amount of time. "Five months seems too short."

"Well, for us it wasn't."

"How did you know?"

"I just knew. You know how they say you just know? It's true, I just knew. He's the perfect man... And besides, he was from Canada so he needed to get his citizenship." Then she gave a short laugh and sipped her Jack & Coke.

I couldn't help thinking that her flip little joke was rooted in truth. It's funny how books and movies try to convince us that Romance is forever at odds with Circumstance. But, truth is, in the real world circumstances can push people together just as easily as they can keep them apart. Kids, houses, wealthy fathers-in-law, and, yes, citizenship, can all make us smile and say "I love you" with just as much zeal as the sound of a midnight pebble against a window.

Meanwhile, Ted happened to be a little boozed and a lot stoned, and although he seemed to be following the conversation in between nachos he never added anything more than a reaction shot.

"So I gotta ask," I began, after taking a healthy pull from a fresh Sam Adams, "last weekend, it didn't bother you that Doug was naked in bed with Taimie?"

"Nope."

"How does that work?"

"We have an understanding," she said, as if that somehow explained everything.

"Oh, well sure, of course," I said, as if I somehow understood everything.

Ted nodded solemnly.

"Besides, we're MarriedCouple.com."

"What?"

"MarriedCouple.com, my website. Well, I have two sites. The other one is Kiradance.com. That's my fan site, but MarriedCouple is my site with Doug. *'Who knew marriage could be good for your sex life?'* That's our tagline. We're sex positive, pro safe sex, pro experimentation. As long as it's safe, sane, and consensual—and you always use a condom—it's all good."

"In France you could run for president on that platform," I joked, albeit feebly.

"And we're ordained ministers so we can marry people."

"Really?"

"Yep. Anybody can do it. You just pay $60 and you fill out a form. Last spring we married two of our friends."

"That's so cool," Ted marveled.

"Wow." This was the stupidest thing I'd ever heard.

"And it's the only place where my fans can see me have hard-core sex."

Ted's hooded eyes widened.

"During the ceremonies?" I joked again.

"No, silly," she laughed. "On the site." Kira explained that she had built MarriedCouple with the idea that her softcore fans would want to pay $20 a month to watch her have hardcore sex with her real-life husband. Technically, it was fairly simple. Just put a camera on a tripod, point the lens at the bed, have sex, rinse and repeat. But I had to wonder how easy it was emotionally. Not to mention what it must do to a marriage.

"I built the site back when I was still dancing."

"You were a dancer?" Kira was a woman of many talents.

"Yeah, at the Wild Goose near LAX." Oh, *that* kind of dancer. "But I quit once the site took off."

I suppose leaving the apartment every night to go strip for strangers while your husband stayed home to rub a pair of pennies together had to be tough on a relationship, as well. But thanks to

MarriedCouple.com those days were long gone. Once those twenty dollar bills started to add up, Kira never had to dance again. So whatever toll fucking on the Internet took, it had to be a welcome reprieve from what had come before. Whether or not marriage was, in fact, good for her sex life, MarriedCouple.com had done wonders for her *overall* life.

And sure, Erotic Webmistress was not the toniest of vocations, but I couldn't blame Kira for using her body to make a living. Of course I didn't ask her that night, but I was willing to bet she didn't grow up dreaming of becoming a stripper. Shit happens, and I suppose for one reason or another dancing around a pole in a G-string must have made sense, just as launching MarriedCouple.com had made sense—under the circumstances. Eventually, Ted, Kira, and I had enough to eat and probably more than enough to drink, and we walked back to the Sheraton.

A little before ten the next morning I went down to the lobby to meet the two founders of Club Relate, Lynda Gayle & her husband Tom. While researching this story I had watched the segment HBO's *Real Sex* had already aired on Club Relate, so I knew what the couple looked like. When I didn't see them I found a seat and went over my notes one final time.

Since getting this assignment two weeks ago, I'd spoken with Lynda Gayle on the telephone so often I felt like I knew her. She was a talker, and I guess I was too. According to her, Club Relate was the only heterosexual masturbation club in North America. They called it a masturbation club because there was no actual fucking, but the members weren't just sitting around in a circle jerk. From what I'd seen in the *Real Sex* piece, Club Relate looked more like a swingers party, or even an oral sex clinic, than a masturbation club. But perhaps Lynda Gayle summed it up best when she said it was "just a place where like-minded folks can cum together."

Unlike Club Kink, Club Relate wasn't actually a physical club at all. Instead, it was an organization that met around three times a month at parties held in various hotel rooms throughout Florida. Usually somewhere between fifteen and twenty-five folks attended each party, and they hoped for a ratio of two guys for every girl. As Lynda Gayle explained, she'd started Club Relate as a woman's club—she was no dummy—and because she knew women usually lasted longer she wanted twice as many men around so the girls never had to wait for a guy to reload.

I happened to look up from my notes just as Lynda Gayle & Tom walked into the lobby. She had to be in her forties, a heavyset woman with long, straight, reddish hair, and although you couldn't say she was conventionally attractive she had a commanding presence you couldn't miss. She carried herself with the purpose and pride of an old warrior who knew well the sweet taste of victory won by the strength of her own hand. Meanwhile, Tom was clearly just along for the ride—and enjoying every minute of it. Also a big boy, he reminded me of a heavier, balder version of the late actor J.T. Walsh.

We said our hellos and headed to the hotel restaurant, where Lynda Gayle had asked her members to meet us. I ordered a round of coffees and tried to relax as the tables we'd pushed together began to fill up with a group of aging men and women—all were at least in their forties, and many seemed well into their fifties or sixties. I shouldn't have been surprised by their age since I'd seen a lot of the same folks in the *Real Sex* piece, but still I couldn't help feeling a little strange. Within an hour the mature individuals I saw before me—many of whom were old enough to be my parents—would be naked and engorged and doing who knows what.

It was a struggle, but somehow I remained focused on the conversation I was having with Lynda Gayle. "So when we get up to the room, I want to keep the meeting as authentic as possible. You guys just do your thing and we'll be a fly on the wall."

"Wonderful." Lynda Gayle enjoyed being the center of attention. But then, who doesn't?

"After we shoot the meeting we'll do your interview, and that's when you get to say all that great stuff you've been telling me on the phone."

"Oh yes, like how I always tell my girls not to do anything you can't wash off." As the members giggled knowingly, especially the women, I spent an unfortunate moment imagining all those laughing ladies with cum dripping off their faces. And then I tried not to wonder if I was really up to this.

Eventually everyone was accounted for—almost twenty in all— and we adjourned upstairs to the Presidential Suite. Right away I got the members into a circle, introduced them to Ted and Kira, and then passed the floor to Lynda Gayle. She began as she always did, with a brief meet & greet session. Ted rolled tape as they introduced themselves and said what they were hoping to accomplish that particular afternoon.

"Hi, I'm Billy and I want to get a blowjob while someone licks my ass."

"I'm Marina and I would like to get my pussy licked by a woman while I suck someone's cock."

And so on.

Next, Lynda Gayle instructed her members to change into something more comfortable—lingerie for the women, boxers for the men—and then she started the first session. I watched as they broke off into smaller groups of twos and threes and fours and found their play area—a bed, a couch, a chair, the floor. Slowly everyone got their motor running while poking and prodding each other with toys and eager fingers. Within fifteen minutes I felt like I was in the monkey room at the zoo. A cacophony of primal sounds came from every corner of the room, the intensity alternately rising and falling, creating a strange sexual symphony dominated by the unmistakable slurping of mouths on genitalia. And the smell was unavoidable. With pheromones flying everywhere, the entire suite was skunked with the animalistic odors of sex.

For some reason my eyes kept settling on Lynda Gayle, where she was reclining with one leg hanging over the arm of on an oversized chair. As she slowly worked a large, red, rubbery, double-sided dildo in and out of her engorged vagina I couldn't help smiling, thinking back to our lengthy phone conversations when she'd revealed some of her deeper motivations for starting the club.

Evidently, her first marriage had not gone particularly well. She'd felt neglected sexually and, like so many women of her generation, she'd been taught not to express her desires. Only after she was divorced did she discover that her situation was not an uncommon one—a hypersexual, super-silent woman married to a "missionary man" who didn't see the point of going down on her. Looking back, she began to realize relationships like hers might be improved if only more women were encouraged to discuss their needs with the men they loved. So Lynda Gayle had set out to create a world, one hotel room at a time, that was full of what her first marriage had lacked—verbal and, of course, physical interaction. It was a place where desires were guaranteed not to fall on deaf ears, even if some members were beginning to lose their hearing.

"Oh this dildo feels soooooo gooooood," she moaned to no one in particular.

Meanwhile, only a few feet away her husband Tom was getting a blowjob from a forty-something brunette—and loving it. "That's just great darlin'. You got it, just like that. Oh, yeah."

Whenever I needed a break from my front row seat at this graphic, geriatric orgy I stepped into another room for a moment or simply stared down at my script, pretending to be thinking ahead to the next stage of the shoot. I felt bad for poor Ted, who was forced to keep an eye on every second of the action. I don't mean to be rude, but the sex wasn't sexy. These were old, out of shape bodies—not that there's anything wrong with that. In fact, more power to 'em. These were real people—amateurs performing for the love of the game, not paid professionals with plastic surgeons on retainer. As far as I was concerned, I was jealous of their balls. Hell, I didn't even like taking off my clothes at the doctor's office. But this story wasn't about me. It was about them.

And because the piece was airing on Playboy TV I did need to raise the beauty coefficient a little bit—at least those were my marching orders from Bruce. So Kira, bless her heart, agreed to put on a show. Her plan was to help Lynda Gayle demonstrate the Club's favorite toy—an "S" shaped, Pyrex glass dildo which they called The Crystal Wand.

While Lynda Gayle lubed up the toy, Kira got ready for her lesson. She'd been wearing a sexy red teddy, and when she took it off it was like the sun had come out from behind the clouds and the whole room was suddenly brilliantly lit. This was the first time I'd seen her naked, and for a moment I swear I couldn't breathe. She was flawless—gorgeous God-given breasts, sleek super-firm torso, a cute well-manicured pussy, and by far the best ass I'd ever seen. I felt myself stirring and tried to look away, but I just couldn't take my eyes off her. Every inch was absolutely stunning. A picture of perfection. And then I noticed something else about her—she was completely comfortable within her own skin. She wasn't shy, she wasn't nervous. Yet there she stood, naked in a room full of middle-aged men and women, all of whom were watching her every move, and many of whom were still masturbating less than five feet away.

When Kira lay on the bed and Lynda Gayle began to ease The Crystal Wand inside her, the entire room went dead silent. As Lynda Gayle worked her magic, Kira began to wriggle and moan, slowly building intensity. Meanwhile, the male members began to inch towards the bed with their hands feverishly pumping their cocks. I was suddenly worried they would all burst at the same time and wind up drowning the poor girl. "Okay, fellas, let's give her some room, alright?" Ever the gentlemen, they stopped advancing, but nothing was gonna keep them from their stroking. This truly was a treat for them.

I suppose it shoulda been for me, too, but somehow I felt conflicted. Sure, she was a beautiful naked woman with a glass dildo in her pussy, but she was also someone I worked with, someone I'd had dinner with. More importantly, this was my *job*. I was on the clock and it just wasn't professional to be getting off on this. And let's face it, it didn't help that all those rock hard erections were so damn close that I was worried about getting caught in the impending crossfire. So I triple-checked my script for what we still needed to shoot while Kira continued doing what she was doing, building and building, until she finally climaxed. And then so did all the guys, who, thankfully, were kind enough to cum into the palms of their hands.

Later, when Lynda Gayle asked if Kira's orgasm had been real, she admitted to having faked the whole thing. Lynda Gayle seemed surprised and even vaguely hurt by this. Kira had been completely believable, but of course she was. Faking orgasms, I assumed, was something she had done hundreds of times as an actress. I wondered if her husband ever had trouble telling the difference between what was real and what was acting. And then I wondered how her husband felt about her being naked in a hotel room with a bunch of middle-aged swingers while a heavy-set woman worked her over with a glass dildo. I knew *I* could never live with that, but then, I was beginning to realize that their relationship was built on a foundation that I could never fully fathom.

The shoot was over around eight, and as the Club Relate faithful packed up to leave I shook hands with everyone, albeit somewhat awkwardly as I couldn't help thinking of where those hands had so recently been. Then I went up to my room and took a much needed shower while Kira and Ted hit the pool.

Drying off I poured myself a Jack Daniels from the mini-bar and gave Jennifer a call. Earlier I'd let her know I'd be done by nine, so now I was calling to check on her progress. She said she was on her way and should be here in a couple of hours. Perfect. I could use some time to catch my breath and downshift from the long, intense day of shooting.

Also, I needed to give my mother a call. It was my habit to keep in touch with her while I was traveling so she wouldn't worry. And because I was her only child, it was her habit to worry. A lot. After letting her know I was okay and that the shoot had gone reasonably well, I mentioned that there was a thirty-nine-year-old woman driving 180 miles to fuck me.

"How much does she cost?" was the first thing out of my mother's mouth.

I laughed, "No, Ma, it's not like that. She's not a hooker, she's a *nurse*." I assured her that Jennifer was a sweet, soulful woman who happened to have had children at an early age and was now separated from her husband. "She's just looking for a good time."

Now it was my mother's turn to laugh, "Hide your wallet."

And then it was almost ten and I was hungry, so I went downstairs to grab a quick bite. Afterwards I joined Ted and Kira in the suite where they had just returned from the pool. Together we all had whiskey drinks while Kira paraded around the room half naked, not bothering to cinch her small silk robe. Of course, I was aroused by her impeccable body, just as I'd been during the shoot. But now I was also uncomfortable, much more so than I'd been earlier. Then it had been business, and there were many others in the room. This was more intimate. It was just the three of us. And we weren't working. We were drinking. Kira's nakedness now seemed inappropriate—uncouth and even rude. Or was it? Was Kira crass or just without inhibitions?

In the end, I didn't know what to think, so I didn't. Instead, I tried my best to be blasé about the situation and allow my preppie charm and versatility to take over. With something approaching grace I attempted to ignore the obvious and carry myself as if she was fully clothed. Ted, however, did not. Instead he paid her boorish compliment after boorish compliment—always a variation of "You're so beautiful." Not that it was a competition, but I think I made a better impression by simply having a conversation. *Oh, you're naked? I'm sorry, I hadn't noticed, I was too busy listening to what you were saying.*

So we chatted, drank, and I was feeling damn good—and why not? I'd successfully produced my second story in ten days, I was developing an excellent bourbon buzz, and very soon I was going to be having fun sex with an attractive older woman.

Around midnight my cell phone finally rang. It was Jennifer saying she'd just pulled in front of the hotel, so I went down to meet her. Stepping outside, I saw her ride and immediately burst out laughing. It was a white stretch "truck-a-zine" with a checkered flag motif painted on the side. After introducing myself to the driver, who was smiling, holding open the back passenger door, I climbed inside. And there was Jennifer, wearing a tight black, low-cut top and even tighter blue jeans. We had a kiss and I told her I was glad she'd finally made it.

Then I brought her upstairs to meet Ted and Kira, who now, thankfully, was wearing clothes. Right away Kira seemed to sense something. "What do *you* do, honey?"

"Oh, I do a lot of things," Jennifer replied. *Hmm... Wonder why she dodged the question?* Why didn't she explain that she was a nurse? Maybe it was just a display of female jealousy and they were simply sniffing each other out. I wasn't sure and it really didn't matter. So I offered Jennifer a drink, but all she wanted was a Coca-Cola. And as I refreshed my bourbon she invited us all downstairs to laugh at the truck-a-zine.

The limo hadn't moved an inch. Jennifer and Kira promptly climbed up on top of the roof as if this was the custom, while Ted snapped pictures and I joked with the driver about the girls and their gymnastic poses.

Naturally we knew we had to take it out for a spin. Once we'd gotten comfortable on the long leather seats Kira tried again. "So what do you do, honey?"

"Uh, I work as a nurse." That's better. There's nothing wrong with being a nurse, no reason to be ashamed whatsoever—"...and I also work for a few of the escort services." *What!?* You do what with the what now?

Kira nodded approvingly, "Right on, right on." Kira had known all along. She had spotted it a mile away. And somehow so had my mother, and she was *four hundred* miles away in rural Alabama! But I hadn't had a clue. And how did I react to this new information? I didn't say a word. I let it sink in. Sure, there was an off-duty hooker in my lap, but c'mon, it's not like I was gonna send her home. It was a three-hour drive. Besides, I wanted to fuck her. Badly. And as long as no money exchanged hands it was all good, right? Right.

So I rolled with it. And we did a few laps around downtown Orlando before heading back to the Sheraton, at which point Ted dimwittedly suggested we go clubbing. But Kira promptly shut him up. "Can't you see those two want to go back to the hotel and fuck?" She wasn't subtle, but, once again, she was dead right.

Back at the hotel I had to pull Kira aside to say goodnight. "You know, you're a damn good interviewer. Jennifer never told me anything about being an escort." With this mildly Machiavellian line I was paying Kira a compliment, but I was also exonerating myself of any prior knowledge of Jennifer's somewhat seedy profession. And, perhaps in my own twisted way, I was asking for her moral permission, as if I needed another woman to tell me what I was about to do was alright.

Kira smiled and gave me her blessing. "Have fun."

When Jennifer and I made it up to my room we chatted a bit before stripping. And as I was taking off my pants I could hear my mother's voice, *Hide your wallet,* which set off a rabid case of giggling in my mind. But still, I made sure to bury my billfold deep inside my suitcase.

Then I joined Jennifer in bed and we kissed slow and soft and wet in the darkness and her body felt trim and fit under my hands and I pressed myself against her and we rubbed and kissed and rubbed and kissed and rubbed and kissed until she whispered, "Go down on me."

Oh, right. I better lick her pussy. Although I hadn't exactly given it much thought, I guess I'd been a little hesitant to get down there. I mean, who goes down on a hooker, right? But then I remembered I wasn't with a hooker. I was with a woman who wanted to be with me. And I wanted to be with her. We'd made a connection and now we were gonna make each other feel good. Besides, what was I gonna do, say no?

So I slid down her body and spread her wide, and then suddenly I realized this was precisely why she'd driven three hours to see me.

"Mmm, that's a good boy..."

And how could I not respect her for that? She knew what she wanted and she wasn't afraid to ask for it. And I wasn't afraid to give it to her. In fact, I *wanted* to give it to her. So I did.

"Such a good boy..."

Around five in the morning, I walked Jennifer down to the truck-a-zine where we found the driver dead asleep. It was still dark and I almost felt bad waking him up. Then I kissed her goodbye and as I watched her drive off into the hot Orlando night I couldn't help wondering if sleeping with an escort—off-duty or not—was the right thing to do. And I didn't mean *right* in any universal moral sense, but rather, was it right for *me*? Was it right for *my* soul? At this early hour I couldn't be sure, but whatever the answer was I knew one thing for certain—my world was rapidly changing.

IV

Just Be Careful You Don't Get Too Close to Your Work

I can't believe you fucked a whore!" Maggie was the other producer at *Sexcetera*, the ex-girlfriend who'd gotten me my initial interview. It'd been almost two years since we'd given up on our May–December romance. Nobody's fault. Just turned out her ten year seniority was an obstacle we couldn't tear down or walk around. But we'd remained friends because our souls still overlapped in a lot of places. And because I was a huge fan of her two adorable Australian Shepherds—Lucy, the super-genius Black Tri who I was head-over-heels in love with, and Lola, the food-obsessed Blue Merle who I liked a lot. So around once a month the four of us would get together for a hike in the Hollywood Hills. "A whore, Ross! She sells her body for money! For money!" While filling her in on my first two weeks on the job I'd figured, as one old friend to another, Maggie would enjoy hearing about a frivolous sexcapade. Wrong.

"C'mon, it's not like I paid her." Previously I'd assumed the fact that no money ever exchanged hands would be an ironclad defense, but now, as I said it aloud, I knew it wasn't gonna hold up in court.

"So what? She's still a whore!"

I wished she'd stop saying that word. Or at least stop saying it so loudly. Lucy was gonna get the wrong idea. "You know, Lucy can hear you."

"Good. She deserves to know what you did. Lucy, your daddy fucked a whore." Maggie still called me Lucy's Daddy because that's the way Lucy wanted it. "Isn't it awful? Look at her, she's horrified."

"But she told me she was a nurse." I never shoulda opened this can of worms.

"Yeah, well, she's still a whore!" I suppose subconsciously I'd been looking for another woman's opinion on what I'd done, and boy was I getting it. As far as Maggie was concerned, off-duty or not, a hooker is a hooker is a hooker. "And you knew what she was *before* you fucked her." Then she added, "I just hope you wore a condom."

"Yeah, in fact I wore two or three," I joked—a good joke too. "Two or three" because we had sex multiple times, or "two or three" because I wanted to be extra careful? But, alas, it was a line wasted on Maggie.

"I can't believe you, Ross. I can't believe you'd put yourself at risk like that. *I'll* never sleep with you again, that's for sure."

"Damn." And I snapped my fingers with mock disappointment. She couldn't be serious. Wait. *Was* she serious? Had she been thinking about fucking me again? Maybe the reason she got so upset was that in the back of her mind she had something riding on it. *Hmmm...* And Maggie *was* looking good—even better than the day she kicked me out of her Hollywood bungalow, and much, much better than all those nights she sent me to sleep on the couch. I had a sudden urge to stop her mid-stride and reclaim those long lost lips. But I couldn't. All because I'd foolishly revealed my romp with Jennifer. *Damn.*

"Just be careful you don't get too close to your work."

"Well, if I can't sleep with the people I meet on the job, then I shouldn't be doing the job." But what I meant to say was, *If I think I'm somehow better than these people, then I shouldn't be doing the job.*

The following day I was back in the office getting my next assignment from Bruce. "You're gonna love this, buddy. Legal has never let us show an erection before, but they're giving us the green light on this one!" I was profiling Sean Michaels, an African-American porn star blessed with an eleven-inch penis. I couldn't help wondering how Bruce, a man well into his forties, had gotten to a place in his life where he was actually excited about putting an erection on television.

But then again, I guess eleven inches was kinda exciting. "Hey, if the story's about a shark, I gotta show the shark, right?"

"Right, but you still can't show the shark feeding."

"Feeding?"

"No insertion, buddy."

Walking out to my car loaded down with a box of videos—the kind that come in the big oversized packaging—I knew this was it. My first story on a full-fledged porn star. When I got home I found Sean's bio on the Internet. He was 41 and had been in more than a thousand scenes during his twelve-year career. Wow. A thousand scenes. And that was just the sex he'd had on-camera. I wondered if you could have so much sex that you actually lost interest? Or was it only possible to have that much sex if your libido was truly insatiable? My guess was the latter.

According to his bio Mr. Michaels was also something of a pioneer. In the early nineties he'd "overcome the racial complexities of his industry" and had "helped create a market for both interracial and all-black erotica." As a result he'd opened quite a few doors for the next generation of black porn stars. Perhaps a dubious distinction, but nevertheless, kudos for Sean.

These days he was also directing and producing his movies for his own company, Sean Michaels Productions, Inc. His bestselling line of videos was a spoof on the James Bond series. The films had wonderfully creative titles like *For Your Ass Only*, *Coldfinger*, and *You Only Cum Twice*—all of which could be found in my brand new box of porn. Sean Michaels played Agent Sean Bond, License to Drill, and, if you believed the box covers, "Nobody did it better." Poor Sean Connery—his cameraman always panned away to a pile of clothes on the floor so he never really had a chance to compete.

But, as I well knew, *Sexcetera* wasn't doing this story because Sean was bastardizing James Bond's good name or even because he might be the Sidney Poitier of adult entertainment. We were doing the story because when Sean showed up for a shoot, his cock needed its own dressing room.

Of course, I had to see it to believe it, so I opened up a copy of *For Your Ass Only*, slapped it into my VCR, pressed Play, and— WHOA!—my eyes went from zero to sixty in a heartbeat as my 28-inch screen was suddenly filled with an extremely tight shot of an enormous black cock pumping in and out of a glistening wet vagina—*phwap, phwap, phwap*. I guess someone else in my office had needed to see it to believe it as well and then hadn't bothered to rewind the tape. When the shot widened out I could see that the cock was indeed attached to Mr. Michaels. Long-limbed and muscular—but not in an obnoxious, over-pumped kind of way— he was a handsome man who obviously took care of himself. At the moment, however, Sean was taking care of his love interest, a young blonde.

Very young. And very beautiful. Spread wide and completely overwhelmed, she got my Lil' Guy stirring, for sure. But not for long. Because I was becoming more and more concerned for this barely eighteen year old girl with her mascara smeared and running like tears down her cheeks as she struggled to take Sean's eleven inches. I just couldn't see the fantasy. Only the reality.

Why would anyone serve up their body like that? Money? Alright, sure. The girl needed money, but why do *this*? How could tomorrow's scars possibly be worth the $500 or $1000 she was getting paid today?

But maybe I didn't deserve to be asking these questions. In all my twenty-seven years I'd never waited a table. The only "tough" jobs I had on my résumé—moving pianos for the Aspen Music Festival and washing windows on Martha's Vineyard—sounded suspiciously like summer vacations. And the alternative to taking those gigs had been living under my mother's roof and maybe helping out with the occasional chore. Not sucking cock on camera.

The first time I saw Sean in person, it was a sweltering day in the Valley. I'd driven out to a house in Chatsworth where he was shooting so we could meet face to face and decide on a date for the shoot. When I rang the bell a woman answered and introduced herself as Sean's office manager. As I followed her into the house I told myself to relax and to pretend this wasn't my first time on a porn set.

"Are they shooting?" I whispered in case they were.

"No, they're taking a break."

I found Sean sitting at the kitchen table, naked except for a pair of white boxers, with an attractive, extremely young and extremely nervous girl on his lap. She was blonde with a European look and wore sky-blue lingerie. A larger African-American man was leaning against the sink, fully clothed in a khaki outfit. He held a small digital video camera by his side. As soon as I walked in, I knew I was interrupting something. The room was too quiet, as if something had just happened, as if the girl was simultaneously being consoled and admonished for shitting on the floor. It reminded me of a Blue Period Picasso, with everyone looking down at their feet.

"Hi, Sean. I'm Ross."

"Ross from Playboy!" Sean beamed a smile. "Good to finally meet you." He remained seated with the girl in his lap, but extended his hand so we could have a shake. "This is Ivette. She's visiting from Prague."

Ivette smiled as I shook her hand. "Nice to meet you. I'm actually going to Prague next month for Playboy." That wasn't a lie, but was perhaps said more to impress Sean than her.

"And this is B. He's shooting for me today."

"Hey B."

"Whaddup Ross from Playboy?"

Sean spoke softly in Ivette's ear. "Excuse me for a minute, okay honey?" She murmured her assent and shifted so Sean could stand. He was taller than my six-foot-one, and as he led me into the next room he moved with patience—deliberate, not slow. My first impression was that this was a charismatic man, even if he was taking a meeting in his boxers.

Right away Sean acknowledged the strange mood in the other room. "Ivette's a little nervous about her first anal scene." Well, I can't say I blamed the poor girl. Eleven inches is, after all, eleven inches. Earlier, while scanning through Sean's oeuvre, I'd noticed that nearly every scene incorporated anal sex. I kept thinking of those stage knives with the collapsible blades, and I wondered if perhaps he was using the same technology. If not, where was it all going?

"Sometimes you got to ease the girl into it, you know?" And he smiled softly. It was a respectful smile, without laughter.

"Oh yeah, of course." I nodded as if I knew a damn thing about anything, and then changed the subject with a compliment. "So Sean, your Bond titles are hilarious. What's this next one gonna be called?"

"Right now we're calling it *Thunderballs*. What do you think?" This time his smile came with a laugh.

"Love it." Soon Sean and I settled on a day, and I was heading for the door. On my way out I heard a flush and the bathroom door opened and there was Ivette in her lingerie. I gave a short wave. "Nice meeting you."

"Yah," she said with an accent and a faint smile.

I couldn't help thinking that, all made up in her brand new lingerie and without a foot-long cock jammed up her ass, she didn't look half bad. "Good luck."

Back at the office I was in the middle of punching up my script when the phone rang. "This is Ross."

"This is Maaaaaagggie..." Mmmm, slow and sexy.

"Hey, how are you?"

"Gooooood." Again with that voice. She was working from home these days, and lately she'd been calling to chat. But now she was calling to flirt.

So I flirted back. "What are you wearing?"

"Oh, just a pair of flip-flops."

"I'll be right over. I'll bring the booze and the barrister's wigs."

She laughed and returned to her normal friendly voice. "Speaking of booze, we should grab a beer sometime."

"Sure."

"Providing you haven't had sex with any more whores."

"No, I've been good. And yeah, I'd love to get a drink. When?"

"How 'bout this weekend?"

"No, I can't. I have plans." I didn't, but a weekend drink sounded like trouble. Too much, too soon.

"Next week then?"

"That could work. But I'm shooting Sean Michaels, so we'll have to see."

"I trust you won't be fucking *him*."

"Probably a safe bet."

The following week I found myself lying in the backyard of a multi-million dollar Calabasas home waiting for Sean. Nearby, my cameraman Max—talented, slightly anal, and extremely affable—kept busy by talking on his cell phone. I'd arrived feeling more than a little nervous about my first full day on a porn set, but now that Sean was running over an hour late those feelings had subsided into something far worse—boredom. The only plus was that the house was perched way up on a hill so I had a panoramic view of the San Fernando Valley, such as it was.

Finally, a full two hours late, Sean arrived with his crew in a caravan of cars. After he apologized for his tardiness there was a flurry of waves, nods, smiles, and handshakes as he introduced his five man crew and the two young actresses—a blonde named Nikki and an Asian named Jade Marsala.

Sean needed to shoot some establishing shots before he got to the sex scene, so while he worked with his crew I used the time to interview his co-stars.

"So Jade, tell me, how does Sean promote interracial sex in the adult business?" I asked, hoping to hear how he always cast a wide variety of ethnicities.

"With advertising," Jade answered. I guess she heard the word "promote" and thought I was talking about promoting his product.

"No, I'm sorry, I mean *promote* as in *encourage*. How does Sean *encourage* unity through diversity?"

"Uh... advertising?"

"Okay, that's great, thank you, that's all we need."

When it was Nikki's turn I asked, "So, are you nervous about the anal scene?"

Her face dropped like a piano in a Laurel & Hardy film. "It's anal!?!" And then her eyes darted around the set in search of Sean. I guess she never got the script.

When Sean was finally ready to get down to business, nightfall was not that far away. To cut costs he'd only paid to use the exterior of the house, so I knew time was going to be a factor. The scene called for Jade, Nikki, and Sean to have a three-way in his Mustang convertible, which was strategically parked so the mansion would be looming in the background.

Sean was standing in the backseat wearing a bright blue, broad shouldered suit. Something about his overall build, attitude, and outfit reminded me of Michael Irvin, the legendary Dallas Cowboys wide receiver *slash* clothes horse—and I bet Sean's hands were every bit as good. Sean called for quiet, made sure his two cameramen were rolling, and before I knew it the game was on. He began by kissing Nikki while simultaneously massaging one of Jade's breasts through her slinky back dress. Suddenly my stomach felt uneasy, like the beginning of a roller coaster ride when you're slowly taken higher and higher and higher and you're already anticipating the drop—*Chick-a, Chick-a, Chick-a...* Here we go, I thought. My first live porn scene.

The kissing and groping flowed smoothly into disrobing. Sean's suit jacket came off and Nikki's dress was pulled down so that her breasts were released into the evening air. Then Sean's shirt fell away and Jade's dress wound up bunched around her waist, exposing her breasts as well as her hairless crotch. When I saw Jade beginning to unzip Sean, I held my breath. And then there it was—The Shark. As I watched all eleven inches of Sean Michaels emerge I wanted to ask my cameraman if we were gonna need a bigger boat. Then, as soon as it appeared, it disappeared into Jade's mouth, or at least part of it did. She gamely accepted as much as she could, but she was only human.

After a minute or two Sean hiked up Nikki's dress and introduced his mouth to her shaven crotch. He gave himself plenty of elbow room, spreading her nice and wide with his big strong hands. Then he unrolled his wide tongue and began lapping her up like a thirsty Labrador after a long summer's walk. When Sean's cameraman went in for a close-up he was accompanied by my man with a handheld spot, so even from where I was standing I could see Nikki's juices glistening under the glare of the bright light.

Before long Sean was standing and pulling Jade's tiny ass up to him. From there he began boring a hole into her pussy, doggie style. Suddenly, without warning, she was shrieking like a wounded animal—presumably from pleasure. Whether feigned or actual I couldn't be sure. But still, wasn't anyone worried a neighbor might hear and call the cops? Or a SWAT team?

By now I'd seen—and heard—more than enough, and I wished I was at home on my couch where I could simply fast-forward through the scene. But I wasn't, so I couldn't. Instead I took a few steps back where it was no longer possible to make out every gory detail. From here I could only see them from their torsos up, which made it a helluva lot easier to digest what was going on.

Of course, there was no way that they were making love, but it also seemed like they weren't even having sex. I mean, sure, they were fucking, but was there really any pleasure involved? It appeared to be purely physical. An action. Like sawing wood. A penis was rubbing against a vagina. Just friction. That was it.

But how could I not be impressed by their emotional distance? What a superhuman trick of the mind it was to boil down the sex act to its bare essence and lose all the psychological trappings and hang-ups that clutter the bedrooms of us so-called normal folks.

And as the minutes passed and the sun began to set I started to wonder what was going through Sean's mind. He must have known that he had a limited amount of time to finish the scene. There wasn't much daylight left, and he wasn't equipped with nearly enough artificial light to compensate for the loss of sun. Did he feel the pressure? And would it affect his erection? A twelve year veteran, Sean had to know there was no room for error. Even without erection trouble he was barely going to make it. Surely a lesser man would have lost his wood under these circumstances. But Sean was definitely not a lesser man.

So he forged ahead. And I gotta say, there was something vaguely impressive about what I was watching. This was a display of both athletic and mental prowess. Sure, it wasn't exactly Mikhail Baryshnikov's performance of *Don Quixote* or Wayne Gretzky's hat trick against the Maple Leafs in Game 7 of the 1993 Western Conference Finals, but it was a show of some kind. Sean had complete control over every inch of his prodigious member and, just when he was about to use up the last few seconds of available light, he finished the scene with the obligatory money shot across Jade's expectant face. Jolly good show, Mr. Bond.

I watched as the crew congratulated him with what they called the "porn star handshake," an elbow to elbow move that eliminated any hand to hand contact. Then, wishing I knew about this maneuver back in Orlando, I tapped elbows with Sean myself and reminded him that we still needed to do his interview.

Once he'd had a chance to clean himself up we sat down together inside the garage. And as we chatted I decided that I honestly liked him—even if he had kept me waiting for two hours. He seemed reasonably intelligent, well-spoken, and remarkably understanding. I was particularly impressed with his take on the racism he'd run into when he was first starting out. "I would encounter women who wouldn't want to work with black men. I could've easily said, 'You bitch, you this, you that, where were you brought up at?' But who am I to judge you? Who knows what you've been through, sorry you feel that way, and, you know, maybe this could work out in the future."

Sean seemed to be enjoying himself, probably because few people ever asked him serious questions about his work. Whether or not he actually deserved to be put in a league with Jackie Robinson, he did want to feel like his twelve years in the biz had amounted to something—something a little more substantial than simply waving his eleven inches around on camera. He wanted to believe he'd done some good. And while he hadn't exactly stolen home in the World Series, he had opened some doors for other African-Americans who dreamed of one day swinging their own cocks around on camera. As I paused between questions he admitted, "This is nice. I'm glad I'm talking about this." And I was glad Sean was glad.

V

I Guess I Won't Be Running for Public Office after This

*T*he following Saturday night I got home around eleven after going to see the Kings play the Flames. It was a good game, which we'd won 3–2 thanks to a late third period goal from Ziggy Palffy. I had a bunch of beers and maybe even a shot of Jack Daniels or three, so I was feeling pretty spry when I heard my phone ringing.

It was Maggie. She was on her cell phone at a wine tasting. "My date's boring." Knowing her, I wouldn't have been surprised if the poor bastard was standing right there next to her. "I'm coming over."

Of course I couldn't say no, and around fifteen minutes later there was a knock on my door. I opened it and there she was, sexy as hell in a snug blue dress. I gave her my best smile. "Ah, there's my devil in a blu—"

But she was on me before I could finish.

A few weeks later I was in the VIP room of the Century Club with my new cameraman, a Brit named Dexter. We were covering a party thrown by the midlevel porn company Elegant Angel Films, and their middle-aged owner, Patrick Collins, was giving what I guess you'd call a press conference.

"This girl really is a slut." Collins was clearly not the most eloquent knife in the drawer. In fact, if you were seeing him for the first time, as I was, you just might think he was a crass, uneducated, foul-mouthed, poorly dressed, piece of shit porn mogul. Whether or not any of that was true in real life, outside of this evening, I'll never know because, thankfully, I'd never have to see him again. I suppose I coulda given him the benefit of the doubt and assumed that he was just playing a role for publicity purposes. But either way, as far as I was concerned, it was guys like him that gave porn—and men—a bad name.

"This girl really is a slut," Collins repeated, in case some of us hadn't caught his spit-laced venom the first time. Of course, he was referring to the bikini-clad woman to his right, Alexandra Quinn.

Best known for her energetic work in the *Slutwoman* series, Quinn was one of the Elegant Angel contract girls—and evidently her contract allowed her to be paraded before the press like a prize thoroughbred on Derby Day. Somehow she was able to smile her way through this degradation, even sporadically cooing, "Oh yeah..." My guess—if her glazed eyes were any indication—was that she wasn't really there, but instead drifting safely in a galaxy far, far away.

The purpose of this party was to celebrate Elegant Angel's latest publicity gimmick, a nationwide screenwriting contest. The company had asked its loyal fans to write and submit their very own sex scenes for Quinn's upcoming installment of *Slutwoman*. The winning author would be flown to LA where he would get to star in his scene opposite Alexandra Quinn. So basically the contest was for a chance to fuck Quinn.

I suppose I could understand the desire to have sex with a porn star, but what I couldn't fathom was why anyone would want to do it on-camera and for a movie that would actually be released to the public. Was Middle America really buying into the Porno Chic myth? Well, I guess so, because hundreds of gentlemen had put their personal fantasies into words in hopes of getting their fifteen minutes of fame with the Mighty Quinn.

"Now look at this body! I'm telling you, it's built for sex!" Collins was obviously enjoying himself. "Look, lemme show you what I'm talking about." And he reached down the front of her G-string, presumably into her cooze. Then, after a moment, he removed his hand and extended two fingers in front of the audience. With the exaggerated air of a pro-wrestler he smelled them, waited a beat, then exclaimed, "She's wet right now!"

I felt for the poor girl, I really did. But even though she'd already been through plenty this evening I still had a job to do. "Ah, excuse me, Miss Quinn?"

"Yeah."

"Yeah, hi, Ross Dale with Playboy TV. How are you?"

"Fucking great!" Quinn barked.

"Are you looking forward to meeting the lucky winner?"

Without hesitation Alexandra spewed, "I'm gonna fuck the shit out of him!"

"Any other thoughts?"

"I'm gonna fuckin' rock his world!" Indeed.

That was about all I needed from this dynamic duo. Now I had to go looking for the mysterious emcee I'd been promised. A few days earlier, Lori—my Elegant Angel PR contact who, on the phone, sounded a lot like a soccer mom—had told me that the big contest winner would be announced that night. But because she hadn't known who was scheduled to be the emcee I was supposed to keep an eye out for anyone holding a microphone.

When I made it backstage and found an ill-fitting excuse for a tuxedo draped over a scruffy looking gentleman in his late twenties I was fairly certain I had my man. As I approached, he was scribbling on a folded piece of paper. "Hi there, I'm Ross with Playboy TV. You wouldn't happen to be the emcee would you?"

"I sure am. William H. Nutsack at your service."

"Ah, okay, Mr. Nutsack, I was wondering—"

"William's fine."

"Okay, William, I was wondering when you'll be announcing the winner? I don't wanna miss getting it on camera."

"What're you talking about?"

"The screenwriting contest. I need to know when you'll be announcing the winner."

"There's a contest?"

Was this jackass fucking with me? He did look a tad stoned. "Yeah, there's a contest. You really don't know anything about this?"

"Fuck no. No one told me shit. Just introduce the girls, that's all." There was a cadre of scantily clad porn stars slowly gathering around us. Soon they would be gyrating on stage as part of the evening's entertainment.

"Alright, it's no big deal. I need you to do me a favor, though. When you go out there, before you introduce the girls, announce the winner right away. Then I can shoot it and you can forget about me and get on with your show. How's that sound?"

"Sounds good. Is the winner here tonight?"

"No, he's in Texas."

"Oh, okay, cool. So what's his name?" Luckily I'd had the foresight to ask Lori, so I knew the winner was a twenty-three year old small town kid named Jon Dudley. I passed this information on to Mr. Nutsack, and even wrote it down for him on his crib sheet so he couldn't screw it up. Christ, what a clusterfuck this was. I was beginning to see that the porn world was not exactly a well-oiled machine, even if that description did hold true for most of the girls.

The next day Lori forwarded me Jon's email address along with his prize winning scene. It was a two page tract about a young kid who gets caught spying on his next door neighbor with a pair of binoculars. But instead of being horrified, she's flattered and winds up inviting the young man inside for a quick shag. That's when our hero lets slip that he's a virgin, which, of course, only excites this gregarious young woman even more. Cue the music and they fuck six ways to Sunday, and, lo and behold, our hero is a virgin no more.

A virgin! Did that mean Jon was a virgin? Or had he dreamt up the virgin angle in order to win the contest? Jon and I needed to talk, so I sent him an introductory email asking for his phone number. The following day I got his response. I couldn't call him at home because he didn't want his parents to know about either the contest or the *Sexcetera* story—probably wise—but I could call him at his work number, so I did.

"Mailboxes Etc., how can I help you?" *Mailboxes Etc.?* Was this the right number?

"I'm looking for Jon?"

"Yeah, this is Jon."

"This is Ross from Playboy TV. How are you?"

"Hey, what's up?"

"Oh, not much, just trying to produce a little television show. Listen, man, I loved the scene you wrote. Bold use of binoculars."

"Thanks."

"I couldn't help noticing that your main character was a virgin. Ah, you wouldn't happen to be a virgin yourself, would you?"

"Yeah, I'm afraid I am."

Oh no. "Fantastic!" *This is gonna be bad.* "This is gonna be great!" *The kid's fucked.* "And don't worry, my friend, you won't be a virgin for much longer."

"Yeah, I can't wait." Jon could not have been any happier about getting this albatross from around his neck. "It's been hard being a virgin. You know, my friends are always talking about their experiences, and I'm just there, you know, minding my own business, not speaking up."

"Well, you're gonna have plenty to speak up about real soon."

"Yeah, I already told a couple friends and they're super jealous."

"I bet they are." *Some friends.*

After chatting with him for only a few minutes I knew without a doubt that Jon was the real deal. And even though I couldn't understand why he would want to lose his virginity on-camera to Alexandra Quinn, I also couldn't help liking him. Part of me even felt paternal toward him. Jon was just a sweet, sensitive kid from Bumfuck, Texas, who didn't know any better. All he wanted was what every other twenty-something virgin wanted—to stop being a virgin. If only he knew that the Mighty Quinn was waiting to fuck the shit out of him. That paternal part of me wanted to tell him he was grounded and that he had to stay put in Texas, but the producer in me knew the show must go on. I could only hope that this wasn't gonna be something Jon would regret for the rest of his life.

I know this sounds hard to believe, but when Maggie first suggested we watch some porn together, I didn't really want to. And I'm not exactly sure why. Maybe it was just a knee-jerk reaction triggered by that damn sheltered bourgeois upbringing of mine. Or maybe it was because I still couldn't stomach all the super-tight, biology class close-ups. Or maybe I was just plain stupid.

"I dunno baby. Why do we need to be watching that?"

"'Cuz it's fun." She didn't think it was so fun back when we were living together. Or if she did, she'd kept it to herself. But I guess now that she'd been working for Playboy for almost a year, she'd become more adventurous.

So why shouldn't I? When I really thought about it, none of my reasons against watching porn made all that much sense. Especially considering my current circumstances. After all, wasn't porn paying the rent?

"What did you have in mind?"

"Early Jenna Jameson." Jenna? How bad could it be? She wasn't one of those girls who'd been chewed up and spit out that I found so depressing. She was one of the good ones—one of the lucky ones who'd gone up against the house and won. "She's fucking hot. You're gonna love it."

"Alright, throw her in." So I smoked some pot and together we settled in on the couch.

Jenna Jameson, cute-as-a-button, was kneeling on a green bedspread in some barely decorated room. The guy was named Randy West and the shoot was from his *Up & Cummers* line. He was older, definitely in his forties, and he had a mullet that I'm pretty sure wasn't even in style back in 1994 when this thing was shot. But Jenna was always in style. She was twenty at the time, and with no makeup and just her natural blonde hair she looked so young and so soft and so pure. But also, not at all. Even at that age and brand new to porn she seemed totally in control—of herself and everything around her. She was nothing like any of the other girls I'd seen so far. You could see in her eyes that she wasn't ever gonna be exploited. And yet it wasn't a hard look. You could just tell she *knew*. Like they say all great hockey players can see the entire sheet of ice in slow motion, she could see it all laid out in front of her. She just knew.

And the way she worked Randy's cock was awe inspiring. So attentive, so caring, she put everything she had into it. I couldn't take my eyes off her. Her hands, her mouth, her lips, her tongue—especially her tongue—all worked together in perfect harmony like a maestro playing an instrument, and it was a difficult piece of music with a lot of notes. She was a virtuoso. A natural. And watching her, I'd swear she'd been a man in another life because the way she touched him it was like she understood exactly how everything she did felt, like she was wired into his pleasure centers, like she was somehow cheating. She was just too good. And you could tell from the tape that even a jaded veteran like Randy West couldn't believe what he'd stumbled upon. I know I sound like I'm exaggerating, but her performance was truly transcendent. Anyone interested in giving a better blowjob should really watch this tape.

Then, when it was time for Randy to fuck her, she gave this adorable short little squeal as he pushed inside her. I'd never seen or heard anything quite like it. And as they went about their business, Maggie and I got down to ours and I paid less and less attention to the tape.

A few weeks later I was on my way to Chatsworth—a part of the Valley I now knew to be the porn capital of the world—where I was finally going to meet Jon Dudley. Lori was picking him up at the airport in a stretch limo and then bringing him straight to the set of an Elegant Angel film. The idea was for Jon to get a taste of a real live porn shoot before tomorrow, when it'd be his turn.

When I saw Jon step outta the limo, he looked exactly as I'd imagined—short and tubby with a terrible small-town haircut, some lingering acne, and the biggest smile I'd ever seen. This was also my first time laying eyes on Lori, and she wasn't quite the soccer mom I'd heard on the phone. She was more of a tweedy, long skirt wearing, clipboard carrying PR type who was probably just trying to stay busy and help her husband pay a few bills.

"Hey Jon, I'm Ross. How are ya?"

"Great! I've never been in a limo before."

"One more thing to cross off your list. Listen, I want you to meet the hosts of the segment, *Sexcetera*'s very own Hoyt & Frank." Of all the reporters, Hoyt Christopher & Frank Gianotti were the only two that worked as a pair. I wasn't sure why, but my boss told me that Playboy seemed to like it that way. I'd seen a few of their stories. They were the quintessential high energy, good-time party guys. Known simply as Hoyt & Frank, they were both blessed with model-caliber looks. Hoyt was a USC blend of surf and frat, while Frank was a hip-hippie from Athens, Georgia. Supposedly, wherever they went girls flocked to them like birds to a pair of pinecones covered with peanut butter and scotch.

Dexter was already rolling tape and, as planned, Frank jumped right in. "Jonnie, no adult star is complete without a stage name. So, what is yours going to be?"

Jon was primed and ready. "My stage name is going to be Dick Fitzwell."

"And does it?"

"I sure hope so," Jon replied with scary sincerity. The kid was alright.

I followed as Hoyt & Frank escorted Jon into the studio, which was basically a long warehouse that had been sectioned off into a series of different sets. By the rough and tumble, dirty-bird look of the place I figured that this space was used exclusively for porn shoots. There was a lounge set, two different bedrooms, an office, and a workout room. The Elegant Angel crew was already in the lounge setting up around a leopard-skin couch.

Today's shoot was part of a series called *Filthy First Timers*, which, as the name suggested, featured girls having on-camera sex for the first time. An established male porn star always did the honors, and, in this case, the cock was provided by someone named Tyce Bunay. We still had a few minutes before they got started so I had Hoyt & Frank ask Mr. Bunay to step into the workout room and give Jon a quick lesson.

This time Hoyt began. "Alright Tyce, how about a few pointers for Jonnie here on the lick-lick."

Tyce smiled. "Okay, Jon, here's what you're gonna want to do. Take your left hand and just kind of reach it around the top and spread her pussy real good. And then you look for the little man in the boat. And Quinn's got a big man in the boat. He looks like he's on steroids. So when you find the little man in the boat—"

"Maybe the little big man?" Frank interjected.

Tyce missed the Dustin Hoffman reference. "Uh, yeah, right. So just polish his helmet with your tongue and you'll do just fine."

Jon had a question of his own. "Tyce, how do I keep from cumming too soon?"

"That's easy. Just think of dead pets."

Moments after finishing his advice, Tyce was called to the set. We followed him into the next room where there was an extremely young, extremely fake blonde sitting quietly on the couch wearing only her bra and panties. As Tyce discussed the scene with the director, a greasy muscle bound type with a ponytail, I couldn't take my eyes off the girl. Not because she was particularly attractive, but because she looked so disturbingly uncertain. And so young.

When Tyce and the crew were all set the director called "Action." Like a high school wrestler hearing the whistle blow,

Tyce wasted no time with his first move. He deftly removed the girl's brassiere and began sucking her left nipple. Within a minute or two his pants were off and he was presenting his erection for her to begin blowing him. Only a few feet away Jon studied the action closely, and he seemed to like what he saw. I thought he might pick up on the scent of the girl's apprehension, but Jon, with his big goofy grin, seemed oblivious. This was just good clean fun as far as he was concerned.

After a minute or two the director said, "Okay, Tyce." This was the signal to spread the newbie out on the couch and get inside her. As Tyce found his rhythm, the poor girl seemed like she was wincing an awful lot. To me it appeared that her disturbing facial expressions were caused from pain instead of pleasure, and it was my further diagnosis that her anguish was more mental than physical. But she was past the point of no return. Tyce had his professional cock inside her and he was thrusting quite vigorously as the cameras rolled only a few feet from her closed eyes. This young girl was now a porn star. Jon was grinning ear to ear, but I couldn't take another strained grimace.

So I stepped into the next room and, like the poor girl on the couch, waited for it to be over. Today was enough to turn me off to porn all over again—and so soon after I'd begun to acquire taste for it. I guess it was one thing to enjoy a thirty dollar steak in your favorite restaurant, and quite another to watch the cow get slaughtered.

That night I met Maggie at the Malibu Beach Inn. She was shooting a story there the following morning and had gotten her hands on their nicest suite. Lately it seemed like we'd been spending a lot of time together—maybe too much. The sex remained stellar, but emotionally I was beginning to feel like we were approaching those old familiar walls we'd beaten our heads against two years ago. And after what I'd seen earlier that day I wasn't feeling all that amorous, and the last thing I wanted to do was fuck. I probably shouldn't have gone to see her, but that had been the plan. Besides, the room was right on the ocean, there was a hot tub on the balcony, and Playboy was picking up the tab, so how could I resist?

After some uninspired sex, some mediocre Chinese food, and way too much Jack Daniels we were sitting in the hot tub drinking champagne and watching the waves crash in the cool November night. It should have been a nice romantic moment, but it was far from it. Instead of the waves, all I could hear were the old arguments rolling in—*Stop chewing with your mouth open... You're too young for me... I want to have a kid... Why don't you love me anymore?*

Funny thing was, I did love her. I loved her a lot. And I thought she'd be a good mother, too. Sometimes I even saw her with my kids. I just didn't see it anytime soon. If only she didn't want so much so fast. Still, there was a part of me that wanted to marry her—it's just the rest of me thought that part was wrong.

"What are you smiling at?"

"Nothing." I sipped my champagne and hoped that she still had some Ambien left in her dopp kit.

The following day we all met back at the same studio for Jon's big scene. When the kid arrived I was about to pull him aside for his pre-game interview when Lori stopped me with a whisper, "Uh Ross, the director wanted me to ask you not to get him thinking too much before the scene. He's worried that Jon's gonna have trouble, it being his first time and all."

"No problem, Lori, just a couple quick questions about how much fun he's having and how great Elegant Angel is treating him, and then he's all yours." Christ, it wasn't like the kid was gonna be disarming a bomb, he was just getting raped by a porn star. He could do this in his sleep.

I brought Jon back to the "office" set, where we were already lit for the interview. "So Jon, what are you feeling right now?"

"I'm excited."

"I bet you are. What else are you feeling?"

"Well, I'm also nervous—nervous about getting in there with Alexandra because, first of all, I don't know what I'm doing. I don't know my way around a woman. And it's just very nerve-wracking hoping that I can sustain an erection for an extended period of time with a whole bunch of strangers watching me. And I'm also hoping that I don't cum too quickly. But mostly I'm just excited about losing my virginity to a beautiful woman like Alexandra."

"You got a lot on your plate there, doncha?"

"Yeah, I guess I do."

"Now Jon, I got to ask you—because this is obviously not a normal, everyday way to lose your virginity—are you worried at all that you might regret this in the years to come?" That was exactly the kind of question they didn't want me to ask.

"Well, say twenty years from now, looking back at it… That's a tough one. Hopefully I'm not going to regret what I do. I don't think that I will. I guess I won't be running for public office after this, but hey, what can you do?" *What can you do?* Well, for starters you can *not* enter a contest where the winner has sex with a porn star!

After I'd gotten what I needed and we'd stopped tape I gave Jon my best stab at a pep talk. "Jon, I've been watching you closely, and I can tell you this right now—you're gonna do great."

"I hope so."

"I know so. So just enjoy yourself." *Christ, I practically told him to win one for the Gipper.*

As we walked on set—for some reason they were using the lounge again—Lori pulled me aside a second time and whispered in my ear. "Listen, Alexandra is going through a tough time, and, well, now she's feeling a little guilty about taking this kid's virginity."

"But she's still gonna do it, right?"

"Oh yeah, she's gonna do it. She just doesn't want to interview with you. Is that alright?"

"Ah... sure. I'll make it work."

"And when she's around try to keep the Hoyt & Frank clowning to a minimum."

"No problem." Suddenly Slutwoman had a conscience. *Who knew?*

Before they got started I spoke briefly with the director—a heavy-set chap in his early forties—and we agreed the less people in the room, the better. So I left my cameraman behind and went into the next room to wait with Hoyt & Frank and all the other nonessential personnel. The consensus was that Jon would only last a few minutes and we'd all be going home soon. Boy, were we wrong. As the minutes accumulated I started to feel like an expectant father in the hospital waiting room, constantly looking at my watch and constantly thinking I heard the door about to open.

Finally, over an hour later, the door did open and we all stood for the good news. But instead we were told they were just taking a breather. Miraculously, Jon still hadn't cum. During the break he paced around wearing only his loose fitting Fruit of the Loom briefs and a pair of dirty white socks. His hairless belly jiggled slightly when he walked. But he wasn't nervous—or at least he didn't appear nervous to me. I believed his pacing was from excitement and that he was having a helluva time. Maybe he knew more than we gave him credit for and he was simply milking the moment for as long as possible, like a kid in his PJs begging to stay up just a little while longer.

When they returned to the lounge to begin round two, I went into one of the bedroom sets and lay down. Closing my eyes, I tried not to think about all the sex that had been filmed on this worn out futon. Instead, I thought back to when I lost my own virginity.

I was almost eighteen. It was right after I'd graduated from Groton and I was spending part of the summer with friends on Martha's Vineyard. I met a girl and we spent three terrific weeks together. Then one night the two of us drove to a nearby Cumberland Farms market. What an exhilarating feeling it was walking down the aisle with a red Gatorade and a pack of Trojans, knowing that this was indeed it. Of course, beyond the IQ test part of it—the round peg goes in the round hole—neither one of us had any idea what we were doing. But what a wonderfully sweet evening we had clumsily rolling around on her Laura Ashley sheets—an evening made all the sweeter because she, too, was a virgin.

My dreaming was interrupted by the sound of applause erupting from the set, which could only mean one thing—Jon's virginity had left the building. I rolled off the futon and sent Hoyt & Frank to get Jon's immediate reaction.

"It feels great! It was pure bliss!" Jon was exploding with energy. "This was the best day of my life, ever! Alexandra, she's a beautiful lady! Beautiful! And sweet—a sweet, sweet girl! It was the greatest experience of my life!" And we all knew he meant it. He was as much of a gentleman as anyone could have been under the circumstances.

After a surprisingly wistful goodbye I left thinking what a great kid he was. But as I drove home I felt my stomach turning. Surely Jon would regret this experience later in life. Or would he? Just because I believed his sexuality was now scarred, did that necessarily make it so? And maybe his sexuality needed a little roughing up. Maybe scarred was a helluva lot better than *scared*. Now that he'd gone toe-to-toe with The Mighty Quinn I knew he'd never again be intimidated by the girl selling soft-serves at the Dairy Queen back in Bumfuck, Texas. So maybe Jon, and even that poor girl on yesterday's couch, weren't quite as damaged as I thought they were. Either way, I just hoped that when Jon and his future girlfriends were swapping their virginity stories he would have the good sense to cowboy up and lie like a man.

VI

What Happens on the Road, Stays on the Road

*Y*ou know, this is only my second time out of the country—
if we're not counting Canada, which I assume we're not."
It was the beginning of December and I was boarding a ten-hour
KLM flight to Amsterdam.

"No, let's not count Canada." Kira—looking both incredible and
comfortable in her snug burgundy velour sweat-suit with no
makeup and her hair pulled back in a ponytail—was following me
down the aisle.

I couldn't believe how lucky I was. I'd been on the job for less
than four months and already they were sending me to Europe.
The only other time I'd been overseas was so long ago that I had
to get a new passport. After finishing high school some friends
and I had gone on a three-week European tour. It had been
proposed as a quasi-educational and cultural celebration of
manhood, but mostly we just drank on trains.

Finding my seat on the aisle I stuffed my carry-on in the overhead and squeezed down next to an elderly Asian woman. "We're
not together?" Kira was glaring at her boarding pass. I knew my
cameraman Max was sitting somewhere in the back, and with the
lady on my right and the seat across the aisle occupied by a

gentleman in a tweed sports coat it looked like the three of us were, in fact, spread throughout the plane.

"I guess not. I'm sorry." Not sure why I apologized—I hadn't booked the tickets.

Kira turned to Tweed Sports Coat. "Excuse me, but I was wondering if you would mind trading seats with me so I could sit with my husband?"

The man looked up with questioning eyes. He didn't understand her. Neither did I. "Doug's coming?"

She leaned into my seat so other passengers could pass. "I'm talking about *you*, silly." Then she asked Tweed Sports Coat once more, this time speaking slower and a little louder, but he replied in another language, probably Dutch. Kira saw the dead end, so she flagged down one of KLM's finest—an attractive thirty-something blonde in a vibrant blue uniform.

"Can I help you?"

"Yes, could you ask this gentleman here if he would mind trading seats so I can sit across from my husband? I'm on the aisle, too, just ten rows back, so it's really the same seat." KLM Blue nodded, and in a bustling thirty seconds Kira got what she wanted.

Soon we were airborne and the KLM Blue Woman Group was performing its beverage cart routine. We each ordered a pair of Heinekens and got to talking.

"Thanks for writing such great scripts."

"Just doin' my job."

"It's so nice to have good things to say."

"Well, thank you. I appreciate that and I'm glad you—"

"That other time you were out of the country, did you go to Amsterdam?"

"No, but just like every other kid who grew up with a water bong, I've always wanted to go." She laughed, but I wasn't just joking. Back at Groton, Amsterdam had captured my imagination the moment I first heard the rumors of this brave old world built on cobblestones, canals, and cannabis.

Whether recklessly liberal, refreshingly open-minded, or just plain practical, the city had balls. Balls so big they weren't satisfied with allowing marijuana to be sold over the counter in neighborhood coffee shops. Nope, they'd also dared to legalize prostitution. Their notorious Red Light District was known all over the world as the ultimate male amusement park—a paradise for penises of all ages.

Of course, all the women I knew back on the East Coast—and not just the unshaven feminists I'd made love to at Wesleyan—had a much different view of the Red Light District. What they saw was the brazen commodification of the vagina—a horrifying marketplace where pussy was bought and sold in full view of the impressionable public. So I was glad none of these intelligent, socially conscious women knew of my latest mission—to celebrate this "hell on earth" and glorify its legalized prostitution in a superficial, salacious, ten-minute segment for Playboy TV.

"How about you?" I asked.

"No, never. But I have been to Prague." As excited as I was about going to Amsterdam it was only the first half of the trip. Our second stop was Prague, where we were profiling an American expat porn director. "I shot a film there a year ago. Sort of a sexy vampire kinda thing."

"And you were the sexy vampire?"

"Yup," then switching to her Transylvania accent, "I vant... to suck... your co—"

"Yeah, yeah, I get it." I laughed and wondered if anyone was listening to us.

We continued to chat and drink until the in-flight movie, *A Perfect Storm*, put us to sleep.

And then we were landing and sleepwalking through the terminal—collecting our bags, stuffing our pockets with Guilders, stepping into a cab—and I was still snoozing well into the drive as the sterile highways turned slowly through my heavy lidded eyes into foreign, yet somehow familiar, suburbs. But with time she unfolded... Amsterdam. Like a dream outside my window and suddenly I couldn't even blink. Every glimpse dripped of romance— the architecture, the cobblestone streets, the canals, the bridges, the boats, the bicycles, the bundled up Dutch women leaning into the crisp December air. Like visiting a museum, it was almost too much—too beautiful to swallow all at once without choking.

Our hotel fit right in—an adorable, family-run, twenty room inn called the Hotel Toren. I paid the fare and got out of the cab with the full intention of helping Max and the driver unload our bags, but I just couldn't. Instead I was caught in the tractor beam pull of the canal. I leaned on the stone railing and looked down at the dark water, and then across to yet another row of gorgeous buildings, and then to the bridge on the right. It was absolutely stunning. And surreal because I was actually here. This wasn't a photograph or an establishing shot in a spy thriller. This was real. This was my job.

Then I heard Kira over my shoulder. "It's so beautiful." She was smiling, but at the same time she looked like she might cry.

Later, after a round of naps, we met my lead interview for a pre-dinner drink in the hotel bar. His name was Gary and although he lived in Montreal he was in love with Amsterdam—at least that's what I wrote in the script to explain why our authority on the Red Light District happened to be from Canada. I supposed he looked about like I thought he would—big and sorta odd, but not in a freak, circus kinda way. More like something was just a bit off. Like his skin didn't feel quite right and instead of going to a tailor he'd just given up, resigning himself to his ill-fitting birthday suit.

The fact that he didn't actually live here didn't appear to be much of a handicap. He seemed to know everything there was to know about the Red Light District—or the RLD, as he sometimes called it—and for the past five years he'd been running a free online travelogue dedicated solely to prostitution in Amsterdam. Besides showcasing some of his own amateur photography (mostly mediocre shots of local Dutch girls posed semi-nude in various spots around town) his site also offered extremely thorough explanations of where to go and what to do. And, because Gary put an emphasis on etiquette, there was also much written about where *not* to go and what *not* to do. In exchange for getting to promote his website Gary had agreed to be our guide, both on-camera and off.

After some small talk we adjourned to a nearby restaurant where we were having dinner with the owners of a local adult modeling agency. It was a modest operation run by a Dutch couple in their early thirties named Martina & Jann, although from what I understood it was really Martina's baby and Jann was just around to change the occasional diaper. Over the years Gary had become somewhat friendly with them while booking their talent for his photo shoots, and he'd arranged for them to help me solve a slight problem of my own. It seemed kinda silly, but as Gary had explained to me way back during our first phone conversation, it was nearly impossible to get an actual prostitute on camera. Even though their profession was completely legal, most of them were hell-bent on keeping it a secret from friends and family. There was even a story going around about a drunk tourist who wouldn't stop taking pictures of one of the window girls until she made him stop by sticking a knife in his gut. So instead of the real thing I was hiring local porn stars to play prostitutes. I was, however, going to film them in actual locations, so the story wasn't a complete fabrication.

The restaurant offered tavern fare and I ordered the duck and a double scotch and we toasted our first night in Amsterdam. Then we watched our new Dutch friends smoke cigarettes throughout the entire meal. This tobacco fixation was the European way and quite a departure from the Californian way where we had recently outlawed smoking in restaurants and bars altogether. But then I'm sure Martina & Jann thought my love of scotch was just as excessive and perhaps just as American by the time I was finishing my third double.

After dinner I steered the conversation toward the subject of coffeehouses, and Jann offered to show me a good one that happened to be close by. Gary and Max wanted to come, too, so at the hotel we bid goodnight to the women and walked on.

When we got there, there was no waitress service, so we queued at the counter. A small chalkboard menu offered coffee, beer, and six different kinds of buds, all with predictably dopey names like "Cosmic Paradise" and "Green Eggs & Wham." Jann ordered us beers, an eighth, and some rolling papers. I gave him a few Guilders and watched with fascination as the clerk reached under the counter and emerged with a glass jar and an electric scale. After weighing out the eighth, he put the buds in a little bag and tossed it on the counter next to our papers. Then he poured our beers and Jann laid down my Guilders and the drug deal went off without a hitch—no annoying European police siren sounded and no one worried that we'd just bought oregano. Just a good, clean business transaction.

We all sat around a small table and Jann began grinding the bud into a small, rollable pile atop one of the papers. I sipped my beer and watched Max watching Jann. He was mesmerized. Was this his first time seeing someone roll a joint? Probably. I knew he didn't smoke and that he wasn't about to start now. Max was a clean-cut kid, for sure, but not the kind that made you feel guilty. Instead, he was just curious about how the other half lived, which was why he'd come along to the coffeehouse. He wanted to see firsthand how things were done and I liked that about him—sometimes it's better to be interest*ed*, than interest*ing*.

Now Jann split open one of his cigarettes and began mixing tobacco with the pot. I was horrified. "What are you doing?"

"This is how we do it. We mix it with tobacco."

"What is it with you people and your tobacco lust?" I kidded. "I bet ya mix tobacco in with your ice cream, doncha? Ben & Jerry's *Coffee & Cigarettes Heath Bar Crunch*—that's real popular over here, isn't it?"

He seemed amused, but he didn't stop rolling the hybrid joint. Then he handed it to me with a warning. "Careful, our pot is much stronger than what you have back in the States."

"Have you ever been to the States?"

"No," he smiled, "but this is Amsterdam."

I didn't appreciate his disrespecting good ol' American kind-bud, and even though I was feeling a touch of drunken patriotism coming on I let it go because it was way too early in the trip to start playing the Ugly American. Besides, I loved this town. So I inhaled deep and long and then let it stream out real slow. And right away I felt that old familiar hateful head-rush of tobacco on a drinking night. It made me a little ill, and my face must have said so.

"Pretty strong, huh?" Jann was smiling again. "I told you."

"Listen, I know this is gonna sound crazy, but would you mind twisting me one of those without the tobacco?"

"Without tobacco?" I could tell he thought I was weak, but he rolled me one anyway.

And it was just right—not too strong, not too light, Goldilocks-middle-bear perfect. So that's what I had floating through my head as I walked along the cobblestones back to the Toren, keeping close enough to the canal to watch the streetlamps dance in the dark waters, and I was damn happy. *Just 'cuz you're in Rome don't mean you have to wear a toga made outta tobacco* is what I wanted to tell Jann, but right then I wasn't quite sure if that actually made any sense.

The next morning Gary met us outside one of the hub offices that managed the nearby window rooms. This was where the girls came to pay their hourly rents and pick up their room keys. We were soon joined by Martina & Jann and two of their models, Susana and Jeffrey. Jeffrey was playing "the john," who, according to my script, we were following on a prostitution tour of the RLD. So together the eight of us loitered while Gary stepped inside.

I was beginning to see that prostitution in Amsterdam wasn't just legal, it was organized. But I guess that's exactly why it was legal—so the government could organize and, more importantly, regulate it. Here in Amsterdam the government cared about the health of even its "lowest" citizens. Near as I could tell their thinking was that since they knew hookers were gonna hook sure as the sun was gonna set, they better make sure the girls and their johns were relatively safe. Instead of pimps the girls had an organized union, crisis centers, monthly blood tests, and day care. And since it was a legal, recognized occupation, they were also taxed on their income. I gotta say, it made a lotta sense.

The office door opened and out came Gary with an irritable looking Dutchman carrying a large ring of what looked like at least a hundred keys. We followed this disgruntled Keymaster down a side street past door after door after door. Each one framed a large, full-length window. In some of them you could only see a dark curtain, but others revealed girls sitting on stools with a bright red neon light running along the perimeter.

When I saw the first girl I felt a flush of embarrassment, like I'd opened the bathroom door at a party and found her sitting on the toilet. But with the second and third and fourth there came a degree of familiarity. And soon I could see them as they were, bored young girls making change in tollbooths. What was a little unnerving was that it was ten in the morning on a weekday, and yet there were still plenty of women waiting for some early bird to catch their worm—or perhaps at this hour there were still late revelers out looking for a quickie on their way home. A damn sad sight. "So this is it, huh?"

Gary was walking beside me. "This is it."

According to him fifty Guilders, or about $19 U.S., got you ten minutes of a fuck and suck. And one hundred guilders, or $38 U.S., got you fifteen minutes of "a fuck and suck." That was the phrase he used—"a fuck and suck." I didn't care for it. It sounded like something you did to your car, or carpet. And the whole process seemed so cold. But, on the hooker spectrum, the window girls actually made out alright. They did a high volume, but because of it they were also the best paid. If you played it out it came to 400 Guilders, or around $150 U.S., an hour. Of course, they're not working every minute, but some come close. Interestingly, many of the girls only worked a few hours a week to supplement their more mainstream jobs as waitresses or sales girls. "It's just amazing to me that this exists, that this is accepted by society."

"Well, I don't think it's as much acceptance as tolerance. The thing you have to understand about this city is that it was once the trading capital of the world. It was built on commerce, so there's a real symbiotic relationship between compassion and cold practicality, and a lot of it is based on currency." I could tell by his delivery this was a speech Gary had given many times before. "There's almost a shopkeeper mentality here that I think breeds that tolerance, the idea being that if it makes money, it's good."

But as I looked at each new face, I wasn't so sure I agreed. Forlorn and far from sexy, this street was definitely sending out some bad energy. However, I wasn't gonna dwell on all that negativity while we were working. "It really is just like window shopping, huh?"

"Yes, that's exactly right. If you see something you like, you just go right in and try it on."

When we got to our window it was of course empty. The Keymaster unlocked the door and Gary whispered, "You should pay him now." I pulled out my wad, gave him roughly $200 worth of Guilders, and he nodded and walked back to his office.

Inside, Gary gave us a tour of the room. As he explained, when a girl has accepted a gentleman caller she turns off the red light and draws the curtain so no one on the street gets a free show. Then, in this case, they step down a short flight of stairs to a small room just big enough for a single sized futon and a washbasin. I had to laugh because, minus the sink, it looked a helluva lot like my freshman cubicle back at Groton.

Gary told us the washbasin was used for washing not just hands, but genitals. He also pointed out several panic buttons placed in various strategic locations around the room—seven in all. Then he showed us the back door and said it led to a long hallway running behind all the rooms on the block and that each room had a similar door. Inside the hallway there were security guards, so if a customer was getting rough with a girl she could press a button and a guard would come bursting in to save the day.

After the brief tour I told my "actors," Jeffrey and Susana, that they should get started because we only had the room for an hour.

Jeffrey looked confused. "What do you want us to do?"

"Well, you know, have sex."

"Yeah, but what positions? For how long? What should we do?"

Oh, right. I hadn't given it any thought because up to now my only experience with porn stars had been shooting behind-the-scenes on someone else's set, where *someone else* had been giving direction. But this was my set so I needed to be someone else and tell them what to do. And fast. So I thought for a moment, then tried to sound as professional as possible. "Let's start with oral and then move to three different positions, each one for around five to ten minutes. Max, you tell them when you have each one covered so they can move on to the next one. How's that sound?"

Max and Jeffrey nodded, but Susana looked up with her sweet questioning eyes. "English?" And then softly shook her head.

Alright, so this wasn't going to be easy. I took a deep breath and sat down between Jeffrey and Susana with hopes that proximity might aid understanding. Then I spoke real slow, with a lot of hand gestures. "Okay, first—" Holding up a single index finger, "I want you—" A point to her, "To go down—" A brief mimed blowjob complete with fist pump, head bob, and tongue in cheek, "On him." A point to Jeffrey. "Blowjob, yes?" Again the mime. "You understand, yes?"

She nodded, "Yes."

Phew. This was actually kinda fun—like X-rated charades. Although next time I should make it easier on myself and just bring a copy of the *Kama Sutra* and a pointer. "Good, okay, next, ah, second—" Two fingers held up, "Jeffrey—" A point to Jeffrey, "Will have sex—" With my left hand I curled my fingers, then joined the tips of my index and thumb so I formed a hole, then I put my right index finger in and out of that hole, "With you—" And a point to her. "Sex, yes?" and I made the same sex gesture.

"Yes."

"In the missionary position." Still I made the same in & out gesture.

"Ah, what is miss-shun-airy?" Kira and Max stifled a laugh.

"You know, missionary, uh... normal," and I pressed my palms together so they were parallel to the ground and began clapping loudly. And now everyone was laughing, probably because I looked more like a wounded seal than a missionary.

"Ross, she doesn't understand." Martina was trying to help. "We don't use that word with sex."

No, of course they didn't. While the Dutch may mix their tobacco with their pot, they certainly do not mix their religion with their sex.

"Alright, so I'm the girl—" and I leaned back on the bed and spread my legs, "And the guy's on top." Then I pretended like I was holding the hips of an invisible man.

More laughing, then Martina spoke some Dutch.

"Does she understand?"

"Yes, now she does."

"And can you tell her I also need doggie style—is that the same here?"

"Yes, it's the same." And Martina spoke some more Dutch and I realized I'd been pretty stupid not to have her translate from the beginning.

"Great, okay, any questions?"

Jeffrey had one. "Should I do oral on her?"

"Well, I'm thinking not. At least in America I don't think a guy would go down on a prostitute." *Although if she happened to be off-duty and had just driven three hours, then maybe...* "Gary, what do you think?"

"No, he most certainly would *not* do that." And he made a sour face.

"Alright, then it's settled. Don't go down on her." I stood up and took Kira with me to the top of the stairs so we'd be out of the way. Max rolled tape and Jeffrey and Susana went right into it.

And as I sat on the cold, maroon tiled stairs of this Red Light District window room watching two Dutch porn stars fuck each other just like I told them to, I couldn't help noticing how easy it was to slip from television producer to porn director. And yeah, it bugged me a bit. This wasn't the job I thought I'd signed on for. But hey, at least I was in Amsterdam.

By the time I was directing my next scene, about twenty-four hours later at a brothel called Ria's, I was just happy the girl spoke English. The room we were shooting in was decorated in the perfect bordello cliché—black, gold, and leopard prints with a round bed and mirrors covering the walls. Gary picked this place for one simple reason—they had said yes. The nicer, top of the line joints like Yab-Yum and Club Elegance had turned him down because they didn't need the publicity. But Ria's was more middle-of-the-pack and they figured a mention on Playboy TV couldn't hurt.

According to Gary all the brothels basically operated the same way. You go to the bar, pick out a girl, then retire to one of the back rooms for an hour-long "private party." This kind of privacy runs you around $150 to $200 depending on the quality of the establishment. From what I'd seen so far, this was easily the most civilized way to pay for sex.

When we were ready to begin shooting I was forced to leave the room. Otherwise Max's camera would catch me in all the mirrors. So I went back to the lounge area where Gary, Martina & Jann were having coffee at the bar. Kira was lying on a couch going over her lines. Sitting at one of the small cocktail tables all by himself was the boyfriend of the Belle du Jour. He wasn't even reading. He was just sitting there, staring into space. I sat on the couch next to Kira and whispered, "Can you believe she brought her boyfriend?"

"You mean you've never seen a suitcase pimp?"

"What's that?"

"Suitcase pimps are the models' boyfriends who hang out at the shoots and show up pulling the girl's suitcase. See, look under his table." Sure enough, at the guy's feet was an overnight bag, the kind with wheels and a retractable handle.

I asked Kira why a suitcase, and she explained that the girls need something to carry all their lingerie and stripper clothes in. And then I remembered that Chainsmokin' Taimie had brought a similar suitcase to our shoot at the Argyle and it all made sense. Although I still didn't understand how anyone could deal with the fact that a complete stranger was fucking his girlfriend—quite loudly, I might add—in the very next room. Amazing what some men will do for love.

By the time we broke for dinner we were almost done with the two-day shoot. I should have been celebrating, but instead I spent the entire meal with an eye on the nearest window to see it if it was still raining. It was.

"How are you holding up?" Kira knew I was stressed.

"It's gonna stop raining," I said, as if I knew. I'd reserved an open-air boat for a three-hour canal ride. The plan was to get beauty shots of Amsterdam as well as b-roll of Gary photographing one of Martina's girls as we motored through the Red Light District. It was gonna be gorgeous footage. But not if it was raining. I checked my watch. We were due at the dock in thirty minutes.

"What if it doesn't?"

"The rain always stops."

"How do you know?"

Max had been listening. "Either way, the girl's gonna be freezing her tits off." He could be too practical sometimes.

"Martina, you told the girl it was gonna be cold, right?" Many times I'd warned her that the boat girl needed to be comfortable getting naked in low temperatures.

"She knows."

"It's gonna stop raining." It had to.

When our waitress brought the check, Max tried to take my mind off the things I couldn't control by returning to one of our running jokes. "I wonder which window she works at."

I laughed and for a moment forgot about the rain because suddenly I was thinking of all those women I'd known back on the East Coast. Maybe they'd been right about the Red Light District. Maybe it *was* a pox on society. But I didn't muddy our dinner by speaking of such thoughts. Instead, with mock *gravitas*, I replied "But don't we all find ourselves in a window at some point in our life?"

As we exited the restaurant it turned out I was right. The rain was slowing down. And it was fully stopped by the time we got to the dock and the twenty-foot flat-bottomed motorboat that was to be our limousine for the evening. Because of the weather it was all closed up. I met the driver, Hilda, a shorthaired middle-aged Dutch woman with a can-do flair about her. I told her we needed the back open, and she got right on it. I liked her already.

Then I noticed Martina's brow was furrowing while she spoke Dutch with the model and her suitcase pimp, and when she turned to me I knew it was gonna be bad news.

"Uh, Ross?"

"Yes."

"She says it's too cold. Is it possible we can do the shoot with the top up?"

I almost laughed, but I was too damn mad. "No, we can't. The whole point of the shoot is to see the city lights behind her. Please explain to her how beautiful it's going to look, and how beautiful *she's* going to look."

Martina translated and there was an exchange. Then, "She says it's too cold. She just got over the flu."

"But I thought we told her it was going to be cold. Didn't we tell her to be prepared for cold weather?" By *we* of course I meant Martina.

"Yes, I told her."

I bet she hadn't.

There was more Dutch, and I knew the model wasn't budging. Martina was beginning to look like she might cry. "I'm sorry Ross, I don't know what to say."

"Can we get somebody else? There's gotta be someone we can call."

Martina & Jann looked at each other, trying to think of something, but I could tell they had nothing. They were in over their heads. I wouldn't be surprised if we had shot their entire stable of girls during the past two days. Hilda had finished converting the boat and was now waiting for us to board. I couldn't believe how close I'd come to a perfect shoot, and yet I was still so far. I was missing a major visual piece of the story. I was desperate. "What if I paid her more money—say double?"

But before Martina could translate Kira jumped in. "Ross, I'll do it. Gary can shoot me."

"Now that's a wonderful idea!" Gary was suddenly beaming. He'd been wanting to see her naked since the moment he met her.

"You sure?"

"Yeah. The boat's gonna be too crowded anyway."

"Perfect." Kira was saving my ass. "We'll shoot Kira." And I told Martina not to worry, that it wasn't her fault, even though I suspected it was.

Martina spoke some more Dutch to the model and then turned back to me. I was expecting her to say the girl had changed her mind, that she was bluffing and now that we'd called her on it she was willing to shoot outside. But instead Martina said, "Uh, she's wondering, can she still stay for the ride?"

And now I did laugh. "Ah... no. If she ain't getting naked, she ain't riding in the boat. But please, don't say it like that. Tell her, you know, thanks for coming and we're very sorry it didn't work out, and we hope to work with her again sometime, yadda-yadda-yadda, but she's gotta go."

As the model and her suitcase pimp slunk away, I put my arm around Kira, and with a big shit-eating grin turned to Jann. "You know, you may have stronger pot, but in America we have stronger girls." And I gave Kira a squeeze.

Then we all climbed aboard, and Hilda showed me the wet bar before pushing off. After passing out some beers I poured myself a substantial scotch and settled in. As gorgeous as Amsterdam was when we first arrived, it was even more breathtaking at night. And this was definitely the way to see it. Everywhere we went the city was illuminated, but subtle and artful, not at all gaudy. Strings of white lights seemed to be hanging everywhere—from the bridges, the other boats, the stone walls. And by the time we were motoring through a particularly amazing stretch called Seven Bridges we were well into our third round of drinks and passing a joint. As I watched Max shooting with a beer in one hand and a smile on his face, I knew this wasn't a bad way to make a living.

Around halfway into the trip we headed for the Red Light District. Which meant it was time for Kira to take off her clothes, and there she was again—absolutely gorgeous. Was her ass actually glowing? The brisk night air had pulled her skin tight, and from where I stood in my cashmere sweater I could see she'd turned all goose-bumpy and nipply. I just hoped the beer and grass were keeping her at least a little warm.

Then, without hesitation, like a gymnast mounting her apparatus, Kira climbed up on the back of the boat and went right into her routine. While Max rolled and Gary popped his flash, I watched in awe. Kira had a big smile on her face and she worked it like the pro she was—holding each pose just long enough for Gary to get his shot, then giving him a different look, each one more flattering than the next. And her eyes were ablaze. You just couldn't catch her in an awkward position. So self-confident, so self-aware. She musta been a helluva stripper, I thought, as she reached for the three-foot red, white, and blue Netherlands flag that was flying on the railing and began incorporating it into her act.

When we reached the heart of the RLD the canal narrowed so the edges were only about ten feet from each side of the boat, and suddenly a small army of gawkers was lining the banks three to five people deep. It was like we were in a single float parade and Kira was the grand marshal, waving the flag as she called out, "Hello Amsterdam! We love you Amsterdam!" And the crowd loved her back, cheering their appreciation as loud as they could.

The energy of the audience turned everything up a notch. I could feel us all get a simultaneous rush of adrenaline and I knew I was witnessing something magical. The freedom and beauty of this wonderful city was merging with the freedom and beauty of this wonderful woman and together they became one—Kira was Amsterdam and Amsterdam was Kira. Where else could this happen? Who else could make it happen? Surely not that chilly Dutch girl we had to send away. No, this was pure Kira, caught in a moment. And, like watching a fabulous roman candle, I knew it would end all too soon. So I held my breath and tried not to blink as I thought to myself, *"Merrily, merrily, merrily, merrily, life is but a dream..."*

By ten the following morning Kira and I were finishing off the previous evening's joint as we stood in line with Max outside the

Van Gogh museum. I'd planned it so that we'd have the whole day free for sightseeing, and this was our first stop.

Inside, we all got the audio tour and criss-crossed our separate ways through the museum. Of course, it was amazing to see all that Van Gogh under one roof, and I enjoyed rehearing everything I'd forgotten from my Art History classes about Vincent and his patron brother Theo. Ironically, one of the reasons I didn't remember so well was that I used to go to those classes fairly high, and here I was stoned again, looking at all the pretty pictures, marveling at Vincent's drive, his stubborn determination, his unwavering will.

Then I felt guilty. I knew the pot was sending me that way but I didn't fight it. It was good to feel. And to remember why I'd come to LA—not necessarily to be an artist, but at least to write screenplays. I'd written for a while, but not nearly long enough. My fingers never bled—they didn't even have calluses. Sure, I needed to pay the bills and that's why I took the job at E!, but then I let that job take me. I stopped writing for myself because I was writing for *The E! True Hollywood Story*. And now I was writing for *Sexcetera*, but both gigs were a sour sellout of the original dream. I was soft and I knew it. So weak and always thirsty and never certain... Best thing you could say was that I'd compromised.

Then I saw Kira walking in my general direction. We smiled and pulled down our headsets like coming up for air in an underwater cave and I didn't tell her what a loser I was. Instead I asked her how she liked the museum.

"I'm so happy we're here," and she went on bubbling over with appreciation. She was particularly fond of the Asian influenced work, and while the famously strange-angled bedroom set didn't do that much for her, she thought it was "so cool" that they had the last painting he'd worked on before he died and it was "too perfect" that he'd painted those ominous black birds in the sky, as if he knew his day was coming and wanted to add his own vultures.

While she spoke I felt a flash of all the East Coast museums of my youth, and I remembered the coffee-bellied warmth of grazing through the MFA and the Met with svelte, autumn-sweatered girls and how their hair fell softly on corduroy jackets. And then I didn't care that I was never going to write anything of consequence. I was just glad Kira was hanging here beside me in this new museum.

Once we had our fill of Van Gogh, we dashed through the Rijksmuseum so we could say we saw it. After all that we still had a couple hours before dinner, so Kira and I headed for a spa that happened to be a few doors down from the Toren. She'd noticed it on the way to dinner our first night in town, and I'd promised to treat her to a massage when the shoot was over as a reward for a job well done. I offered to pay for Max as well, but he opted for a nap in his room. Me, I'd never gotten a professional massage and I was excited to see what all the hype was about. Although I have to admit I was a little nervous about having a stranger laying their hands on me. But it was just a massage. How bad could it be?

When we got there the woman at the front desk told us the masseuse had gone home for the day—perhaps she had window reservations—but the spa was still open for another two hours so we could use the saunas and the jacuzzis. I handed over some Guilders and she gave us a pair of towels that were so small they looked like they were for drying dishes. "The changing room is over there." She pointed to a door behind her. The changing *room*—as in one single room?

Kira must have seen my quizzical look. "It's unisex."

"Oh."

I let Kira lead the way, and we walked into a long row of lockers with seven or eight men and women in various stages of disrobing and re-robing. Kira stopped and casually began taking off her clothes. I turned away and rather rigidly took off my jacket. *I couldn't fucking believe it.* Kira Reed was about to see my Lil' Guy. And it was cold in here. Sure, I'd seen *her* naked—just last night, in fact—but what's good for the goose isn't always good for the gander. Especially this gander. I mean, she was a model, Grade A goose. And me? Well, I was just me. An average looking gander. Maybe slightly above average with a tan. But not only did I happen to be extremely pale at the moment, I'd also been doing a lot more drinking than working out. But what could I do? Claim I had a sudden attack of irritable bowel syndrome and run back to my hotel room? Actually that might work... No. No, I had no choice. I had to walk this plank. So I did.

My fingers began taking off my clothes, and then there I was— naked, standing right next to her, sucking in my gut the best I could and holding my tiny towel in the general vicinity of my crotch to give me some semblance of modesty.

"Ready?" Kira was waiting with her towel over her shoulder.

"Yep," I lied.

I followed her into the big open bathhouse. There were saunas on the left and hot tubs and cool pools scattered throughout the room. She headed for a sauna, so I beelined to the first empty tub I saw. Stepping into the still water I was a little surprised to find it lukewarm—not hot, not cool, just kinda tepid. And shouldn't it be bubbling? Well, at least my heart rate was dropping back to a somewhat normal level. Then, just when I was almost comfortable, a naked woman with a trim, European build climbed into the tub with me. I smiled an innocent nod at her. *Oh Jesus.* Now I was naked with a stranger—and she was close. And she was leaning toward me. What was she doing? *Holy shit!* Her hand was heading right toward me. And then she reached past me and pressed a button over my left shoulder. Suddenly the tub erupted as the air-jets fired up and the surface of the pool was covered with bubbles. *Oh... Okay.* I smiled another nod as she retreated to the opposite corner. This was better. Much better. Not only did the bubbles conceal my nakedness, they actually felt good. And the water was even warming up. I closed my eyes and tried to enjoy the moment. And I did, for a few relatively relaxing minutes, until I heard someone else getting in beside me.

It was Kira and *damn* she was a whole new kind of sexy, all sweaty and glistening. "The sauna feels soooooo good."

"Oh yeah? I better try it," I said, thinking I could go hide in the steam room while she stayed behind in the tub.

But my plan was thwarted. "C'mon," and she stood, and then I had to stand, and together we got out of the tub and I was naked in the room once again. And, once again, I was left clutching that ridiculous towel as I followed her world-class ass to the sauna. Then, for a sudden moment, I felt myself outside of my body and laughing hysterically. *Where the fuck was I? And what was I doing naked? And when did everything get so damn sophisticated?*

When we got inside the sauna there was so much steam I could barely make out the horseshoe of tiered benches. Kira sat on one of the higher levels and pointed to her feet. "Sit here," and I did. Alright, this could work—my back was to her so she couldn't see my Balzac, and all the steam was much better cover than a skimpy towel. Then I felt her hands on my shoulder. *What was she—Ohhhhhh... She was giving me a massage.* And a damn good one. For the next ten minutes Kira gave me the best backrub I'd ever had. My tired muscles were putty in her practiced hands, and before long the sweat of all my accumulated toxins was pouring out of me like mountain stream water through a mining sieve. When she was done she left one hand on my shoulder and leaned toward me so that I felt the unmistakable brush of a breast against my back, as she whispered, "Did that feel good?"

I whispered back, "Yeah."

"Let's go get cooled off."

She stepped past me and I followed her back toward the tubs. And I would have followed her anywhere. On the way I realized I'd left my towel behind, but now I didn't mind. Was I even naked? Kira found us a cool pool and I loved the invigorating rush that came with the sudden change of temperature. Wow, the Europeans sure knew what they were doing. I bet this did wonders for the pores.

After a cleansing minute or two we got out. I didn't have a towel so Kira patted herself down, then gave me hers. Then she went to find another and came back with bathrobes. She led me out into the lobby where we sat down in a pair of ergonomic reclining chairs. I leaned back, put a towel over my head, and closed my eyes. This was bliss. My body and soul had never been more aligned. Total harmony.

After a nap that felt like a million years I awoke to Kira's soft voice. "You want some water." Pulling the towel away from my eyes I saw her gorgeous, almost surreally pretty face framed with a halo. I knew it was caused by the overhead track lighting and my squinting through blurry contacts, but still, she looked like an angel. She was dressed in her street clothes and was offering me a tall glass of water.

"Thanks."

"They're about to close."

I didn't want to move, but I did. I went back into the locker room, which was now empty. As I changed, besides feeling incredibly relaxed, I also felt a strange sense of accomplishment. Like some sort of NOLS or Outward Bound-style training, I'd overcome my anxiety and even managed to have a good time in the process.

It seemed ridiculous, but being naked in front of strangers—and in front of Kira—had made me a stronger, more confident person. At least today.

"Why don't you two just have sex?" Max was only sorta kidding. We were having our last dinner in Amsterdam and Kira had just left the table to go to the bathroom.

"C'mon, she's a married woman."

Kira and I had been dominating all recent conversation with talk of going to one of the best brothels in town, Club Elegance. Max was extremely practical, some might even say frugal, so he was suggesting that instead of paying a brothel Kira and I should keep our money and simply fuck each other.

"How do you know the prostitute isn't married?"

"You're right, I don't. But I do know Kira. And I know her husband. It's just wrong." This was a ridiculous conversation. "Besides, I'm the last guy that Kira would want to fuck. And really, it isn't even about the sex. It's about going to a brothel."

Kira had been pushing the idea all night. Not so much because she was dying to fuck a woman, but because she was a trouble-maker who always fought for the experience even if that meant battling against the current. And on this occasion we were simpatico. Brothels just happened to be the main attraction here. If we were in Chicago we wouldn't be trolling for hookers, we'd be eating pizza and going to a blues club. And if we were in New Amsterdam we'd catch a Broadway show. But we were in Old Amsterdam, and we'd already been to the coffeehouses and the Van Gogh Museum, so now we were going to a brothel. "I mean, with your logic, we might as well stay home and masturbate."

"Well, that was going to be my next suggestion."

Kira came back to the table, which put a quick end to the debate. "Shall we go?" We said our goodnights to Max, and then we were in a cab and on our way.

When we got there, the front door was large and wooden with a tasteful plaque that read "Club Elegance." Inside was a muscle-bound black man with a British accent bulging inside a tuxedo. He would have made a great movie henchman. "I'm sorry, but I'm afraid we don't offer any male companions for the young lady." We told him we already knew that, and then he explained, "If you desire a threesome, you'll both still have to pay full price."

A threesome? Me and Kira and another girl! I knew my face must have turned twenty-one shades of red as the thought sprinted through my mind, but then I recovered. "No, no. We don't desire a thr—a thr—" I couldn't even say the word, so instead I spat out, "We each want a girl."

Kira smiled. "Yes, we each want a girl." Then she generously paid our door fees, which were around $50 U.S. and included a handful of drink tickets. The Henchman directed us up a staircase to a lounge. It looked just like an upscale brothel should look—Victorian décor, old furniture, ornate woodworking, with lots of paintings of naked ladies in repose, odalisque style. We saddled up at the bar and began trading in our drink tickets—Jack & Cokes for the lady, Tanqueray & Tonics for the gentleman.

After round two Kira asked, "See anything you like?"

"No, not yet." I could tell she was beginning to think I might chicken out. And I had a hunch part of her fun tonight was testing me, seeing how far her prep school producer would trespass over the line. But I wasn't having second thoughts. I just wasn't all that attracted to anyone I'd seen so far. I suppose I'd been naïve, but since this was a high-end establishment I'd expected to find a bevy of Stephanie Seymour look-alikes prowling about. Instead, all

I saw was four or five average looking girls chatting with two or three older men in cheap suits. Still, I wasn't too worried, and I certainly wasn't in a hurry. I just needed to put together an appropriate buzz for the occasion and then I could make my choice. And sure enough, after another round I saw a slender blonde sitting on the couch in the corner. "How about her?"

"Yeah, she's the one I'd choose. Let's go talk to her."

Getting off the barstool, I was suddenly a lot more nervous than I thought. *Was I really going through with this?* Yes, I guess I was, but as I made my way over to her something didn't feel right. This wasn't a sportsman's outing. This was like shooting deer with a machine gun. The game was rigged. I hadn't even said hello and I already knew I was going to be fucking her within the hour. And not because I was so damn charming, but because I had a machine gun—my machine gun in this case being around $200. However, instead of ruining the whole evening right when it was about to get interesting, I told myself that I was back at Wesleyan and at a party. I'd just recognized a girl from my Domesticity and Gender in 18th Century American Literature class. We'd been trading eyes for the past three weeks and now I was about to introduce myself.

"Hi there, I'm Ross." And the rest was easy. A slightly heavier girl appeared and together the four of us drank and laughed and made silly small talk. My girl was named Sophie, and she was from some other place in Holland that ended in "dam." I told her where we came from, what we were doing in town, and then we discussed how cold it was here compared to sunny Los Angeles—so cold, I said, that if I wore underwear, which I didn't, I'd be wearing a pair of flannel boxers with a plaid pattern. After another round Sophie asked if I wanted to get a room. Wow, this was one great party.

Kira and I were told to see the manager by the bar, where we handed over our credit cards. This linebacker of a woman explained that we had the rooms for one hour, and after it was up if we wanted more time we'd be charged an additional hour. This little business transaction momentarily interrupted my college party conceit, but I got it back by ordering a couple more G & Ts. And then the four of us made our way down the hallway into a medium sized room. As soon as the door shut I was aware that I was officially on the clock—59 minutes, 59 seconds and counting.

The room looked a lot like the lounge, except there was a large bed and a tub big enough for two. I lit up a joint and passed it around and we all got a little stoned, and I worked on one of the Tanquerays. After the joint was done I checked my watch and saw I had about 45 minutes left and my buzz was right on time.

"Alright, you two better get outta here," Kira and her girl left for another room, and immediately Sophie started to run a bath.

I undressed her, and she was a beautiful young Dutch girl. Then we had a kiss and she took off my sweater and my shirt and we had another kiss and I was aroused. And the last place I wanted to be was in that damn bathtub, which was so big it was taking way too long to fill. Forty minutes left. As I sipped my last drink I started to think that this bath idea was all about wasting my allotted hour. *Was Sophie trying to delay the sex as long as possible with hopes that I wouldn't be able to finish on time and then would be forced to buy a second hour?* Well, there was no way I was gonna pay double for something I shouldn't be buying in the first place. So at the thirty minute mark I put the kibosh on the bathtub gambit by turning off the faucet myself.

Sophie seemed disappointed. Or surprised. Maybe even upset. I wasn't sure of the translation. So I tried to say something sweet to change her expression. "Listen, Sophie, it's important to me that you—" a point to her, "enjoy it. That *you* have a good time." But it wasn't that important, I thought, because money was most definitely changing hands. And Sophie hadn't just driven three hours to see me. *So there was no way that I*—a point to me—*was going down*—waving my tongue through two outstretched fingers—*on her*—a point to her. But I didn't say or mime all that. Instead, I finished my drink and took off my pants.

And then she giggled. *Could she be laughing at my Lil' Guy?* "What? What's so funny?" But I wasn't upset. Not yet. Surely there had to be some mistake. Hadn't she seen *Unforgiven*? Didn't she know this was how whores got cut?

"You were not kidding."

I wasn't kidding? About what? Oh, maybe about it being important that she enjoy it, but my erection seemed to be more of a sign that *I* was enjoying it—at least, so far so good—so that explanation didn't really work. "I don't understand."

"You really do not wear underwear." And she giggled again.

Now I laughed. And smiled and kissed her like I meant it. And I did, sort of, because her giggle was a sign that she'd been paying attention to me earlier. She'd actually listened, and not only had she remembered what I'd said but it had honestly made her laugh.

At the twenty-five minute mark I dove in and started swimming my laps. And yeah, maybe I was a little obsessed with my time, but only because it was money and I was scared of finishing too late. But I also didn't want to finish too early, either. The way I saw it, leaving too much time on the clock was just as bad. So to get the full bang for my buck I needed to draw the whole thing out at a nice leisurely pace and use every last minute. At least, that was the plan.

With ten minutes left, the phone on the bedside table started to ring. Startled, I answered it and heard the manager's voice giving a brothel version of a wake up call. "Ten minutes left."

"Yes, I'm quite aware of that, thank you very much." And I hung up. The final ten minutes I felt something like John Elway running the two-minute drill—methodically marching up the field, managing the clock, and then crossing the goal line just as time expired. Alright, maybe I had a minute or two to spare, but it was close enough to feel like I won the game. Then the phone rang again, and this time the manager asked, "You want more time?"

"No, that won't be necessary. I'm all set." Then Sophie and I got dressed with more small talk and pretended that we liked each other, which was the perfect end to my little college party fantasy.

Back in the lounge I found Kira chatting with her girl.

"Have fun?" she asked with a bright smile.

"Ohhh yeah."

"Ready?"

"Yeah, let's get outta here."

Downstairs, the Henchman had the house car waiting to take us home. We got in the back of the black BMW sedan and, as soon as the driver shut the door behind us, we both broke out laughing. Then I asked, "So what'd you do with yours?"

"I had a hot bath and she gave me a wonderful massage."

"Perfect. You got your massage after all."

As the BMW rumbled over the cobblestones I suddenly realized how tired I was. We drove in silence, and soon I was wondering why I wasn't at all bothered by the fact that, for the first time in my life, I'd just paid for sex. Even sleeping with that off-duty escort back in Orlando had been a little unsettling. But now, nothing. It was just something I did. And something I hoped no one back in the States would ever find out about. As we neared the Toren I broke our silence, "So ah, this is just between you and me, right?"

"Don't you know anything?"

"Whaddaya mean?"

"What happens on the road, stays on the road."

VII

Stačí, Stačí

*B*y the time our plane touched down at Prague's Ruzyne Airport I was no closer to deciphering the *Ceske Noviny* sports section than I'd been an hour earlier when I stepped on board and was first handed the damn thing. Of course, Kira and Max were no help. So, sadly, it was without the news from last night's NHL action that I made my way slowly down the aisle.

But when I stepped onto the skyway, I was suddenly too shocked to give a damn about hockey. Instead, I only cared about myself and the sight of my own name—a small, handwritten sign that read, "ROSS DALE." It was held rather rigidly by a middle-aged Czech woman in an official-looking uniform. And she wasn't happy. *Was I in trouble?* Was there leftover Amsterdam pot in my bags? Or in my pockets?!? I had a flash of the *Midnight Express* tarmac scene followed by a fast sinking feeling. But then I noticed the man standing next to her. Ashen hair, a weathered brown leather jacket, and equally weathered skin—he was most definitely *not* official-looking.

"Richard?"

"Welcome to Prague!" This was Richard Mailer and his easy going drawl. He was the subject of my story—an American ex-pat who'd been producing and directing porn here in Prague for the past five years. We all shook hands, and he introduced us to a portly gentleman in sweats and a puffy winter jacket. "This is Petr. He's the bank." Then Richard and the Czech woman led and we followed—not down the ramp, through the gate, and on to the baggage claim with the rest of the passengers, but instead out the side door, down the stairs, and onto the icy tarmac where a small shuttle bus was waiting just for us.

Climbing on board, Kira and I exchanged smiles that said, *This is so fucking cool!,* while Richard and I made easy, ping-pong small talk—playing for the volley, not the point. Soon we were stopping and walking inside a large, almost empty VIP courtesy lounge. Right away Richard asked for our passports with a nod to the same hovering Czech official. "She needs 'em to get your bags and get you through customs. And take it from me, you do not want to wait through Czech customs." Petr snorted a laugh as we handed them over.

Once we'd all found a seat I asked, "So where's the best place to exchange money?"

"Petr, they want to exchange some money."

Petr turned serious. "How much?"

"Oh, I dunno, I guess $500."

Petr unzipped his bulging fanny pack and pulled out his cell phone. As he dialed I suddenly understood why Richard had called him the bank. His fanny pack was stuffed with all kinds of colored currencies, neatly organized with paper clips. It looked like he had the entire set of Monopoly money. Petr spoke tersely in what I assumed was Czech, then hung up and told me the current exchange rate. "It's 39.67 Korunas to the Dollar."

Which sounded right—although he just as easily could have been asking his wife what was for dinner—so I pulled out my wallet and handed over $500 to this large, fat man wrapped up in a parka and a fanny pack. Upon receiving my own stack of Parker

Brothers Korunas I looked around to see if anyone had scoped our transaction, but there were only two others in the room—a bundled up woman chatting with yet another rotund gentleman. However, this one wasn't wearing a parka or a fanny pack. Instead he was dressed like a Ritz-Carlton doorman.

"That's a Russian five star general, if you can believe it." Richard had caught me staring. "His name is Igor Khartov."

"You know him?"

"I know *of* him. He keeps a girl here in Prague. A young one. I see him out at the clubs whenever he's in town."

The Cold War was over and Russia was a shadow of her former self, but the uniform still had to impress the ladies. It certainly impressed me. It was wild to think that ten years ago this could have been a scene in a spy thriller, but now it was just a prologue to a porn shoot.

When our bags materialized, we followed Richard out to a private parking lot and piled into Petr's black BMW sedan. Kira, Max, and I squeezed into the back, with Kira in the middle, and as we sped away from the Ruzyne Airport I liked being pressed up against her. As entertaining as all this was, it was even better to be able to share it with someone—with her, with a friend.

Richard and I continued to chat, but now we were discussing our dinner plans, which were more important than usual. While I was here Richard wanted to shoot a sex scene in a local cathouse called The Red Light. It was, as he explained, a working man's brothel, and the reason Richard wanted to shoot there was not because it was such a wonderful location but because he had an in. He knew the owner, another American ex-pat, who'd granted him permission to use his club on one condition—that he and his young boy-toy be wined & dined by the Playboy people at one of the finest restaurants in town. Seemed fair.

"They have an expression here that means 'correct'—it's important to be correct, to do things right," Richard explained.

"I know it sounds kinda silly, especially since the club owner and I aren't even Czech, we're just a couple of Americans for chrissakes, but that's the way things are here in Prague sometimes—silly and *correct*."

They dropped us off at our hotel, a big boxy Hilton that once upon a time was probably some form of communist housing. After checking in and washing up we hurried over to Richard's nearby apartment for a quick drink before dinner.

"Sorry, guys, the elevator's broken." As I made my way up and up Richard's extra long, extra wide marble staircase I could see a tuft of white hair leaning over the edge of the fourth floor. "Actually, the elevator hasn't worked since I moved in three years ago."

"Ah, the sour aftertaste of communism, eh Richard?"

"You got it, pal."

Stepping into his foyer, I stumbled over a pair of beat up cowboy boots. They were part of a large collection that was meant to be neatly lined up against the wall, but, because of an obvious lack of a proper maid service, was not. There was also a pair of six shooters in a western holster slung over a coat hook, which I assumed were fake because that's what they would have been if they were in my apartment. They reminded me of one of our earlier phone conversations. "Prague is sort of the Wild West," Richard had said. "Even though it's a very safe town to walk around and do anything you want, life is still kinda cheap here. Literally you can have a man killed for $175, and that's not a problem at all." Maybe those guns were loaded after all.

"Marketa?" Richard called out in a friendly tone. "Come meet the Playboy people." Marketa appeared and Richard introduced her as his assistant. If she was older than eighteen it wasn't by much. "She takes care of everything." She was not ugly. Even pretty. And warm. The kind of girl that grows on you—fast.

"Can I get you something to drink?" And her English was excellent.

"Absolutely."

"Yeah, what are you guys drinking?" Richard asked.

"What are *you* drinking?" I volleyed.

"Vodka & Red Bull."

"Well, then it's Vodka & Red Bull for me, too." Kira and Max agreed.

"Good," Marketa smiled with a look of mock relief, "because Vodka is all we have."

"Well lemme give ya the tour," Richard said. We were standing in a long hallway that appeared to run the length of the apartment. He led us first into the wide-open living room with a sprawling overstuffed L-shaped couch that belonged in an opium den. The adjoining office was a mess, which I took to mean he actually did a lot of work there. Polaroids of young naked girls standing at attention were strewn all over his office. Each one had a different Czech name handwritten in black sharpie.

"Your girlfriends?" I asked.

"Some of them." Richard pulled off a wink, then explained that they were casting shots—the porn equivalent of a headshot—which directors and producers used to choose girls for their movies. I guess the guys' shots stayed in the drawer.

Next on the tour was a smallish bedroom. "This is where Marketa sleeps. We used to date, but now she's just my assistant."

"How old is she?" I had to ask, but I tried to sell it with an admiring whisper.

"Nineteen." He smiled. Richard was fifty if he was a day. "She's tremendous. I don't know what I'd do without her." But he wasn't trying to be funny or anything close to lewd. And it struck me that, for Richard, Prague *was* like the Wild West. He was free to do whatever he wanted.

Just then Marketa came with our vodka and we toasted and sipped and then continued our tour. Eventually we wound up in the kitchen, refreshing our drinks.

"I love your place—it's gigantic!" Kira was impressed.

"I've been told it's one of the biggest in Prague, but I don't know if I believe it. Ol' Wenceslas has got a pretty big spread too."

I didn't know who Ol' Wenceslas was, but Kira sure did. "The palace! Oh, we have to go the palace." Then to me. "We have to see it before we leave." Excited, her voice rose like a child's.

I spun the conversation back to our host. "You know, Richard, I'm not saying it's a competition, but I think it's safe to say that we already like you a helluva lot better than the guy we did the story on in Amsterdam."

"Oh really? What was wrong with him?"

"Well for starters he never gave us vodka," Kira said

"And he sure as hell never picked us up at the airport. Not even once," I added.

"Yeah, that was so nice of you," Kira added

And Max echoed, "Oh, that was the best."

"*Stačí, stačí.*" Richard was smiling and I knew he had enjoyed picking us up as much as we had enjoyed being picked up.

Then Marketa mimicked his American accent, "*Staaah-chee, Staaah-chee,*" and they shared a laughing look. I assumed it was some local phrase Richard had picked up, but before I could ask, Marketa reminded us it was time to go to dinner. We were five and Czech cabbies were only allowed four, so we had to call two.

Downstairs, Kira and I took the first car while Max stayed behind to continue chatting with Richard about the latest advances in digital video technology. The moment I shut the door I knew I'd forgotten something. I rolled down the window. "Ah, Richard, where are we going?" He laughed, and Marketa spoke to the driver in Czech.

As we sped away I suddenly realized how naked I was. I had no knowledge of the local language and, because my cell phone didn't work overseas, no way to call for English speaking help. But then I looked over my shoulder just as the second cab was pulling up, and I felt much better knowing they'd be close behind. *Why was I on edge?*

The cab dropped us off in front of a rundown building. Above the doorway there was a cheap, backlit sign that read "Aqua 2000." I'd promised Richard that we'd wait for him outside—this way we could be *correct* and all go in together—so despite the freezing cold we stayed on the sidewalk. Then I heard the silence. The street was almost deserted. The temperature might've explained the lack of foot traffic, but I didn't see any cars around, either.

"I thought this place was supposed to be nice," Kira said.

"I'm sure its lovely inside." *Why did I say lovely? No one under sixty says lovely.*

"I hope so."

"It's just the communism. Those were hard years. They took their toll and the face of this city is worn down. But on the inside—on the inside lies the heart and soul of a beautiful people." *What was I talking about? I sounded like a fool.* "Just like the inside of this restaurant. I'm sure there's gonna be great food and really mellow lighting."

"Yeah, well, I was here just last year and I ate in plenty of places that were nice on the inside *and* on the out—" Then *wham*, the unmistakable sound of a car crash. Kira grabbed my arm as we spun around to see what happened. Yep, across the street and diagonally down from us a car had hit a street sign. And the driver wasn't getting out to survey the damage. Instead he backed up as fast as he could, switched gears, and screeched outta sight.

"Isn't that leaving the scene of an accident?" Kira asked.

"I'm not so sure they have that law here."

"He musta slipped on the ice."

"The ice in his vodka, maybe."

"Let's go inside and wait. It's cold." She was right. It was. And Richard shoulda been here by now.

We went through the weather-beaten entrance and up a staircase onto a seedy landing with another Aqua 2000 sign. A man in a tired suit was sitting on a barstool behind a peeling Formica maitre de table. He appeared to be guarding a dirty burgundy curtain.

"Ah, hi, Richard Mailer? We're meeting Richard Mailer?"

The man shook his head.

"Is this Aqua?"

"Aqua," he repeated evenly, without inflection. Then he said something else in Czech and nodded solemnly.

"Is this Aqua, the restaurant?"

"Aqua," he repeated again.

"Aqua? Rest—tur—rant? Food? Eat?"

"Aqua. Aqua."

Maybe he was just thirsty. "English?"

Now he shook his head. "No English."

"Food? Eat?" I pointed to my mouth and hoped to hell my eating mime wasn't too much like my blowjob mime. He looked at me like I was crazy, and for a moment I considered pushing past him and going to look for Richard on my own. The burgundy curtain behind him was parted slightly and inside I could see a garish bath of blue and red lights.

"Ross, it's a strip club." Kira was right again. Through the curtain I could now make out flashes of sequined limbs moving in and out of my sightline. We were definitely in the wrong place.

"Do you have a phone? Telephone?" And I gestured with my thumb and pinky finger extended.

Again the man shook his head. I looked around the landing but I didn't see a phone anywhere. Just then a group of paying customers started to push past us and we moved out of the way. *Fuck.* We were lost in Prague.

"So what do we do?" she asked.

"We find a phone." And we went back out to the deserted street and started walking. Several doors down we came to a big neon sign with flickering Czech letters, which I had a hunch spelled something close to "Dive Bar." Before going in I opened up my wallet and pocketed what I hoped was the equivalent of $20 U.S. and not the rent on Marvin Gardens. In case I needed to pay someone for the use of a phone, I didn't want any ruffians seeing my bankroll.

"Stay close," I said, and Kira grabbed my arm. I wasn't scared exactly, just alert and cautious. I had a hunch we were in a tough part of town and I couldn't be sure what was waiting on the other side of the door. And there was a beautiful young woman on my shoulder—which in the wrong kind of place can attract the wrong kind of attention.

Inside, I was relieved to see an all too familiar site—a bar like any other bar back in the States. Loud music, loud talking, loud drinking. The clientele might have been a little rough around the collar but this didn't look like the kind of crowd that would jump us for no good reason—as long as we didn't linger. I squeezed forward and got the attention of the bartender, a big messy-haired biker-looking thug. Leaning over, I shouted above the music, "Do you have a phone?"

He shook his head.

Here we go again. "Telephone?" And I made the telephone mime.

And then, like clockwork, came the shake of the head.

"English? Do you speak English?" Now he just turned away and took somebody else's order.

"Fuck," I muttered. And then there was a minor miracle—a cell phone was thrust in front of my face.

"Here, you can use my cell phone." English! A longhaired American had come to the rescue.

"Really? You don't mind?" Then I added quickly, "It's local."

"Go ahead."

We all stepped into the hallway where it was a little quieter and I dialed Richard's cell.

He picked up right away. "Where are ya, pal?"

"At Aqua, but I don't think it's the right place. It's not a restaurant."

"Are you sure you're at Aqua?"

"Yeah. The sign said Aqua 2000."

"Aqua *2000*?"

"Yeah, Aqua 2000."

"Oh." I heard Richard stifle a laugh. "That's not a very good place to be." He told us to sit tight, another cab was on the way. Then I gave the phone back to the longhair and thanked him profusely.

"No worries."

"Please, take this." I offered him the money I had pocketed earlier.

"*Stačí*. It's no problem." And he turned around and disappeared behind the black curtain. I never thought I'd be the type to depend on the kindness of strangers, and yet there I was. But I didn't point this out to Kira because I felt a gentleman quoting Miss Dubois might come across as a touch effeminate.

"Oh, you're so good," she said and hugged me close. No, just lucky.

Soon, but not soon enough, we were following the maître d' to our table at the real Aqua, which turned out to be a nice restaurant on the inside as well as on the outside. As happy as I was to be here, I was also worried about being an hour late for what had been billed as a political dinner. Had I put the entire shoot in jeopardy by being so miserably incorrect? But once Richard introduced me to the owner of The Red Light and I saw he was wearing a big round smile to match his big round body I had a hunch everything was gonna be alright. Sporting a beret and a thin beard—the kind that chubby faced people grow because they it think slims their jowls—he was central casting for an ex-pat club owner and if he swapped his beret for a fez he could have bought the Blue Parrot across from Rick's Café American.

Immediately I apologized for being late, even though it wasn't really my fault. Then the table apologized for my cab driver, even though it wasn't really their fault. And we all laughed and agreed that someone who knew more Czech than I did should have been in the cab with us. The whole time Blue Parrot was smiling wider and wider, like he was waiting to say something he thought was quite amusing. And here it came, "So how'd you like Aqua 2000?" The whole table guffawed. Everyone except me and Kira. Even Max joined in. But the biggest laugh by far was from Blue Parrot's manservant, a twenty-something Czech with amazing skin.

Richard explained. "*Aqua 2000* is one of our more popular tranny clubs, while *Aqua* is one of the best restaurants in town."

Then I laughed, too. "About as different as the lightning and the lightning bug," and I was pretty sure no one knew I'd stolen the line from Mark Twain. As my double Johnnie Walker arrived I launched into what I hoped was a humorous version of what Kira and I had just been through, and I could tell Blue Parrot got a kick out of it. When I got to the part about the Good Samaritan I went ahead and used the "kindness of strangers" line because I knew there wasn't a gay man alive that didn't appreciate a nod to Tennessee. And he did, and we got along swimmingly—laughing, eating, and watching the liquor flow.

The next morning was cold, but of course it was. It was Prague in December. I wasn't sure why I hadn't packed my hat and gloves, but I hadn't, so I pulled the sleeves of my sweater down over my hands and walked on. We'd come to the Old Town Square to shoot a few stand-ups, some city b-roll, and eventually meet up with Richard at a café. So Max rolled, Kira took pictures in between her walk & talks, and I directed a bit, but mostly I just marveled at the muted pastel colors of the 13th century architecture all around me.

My history teacher mother had explained that one of the advantages of laying down for the Nazis, and later the Russians, was that the town had never been bombed. Not once. So these streets were the same as Kafka's. It was like traveling back in time—but not in a silly colonial-town-museum kinda way, where the blacksmith won't tell you where the bathroom is unless you use the word outhouse. No, this felt like the way it was, and is, and always will be.

Passing along a line of horse drawn buggies I admired their well-worn, Old World leather. And the drivers' faces, so rugged and weather beaten and Cold War downtrodden—I bet these guys had chunks of New York City hansom cab drivers in their stool. There was also a row of street vendors cooking meats and roasting nuts. I could smell their old iron grills and they reminded me of my Alabama Grandpa's favorite skillet and how everything he cooked carried with it the taste of everything that came before.

And then I heard Kira's voice. "Here." I turned around to see she was offering me a brand new pair of gloves. "Put these on."

"Thank you." What a sweet gesture. And completely unsolicited. She'd just known.

So it was with warm hands that I called Max over and together the three of us slowly made our way through the winding maze of Old Town streets. Because Kira had been here before she led the way, and within minutes we arrived at the famous Charles Bridge.

According to my guidebook it was built by Charles IV in 1357. And it was long—570 yards spanning the width of the mighty Vltava River. *That's almost six football fields to you and me, Russ.* Walking on it was damn near sacred. And the statues of the saints were infinitely more powerful in person than when I'd seen them staring down at Daniel Day-Lewis in *The Unbearable Lightness of Being.* I don't normally believe in this kind of mystical hocus pocus, but I swear they were emitting some form of energy—like the rocks at Stonehenge or the parquet at Boston Garden, there was something passing through the air. I felt electric. And romantic.

"That's King Wenceslas' castle over there." Kira had drifted toward me and was pointing across the bridge to an enormous palace up on the hill.

"I wish your husband was here." My, that was a strange thing to say.

She agreed. "Why?"

"So you could have a kiss." Was I *flirting* with her? Odd way to do it if I was. "This is a kissin' bridge for sure." And I swear something flashed from her eyes to mine.

"Who do you wish was here for you to kiss?"

I didn't say *You* and lean in all puckered up to plant one on her like it was the big finish of a mediocre romantic comedy. Although I wanted to.

Just then I saw Max walking toward us, and I was damn glad. He had on a big smile—but of course he did. He was getting paid to shoot this gorgeous bridge.

"Max," Kira asked, "Will you take a picture of us?" And she handed him her digital camera. "You just gotta hold down the—"

"I know, Kira," he teased, "I am, after all, the cameraman."

"Say 'cameraman.'" I said.

Kira and I said "Cameraman!" in unison, and Max took a picture to capture the best kiss there never was.

Three hours later Max was setting up the lights for Richard's interview while I was sitting on his big L-shaped couch enjoying his well-worn Prague-isms. "Prague is the only place that you can find Claudia Schiffer working at a Kentucky Fried Chicken."

Kira, all tuckered out from our afternoon wanderings, was asleep on her side with her feet in my lap. Before closing her eyes she'd asked me to give her a foot rub, so that's what I was doing, massaging her tiny feet through her bright white cotton socks. And I was doing a good job, which only made it harder to pretend that giving a foot rub to a married woman while having a conversation with Richard was a perfectly normal thing to do. I could hear Tarantino's Vincent & Jules, loud and clear, discussing the sexual undertones, tacit intimacy, and overall inappropriateness of an extramarital foot massage. Before I could add my personal belief that a *bare* foot rub was a much greater trespass than a *socked* foot rub, Richard interrupted, "Everywhere you look there's a supermodel. And you never see silicone. You know, I never cared for silicone. It's just... not so good"

"I agree. Silicone is not so good."

I could tell Richard liked living in Prague, especially the part where he got to be an ex-pat. And then he actually said it. "You know, I love being an American who doesn't live in America. It extends your life, not in terms of years, you know, but in terms of thinking. It seems kinda funny, but outside of America you have to learn to think in different ways, to *see* things in different ways, that at the outset seem ridiculous to you."

Richard had already told me that he'd been out of the U.S. for the better part of the past two decades. Before Prague there was Cuba and Costa Rica. And because he had a certain Bogie *je ne sais quoi* about him, I couldn't help wondering if, perhaps, there was some dark reason why he couldn't go home. But whatever his original motives he was here now and I liked him. He was a warm and gracious host without trying too hard. But not effortless, either. He was, without a doubt, trying—as he should. And certainly as I would.

"For example," he continued, "they have a kind of national hero here named Sergeant Scweck that I think reveals a lot about the Czech character. He's from a book called *A Soldier's Story*, and basically he's this sneaky, sly guy who pretends to be subservient all the time but really he's out for himself, you know, always putting something over on somebody. He's literally a national treasure—there's a word, *scweckism*, and what it means is being sneaky, pretending to be stupid, while the whole time you're really wagging the dog. And people proudly admit to *scweckism*, and you wonder why they think this is a cool way to be, and then you look at their history and you can understand. When I first came here to make movies I faced a lot of *scweckism* myself, but, you know, I did my Jeremiah Johnson bit, I killed my Indians and did what I had to do to get started."

When Richard had arrived in Prague it was 1995 and only six years after they'd bounced communism and elected the playwright Vaclav Havel as their first president. I knew he liked living close to that history. It fascinated him. "Prague has taught me how quickly a country can change," he said and suddenly it all made sense. This city was a lot like he was—old, yet young. I bet for him moving here was like electing his own playwright, a rebirth into a whole new life, a fresh start at the age of fifty.

I found myself envying Richard for his apartment and for his Prague and for his sprawling L-shaped couch. It felt like one of the greatest places on earth—so right, so warm, chatting with Richard and rubbing Kira's feet. And being rubbed right back by Prague itself.

That night after the interview we all walked to a nearby Middle Eastern restaurant, and, although I wasn't always entirely sure what I was eating, the meat was good and the G & Ts went down easy. Back at our boxy Hilton Max said he was exhausted and headed for the elevators, but Kira wanted a nightcap and naturally so did I. Traveling like this reminded me of Wesleyan and how I'd never wanted the night to end and was almost always afraid to face my room alone.

On our way to the lobby bar I noticed a lot of cheap looking girls wearing cheap looking dresses sitting in cheap looking clusters. "Are those—?"

"Yup." Kira confirmed my suspicions. "Didn't you get enough in Amsterdam?"

"No, I didn't mean—"

"I'm teasing."

We ordered beers and got to talking. The fact that we were friends now only made me more curious about her. She musta been a beautiful baby, for sure, but how exactly had she grown up to be Dean Moriarity with tits? And such nice tits. So I seized the opportunity to ask her a bunch of invasive questions about her formative years. And as the answers came, they explained what a hard time she'd had of it.

Her biological father never married her mother and was never in the picture for more than the occasional postcard. Like one of Tennessee's telephone men who'd fallen in love with long distance, he'd just said "oops" and gone on his merry way. But it didn't take long for her mother to find another man—this time the marrying kind—and Kira was soon joined by two half sisters and two half brothers. The new man, Daddy Steve, was beloved by all, even though he wasn't the best of breadwinners.

"When I was twelve we lived in the back of Daddy Steve's truck. All of us did. He was working as a carpet cleaner in Vegas, so he had one of those delivery-style trucks and at night we'd just park at the casinos and stay there like it was an RV or something. But it wasn't an RV. It was a delivery truck." *Wow, whaddaya say to that?*

"You know, it's kinda funny, but when I was thirteen—which I believe woulda been the exact same year you were just talking about since you're a year older than me, right?"

"Yeah, I guess so."

"Well, that was the year my mom and I finally left my dad. He went to Europe for a couple weeks, and while he was gone we packed up the car with as much as we could fit—including the dog, of course."

"Of course. What kind of dog?"

"An Airedale. And then we got the fuck outta there. But, divorce laws being what they are, we had to spend most of the summer hiding out in a shitty little motel room outside of Syracuse waiting for the judge to give us a restraining order and say it was cool for my mom to take me outta the state and down to her folks' place in Alabama."

"Wow." She laughed just the right laugh. "Guess it was a tough summer all around."

"Yeah." And I laughed too. "He was a real cocksucker—drank, knocked my mom around, all the cliché shit."

"Did he ever hit you?"

"No. Well, once, but I just locked myself in my room. Wasn't a big deal. Mostly he went after her."

"Where is he now?"

"I don't know." I rarely spoke about my childhood or my father—with anyone—but now, with her, for some reason I really wanted to. So I kept going. I explained how that same summer my father's crazy aversion to paying his income tax finally caught up with him in the form of a federal arrest warrant. He'd fled and gone underground. Fake passports, Swiss bank accounts, the whole deal. I hadn't spoken with him since, but wherever he wound up I'm sure he turned out just fine. As did my mother. She'd returned to her childhood home to take care of her parents and to go to grad school to become a teacher, while also working part-time at a veterinary clinic. Real saintly stuff. Meanwhile, I got to leave all the madness behind and reinvent myself at one of the best high schools in the country.

I'm not sure if *impressed* was the right word, but I could tell Kira was glad I was sharing. Still, I'd rather be listening. "So, was it weird having a stepdad?"

"Not really. Daddy Steve was really sweet and he always did his best. The tough part was having to take care of everyone else, 'cuz, you know, my mom, she had polio so it was hard for her to get around." *Kira was friggin' Cinderella!* "And lemme tell ya, I have no interest in having kids because I already had them. I changed enough diapers for a lifetime."

"So how'd you make it out to LA?"

"Well, after Daddy Steve had his heart attack and died, Mom moved us all to Kentucky, but the moment I turned sixteen I got outta there and headed back west. I bummed around California for awhile, then stripped my way through UCLA, and now here I am having a beer in the lobby bar of the Prague Hilton."

As she spoke, her words were seasoned with the salt & pepper pride and desperation of a woman who'd made it on her own, but only by doing some things that weren't easy to live with.

Then Kira changed the subject. "Wanna smoke a joint?"

After getting another round for the road we headed upstairs. Her room, like mine, overlooked the lobby from high up on the 16th floor. I cracked open the suicide-proof window the few inches it allowed so we could sit on the wide sill and exhale into the atrium. She handed me a well-rolled joint and I lit it from a matchbook I'd grabbed down at the bar.

"Is this from Amsterdam?" I asked in that voice you get when you speak while trying to hold in the smoke.

"No, it's from home. I had Doug roll me three joints before I left."

I exhaled. "Aren't you scared to travel with it?" As soon as the question followed the smoke from my lips, I figured Kira wasn't afraid of anything.

"No, I do it all the time."

"How? Where do you hide it?"

"I just put it in a condom, then put it in me."

In her? "Front or back?"

"Front."

"Good." And we both laughed.

Then we talked some more and I was feeling pretty damn groovy. But soon I started to notice her hand was finding ways to touch my arm during our conversation. Was that on purpose? Was she coming on to me? No, she couldn't be. She was married. And her kind husband—the perfect man, as she called him—had even rolled the joint we were now smoking. Yet she was looking at me like she sure wanted to be kissed. *Should I kiss her?* I wanted to kiss her. I'd wanted to kiss her back on the bridge, and now her tight jeans and low-cut top were reinforcing this desire. Of course, the pussy-laced dope and cold draft beer weren't arguing a bit. And wasn't she the one that had said whatever happened on the road, stayed on the road? So why not kiss her? A kiss was just a kiss, right? So I looked her firm in the eyes and said, "I better go."

"Nooo." She frowned her disappointment like a child being told it was bedtime.

"Yeah, it's late and we got a long day tomorrow." *What the fuck was I saying?* Long day tomorrow?!? I should be kissing her!

Kissing her!!! Not saying goodnight. But for some reason that's exactly what I said. "Goodnight."

"Night," she said, with what had to be a bit of bewilderment.

Then I was standing alone in the hallway. And I realized how drunk, stoned, and confused I was. *Why did I just turn down what would have no doubt been the best sex of my relatively young life?* What kind of man was I? Well, she *was* a married woman, so maybe I was just a good man. A good man who knew well the boundaries of good taste. A good man who respected his fellow man. A good man who refused to covet his neighbor's wife. No, that didn't sound like me.

I keyed myself into my room, stripped naked, and got under the covers. By then I figured I'd made the smart play, but damn, I sure wished I was rolling around with her right now. So I imagined I was.

By noon the next day all was forgotten and we were back on the job at Blue Parrot's brothel, The Red Light. As the day progressed I saw that when it came to shooting sex Richard had a hands-off approach. After setting up each scene he would turn the set over to his cameraman. Interestingly, I was essentially doing the same thing. By now Max knew what to shoot and he didn't need or want me standing over his shoulder. So Richard and I spent much of the day talking and drinking Red Bulls at a bar that shared the same lot as the Red Light. By the third round I was starting to feel all weird and tingly and had to stop, but Richard kept on guzzling. "I don't like being on set much," Richard confided. "I try to let my cameraman handle as much as possible. After so many scenes it's just not interesting to me anymore."

"Yeah, I can imagine. I haven't been doing this that long, but from what I've seen porn sets aren't that exciting. Mostly it's just 'hurry up & wait' and sometimes it can be hard to watch." I told him about being on the *Filthy First Timers* set.

"You know, I have never done that. Never. I won't shoot a girl for the first time. It's funny, people always ask me, 'How do you talk these girls into doing this?' But I don't. And it disappoints them when I say that, but it's true. I only use girls that have already done something. I don't want to be the one that gets them into this. It's like a tattoo, it's on their record for the rest of their life. Now, if she chooses this, then yes, I'm here to make the movie, but I don't ever say, 'Oh, gee, this is a wonderful field to go into.' It's not a bad field, but it isn't something I would necessarily encourage a girl to go into."

Naturally the shoot ran long—evidently porn star time was the same all over the world—and afterwards Richard took us all out for dinner at a Moroccan restaurant. By the time we got back to the hotel I could see the old Czech bartender in her dark navy uniform locking up the booze and I knew we were less than five minutes too late, which I didn't like one bit.

Then Kira said a wonderful and dangerous thing. "I've got some vodka up in my room."

Upstairs we said goodnight to Max, who was wisely going to bed because it was almost two in the morning. Then I filled my ice bucket and joined Kira in her room. I spun us up a couple of drinks—she even had orange juice—and we toasted another successful shoot.

"By the way, where'd you get all this?" The rooms didn't have mini-bars and I hadn't seen her buy anything during the day.

"This morning at the gift shop." And suddenly I loved the gift shop for selling vodka and orange juice but not nearly as much as I loved Kira for her foresight.

By our second Stoli & OJ she was lighting what was left of last night's joint and I was telling her a story about how screwdrivers got their name during the California gold rush. "They had all those oranges and all that vodka, but they didn't have anything to stir with."

"Didn't they have swizzle sticks?"

"Swizzle sticks? Yeah, sure, the city slickers had them back east in St. Louey, but they didn't have no stinkin' swizzle sticks in the mining camps."

"Oh, of course, what was I thinking?" She smiled.

"But you know what they did have?"

"Can I guess?"

"No, better not. Better I just tell you. What they did have, what they happened to have an abundant supply of, and what just happened to be perfectly suited to the task was... the screwdriver!"

It was a story I'd told so many times over the years I honestly couldn't remember if it was true or if I'd simply made it up for some forgotten reason. Though I kinda suspected that I'd made it up because why would frontiersmen be drinking vodka? Wouldn't it have been whiskey? And even if they did have vodka, why would they need a mixer? Weren't they tough enough to take it straight? But it didn't really matter. It was just a story I told to steady a boat that had become a little tipsy.

And it bought me a second to recognize where I was—to see Kira looking at me hard, then soft, and brushing against my arm. And to realize I was in the exact same place I'd been last night. Except now I was plenty drunk enough not to care about whatever it was that had made me stop short before. And now I knew. I knew for sure. And she knew I knew. And I knew she knew that I knew she knew.

So I kissed her. And then I kissed her again. And again and again and we were kissing. Then we were on the couch pulling each other's shirts over our heads. She wore a black bra, a nice one too—but not for long, I thought, as I reached behind her hoping to hell I was going to be able to perform a one handed unhook, preferably on the first try. But she stopped me. "No, it's on the front." The front? Of course, the front—a tiny plastic hook through a cloth loop—brilliant! Why weren't hooks always on the front? And why weren't breasts always this nice? These were old school, all natural, Playboy Tits—the kind my generation grew up idolizing before plastic surgery and Photoshop waged bloody war on our notion of perfection. And they were in my hands. I thought about how I'd been so worried about them being cold on the boat in Amsterdam. But how warm they felt now.

"Do you want to fuck me?"

"Yes," I said, hoping for just the right balance of enthusiasm and restraint.

"Oh, good," she said, with what sounded a lot like mock relief. She might as well have asked, *Is the earth round? Yes. Oh, good.*

I excused myself to go to my room for condoms, which, like all good Boy Scouts, I kept in my dopp kit. In the bathroom I stopped and had a moment with the mirror. I realized I was back on the threshold and that it wasn't too late to tell her this was a bad idea. I could return to her room, pick up my shirt, and leave like I did the night before. Better yet, I could just call her. Just pick up the phone. *Hi, uh, it's me, listen, I think you're swell, but this is a mistake, you know, it's just, it's just not fair to your husband, and I'm sure you're gonna regret it in the morning, and it's just not honest. I mean, I need to do the thinking for the both of us, and look what a noble sonofabitch I turned out to be, and blah, blah, blah*—Bullshit! I was on the precipice of some kind of paradise and I wasn't about to turn back now.

A heartbeat later I was I knocking on her door and hoping to hell her mirror agreed with mine. When she opened up, her hungry eyes told me we hadn't missed a beat. We were both more than a little boozed and this was our first bout so it took some time to find our positioning and rhythm, but when we did, it was good. And when she said she wanted it harder, I obliged, and then we were making what I thought had to be a considerable amount of noise. It was past 3:00 a.m. and Max was asleep on the other side of this very wall, but if a Commandment couldn't deter me, then neither could a sleeping coworker. I didn't care if we knocked down the whole cheap communist constructed wall.

As I took her from behind my eyes were transfixed on that world class ass—an ass I'd put on a pedestal as completely unattainable only three months earlier in Orlando, and now, seeing myself enter her, I couldn't believe my good fortune. So this was how it felt to fuck perfection... And right then there was a thundering wooden crash that got our attention real fast. We'd actually knocked the headboard off the wall and it had fallen hard to the floor behind the bed. Evidently, it'd been hooked on a pair of screws like a picture frame. We both laughed and continued in a new position. And this went on as long as it could and then we fell asleep.

VIII

I Know What You
Did in Europe!

I'd barely been back in LA long enough to get over my jet lag when a small piece of the road showed up at my doorstep. It was a package from Kira postmarked less than twenty-four hours after our plane touched down. Perhaps I should've recognized it as the harbinger it was—a sign that what happened on the road did not, in fact, stay on the road, but instead stuck like a piece of toilet paper to the bottom of your shoe, and at what point someone was gonna notice, you never knew. But I didn't. I was just curious about what she'd been in such a hurry to send.

Tearing into the padded manila envelope I found a VHS copy of a film called *Forbidden Highway*. On the box cover there was a picture of Kira in a sexy dress superimposed over a desert highway with the single phrase, "Take a ride on the road to desire." Ah, yes, I knew that road. There was also a day-pass to the Sports Club LA and a short, handwritten note. "Thanks for taking care of me in Europe. Kisses, Kira."

As I reread her words, they came back in her sweet trouble lovin' voice, "Thanks for taking care of me," and immediately I thought of the remarkably bold thing she'd said after we'd awoken and wriggled into a round of morning sex. "Mmm, thanks for the fucking.

My pussy is purring." How magnificently alluring and utterly vulgar those words had been—honest words that had set the tone for a dishonest day. And yet what a natural and surprisingly guilt-free day it had been—ordering up a slow breakfast in bed, stealing as many kisses as we could whenever Max wasn't looking, rubbing her white cotton feet for almost the entire plane ride home, and then finally saying a slightly sad goodbye on the other side of customs.

But now, for the first time, I *did* feel a shudder of guilt as I flashbacked to another voice in my mind's ear, the voice of her husband. The voice of *Doug*. "*Take care* of my girl over there." That's what he'd said when I picked Kira up on the way to LAX. And I'd looked him in the eye, shaken his hand, and given him my word. "You got it." What an unmanly lie that had become.

At the very least I was due a good punch in the nose. Or was I? Maybe Doug wasn't all that worried about me fucking his wife. After all, they'd turned their love life into a commodity by selling it online, so how could sex possibly mean the same thing to them as it did to mainstream America? Kira certainly didn't seem too concerned about it, so why should I suffer any lasting shame?

To be honest, mostly I was just feeling groovy—nothing like a trip to Europe and some stellar sex to get your juices flowing. And I was damn curious about her *Forbidden Highway*, so I slid it into my VCR and poured a few fingers of scotch. Watching the opening credits roll over her naked perfection, I had to pinch myself to believe that I'd actually been with her. Little ol' me, who was left to dance with the teacher in all my grade school ballroom classes, who never got near the girls he wanted at Groton, who finally got the girls he wanted at Wesleyan only to find he didn't quite know what to do with them—this little ol' me had actually gotten his mitts on a softcore queen.

I was just sorry that it had to be a one-time thing. Although it was never voiced, I knew there was no way a woman like her would ever want to fuck a guy like me again. While I may have been a fun new toy for her to play with overseas, back here in the States we were in the real world and she was way outta my league.

And because I was so sure we were one & done I was just shy of shocked to get an email from her only three days later. She wanted me to meet her and her friend, Ken Marcus, at his Melrose Avenue studio. An erotic photographer best known for his Playboy center-folds back in the seventies and eighties, Ken was now shooting fetish and bondage photography for his pay website, KenMarcus.com—information I only knew because just yesterday I'd been assigned to produce a story on him. Since they were pals Kira was gonna host the segment, so I suppose she had reason to email. But what was so surprising was the timing. The shoot was still at least a month away, sometime in late January, and with the holidays around the corner nobody was thinking that far ahead. Yet here she was, asking to get together "around six-ish to discuss the shoot." Strange.

And stranger still was the way Kira, alone, opened the back door to Ken's studio—a bundle of dynamite in a snug black dress, with a glass of white wine in her hand and a whisper on her lips. "Kiss me." Sadly, since I was in the process of swallowing my tongue, all I could manage was a polite, uninspired peck on the lips. Did I actually hear her groan at my lackluster effort?

Following her into the studio, I found myself on suddenly shaky ground. I wasn't ready for this—not here, not now. *In 90 minutes I was meeting Maggie for sushi, for chrissakes.* Then I felt a hot flash as I wondered if this whole scenario was really just a set up. Was Ken even here? Not that I woulda put up much of a fight, because she looked sexy as hell in that dress.

But then we turned the corner and there he was, Ken Marcus—early fifties, black t-shirt, black jeans, salt & pepper ponytail, and a sharp pair of eyes behind rather large framed glasses. "Ross, this is Ken. He's been like a father to me. In fact, he almost gave me away at my wedding."

And as we shook hands I was damn glad to have a chaperone.

"How's your *girlfriend*?" I was a full fifteen minutes late for my dinner with Maggie. A lotta time to keep a lady waiting. I'd found her at the bar with a glass of champagne in her hand—hardly touched, so it had to be her second.

"Baby, don't be ridiculous. She's a *married* woman." Big mistake letting her know about my meeting with Kira and Ken. Ever since I'd been back in town she'd sensed a sea change in me and it wasn't enough she didn't like it, she wanted to know the cause. "And I told you, it was for *work*."

"What did I tell you about getting too close to your work?"

"Listen, I'm sorry I was late. I'm an ass. But please, let's get past that and have a nice dinner, alright."

"You're not so smart. I know what you did over there."

"Oh yeah? What did I do?"

"You fucked Kira."

Whoa! I didn't want Maggie to see the panic on my face, so as nonchalantly as possible—which was probably pretty damn chalant—I spun around to face the bartender. I needed a Tanqueray & Tonic, and fast. She had to be bluffing, right? Right. After placing my order, I turned back to her. "No, Maggie, I did *not* fuck her," I lied. "She's *married*."

"So?"

"So what kind of guy do you think I am?"

My drink appeared and I took a healthy pull, and that's when she actually said, "Why don't you love me anymore?"

Why was she busting my balls? We weren't even a couple. *Were we?* No, we were just good friends that got together once in a while for dinner and sex. Sure, we loved each other, but we weren't supposed to be *in* love. That ship had sailed and sank just a mile or two offshore. If this was the way dinner was gonna go, I didn't want any part.

Leaning in close, I whispered as hard as I could, "Go to the bathroom, powder your nose, and come back in a good mood or I'm gonna walk right the fuck outta here." And I meant it. Her eyes flared as she calculated my resolve, then, sensing I was dead serious, she surrendered her now empty glass of shamps and made a beeline for the bathroom.

While I drained my drink and ordered us another round it dawned on me that finally, for the first time in our relationship, I hadn't rolled over. I'd actually asserted myself. And won. Sure, it was just a skirmish, but a victory was a victory. When Maggie came back I was still charged up and kinda hoping we'd get to lock horns again, but she was all smiles. So we took our seats at the sushi bar and enjoyed the best spicy tuna rolls in town.

After plenty more gin, shamps, and raw fish, we somehow drove our separate cars back to her place where all the power and freedom I'd felt at dinner inspired some of the best sex we'd ever had together. Or maybe it was the porn. She had a brand new box-load in her living room because she was working on a story about a director named Jim Gunn and his ongoing *Lesbian Cheerleader* series—why it wasn't titled *Smells Like Teen Spirit* I have no idea. She picked a winner and we stripped our way into the bedroom.

Her room was so small and her television so big and my belly so full of gin that it sure seemed like these adorable, all natural blondes were right there in the bed with us. And the best part was they didn't look bored. From what I'd seen so far in the gay-for-pay world of girl-on-girl action, too many young ladies seem to be sleepwalking through their roles. But not these peppy cheer-leaders. They pulled off each other's ill-fitted generic red uniforms—kissing, licking, caressing, getting hotter and wetter as they went along. And we followed as best we could, stroke for stoke, trying to match their deliberate, incredibly thorough, and occasionally quite intricate maneuvers. By the end all four of us were completely satisfied, and I didn't even have to buy the cheer-leaders sushi.

Three days later I was on my way home after playing hockey with my men's league team when my cell phone started to ring. I was pushing 80 on the 101 and should have let it go to voicemail. But I didn't and it was her. "I know what you did in Europe." *Again?* Maggie really wasn't gonna let this go. She was like Nancy-fucking-Drew with this thing.

"Baby, you gotta stop." Female intuition was a powerful thing for sure, and maybe it could even reach across the ocean, but in the end intuition was just intuition. A suspicion. A conviction was hard evidence and there were only three people that coulda had any of that—me, Kira, and possibly Max, and there was no way any of us had squealed.

"I shot with Max today. He told me what you did."

Fuck. Could he have told her? No. No way. But then again, maybe. She coulda tricked him into saying something. She coulda told him I'd already confessed. I was caught in the classic Prisoner's Dilemma. "Baby, I didn't do anything."

"He told me."

And if he did tell her, *what* did he tell her? The brothel or the adultery? Max couldn't be absolutely positive about me and Kira, but he certainly could have suspected. After all, we had knocked the headboard off the wall in the adjoining room. "What did he say I did?"

"You know. You tell me." Surely this was a trick. Or was it? "Tell me. Or are you gonna be a liar? I can't trust a liar and I certainly can't fuck a liar."

I doubted she could fuck an adulterer or a whoremonger either. I had no idea what to say next. So I did the only thing I could do. I lied. "Hello...? Hello...? Can you hear me?"

"I said I can't fuck a liar. Are you a liar?"

"You're breaking up. Can you hear me now?"

"Don't be a liar!"

Borrowing Chevy Chase's press conference move from *Spies Like Us*, I began dropping syllables to fake a bad connection, "I... an't... ear... ewe. Oh... ervice. Anging up... ow." Then I ended the call so I could start thinking my way through this thing.

Of course, the obvious thing to do was to call Max and find out what he'd said, but it was already after eleven and he lived with his longtime girlfriend. Waking them both up to ask if he'd caved under interrogation seemed a bit extreme. *Had Maggie purposefully waited to call me until she knew it would be too late to call him?* Shrewd shrew she was, maybe so, but either way I was on my own.

Conventional wisdom was to deny, deny, deny, and then deny some more. But I knew Maggie. She wasn't about to give this up and another denial would only prolong the agony. Besides, I wasn't supposed to care. Sure, my natural knee-jerk reaction was to do whatever it took to keep the thing afloat, and the gamesman in me delighted in trying to come up with a way out. But the fact was, this whole thing was turning into a toothache and it needed to be pulled. Besides, I loved her, and if my European mystery was really bothering her this much then she deserved to know the truth.

Or at least the partial truth. Copping to the sex with Kira was out of the question because that could hurt Kira. I'd be taking that to the grave. And if that happened to be what Max told her, then I guess I'd be playing the deny card after all. So it was settled, and when I got home I called her back.

"Are you gonna tell me? Or are you gonna be a liar?" On the surface she almost seemed amused, as if she was toying with me.

"No, I'm not a liar," I lied. Deep breath. "Kira and I went to a brothel together."

"And you fucked her." It wasn't a question.

"No, I didn't fu—we did not have sex. Not with each other, I mean." Then I gave my best Bill Clinton, "I did nooooot have sexual relations with that woman."

"That's not funny."

"But it's the truth. I just had sex with one of the brothel girls."

"With a whore. You fucked another whore."

"Yeah, I guess I did."

"And she wasn't off duty this time, was she?"

"No, I guess she wasn't."

"I can't believe you. I hope you used a condom."

"Yes, I used—listen, if it makes any difference, it was a nice brothel. Really upscale. It wasn't some skanky—"

"That's it. We're through." She hung up and that was when I finally realized Kira was wrong. What happens on the road actually comes home with you. Then I thought life was a little like it was on the ice—regardless of intent, a player is always responsible for the actions of his own stick. Then the phone rang. It was Maggie. "I want all my shit back. I'm coming down."

I barely had time to gather her stray belongings before I heard her knocking on the door. I opened it, and there she stood like a rain-soaked Mrs. Robinson watching Benjamin confess their affair to Elaine. Only it wasn't raining in Hollywood.

"You wanna come in?"

"No. Just gimme my stuff."

I did. And as she turned to leave, so badly I wanted to lighten the mood by saying, *What, no break-up sex?* But instead I went with, "Sorry." She didn't turn around, but still, I was glad I said it. Because I was. Because it was the end of something. Although it certainly wasn't the end of everything. I'd known her too long and watched her walk away—or been sent away myself—far too many times to believe this was the absolute end. After all, we still worked in the same office. But it was most definitely the end of something.

IX

How Can We Be This Lucky?

*A*s always, I spent Christmas with my mother. And, as always—because Opelika, Alabama, is no place to party—I was heading north to be with my friends for New Year's Eve. I arrived in New York the day before the big night and took a cab straight to my friend Oliver's apartment at the Dakota. These days he was actually living in New Jersey, writing for the *Star Ledger*, but this was where he'd grown up, and this was where I'd visited him so many times over the years—even lived here myself one summer while taking film classes at NYU—and this was where we were gonna throw one helluva party tomorrow night because Oliver's wonderfully considerate parents were conveniently off skiing in Aspen.

Now, riding up the interminably slow vintage elevator I had my usual thoughts of John Lennon standing in this very same place. And how much I've always loved his music, especially his solo work, and how nice it would've been to have had him around just a little bit longer. Mark David Chapman. What a crazy fucking bastard. Who does that? A politician sure, but a musician? An artist? Hard to believe. And hard to believe Oliver had actually heard the shots from his bedroom window. And perhaps hardest to believe was that, after coming here for more than a decade, I still wasn't smart enough to take the stairs. Christ, I hadn't even made it to the third floor yet!

As I continued to climb, slowly, my mind wandered back to that first invitation. It was for Fall Long Weekend. Oliver and I were in tenth grade—or, as us preppie fucks would say, Fourth Form—and not knowing how large he lived I'd naïvely asked if he was sure he had enough room. And I'll never forget how he responded with complete humility that, in fact, they did have enough room for a weekend guest. No sarcasm, no smile, only sincerity. If anything there was a prescient pregnant pause where perhaps he foresaw my shock and awe at the size and sheer splendor of the home he hadn't earned, but was born into. Maybe he even anticipated the embarrassment of his riches and worried that I might think less of him after his unmasking. But the reality was just the opposite. The day I first walked into the Dakota was the day I began to fully understand what a rare soul Oliver was. Not because of his wealth, but because of the way he wore it—with warmth, generosity, ambition and the difficult understanding that *deserve's got nothing to do with it*, this was just the card he'd been dealt.

If pressed, I'd say he probably had a bit of a chip about that card. He certainly kept it close to his chest and there's no way you'd ever catch him playing it. Instead he seemed determined to show the world—and himself?—that he was his own man, that he was worthy. At Groton I watched him work his ass off every single day. He took all the toughest classes, graduated Magna Cum Laude, captained the lacrosse team, and was even Vice President of our class. And I had to love him for that.

Meanwhile, I finished with the sixth worst grade point average (that's right, only five students finished below me, and incredibly one of them went to Princeton), I only played one varsity sport (three years of hockey), only had one meaningful extracurricular (a somewhat subversive column for the *Circle Voice*), had long hippie hair (embarrassed to say, my Jim Morrison phase), and was well-known to students and faculty alike as a partier (which, in preppie terms, meant I spent my Saturday evenings pulling tubes and drinking warm shots of Smirnoff with a Coca-Cola chaser).

Without a doubt I could've made more of my four years at Groton. On some level I suppose it was a wasted opportunity, but under the circumstances I think things went down pretty damn well. Of course, I didn't understand it at the time, but when I first filled my suitcase full of Brooks Brothers and headed back north I wasn't looking for a stepping-stone to Harvard. I was just trying to find a home and a family.

When I finally stepped off the elevator the apartment door was ajar, so I went on in. "Oliver?"

"Yo Ross-coe!" I saw him coming out of the darkness of the long hallway.

"Ollie-boy!" He was already wearing his puffy down jacket.

We shared a big hug, then, "C'mon, we're going to Evelyn's. Benji's already there."

Benji was the third part of our holy triumvirate. Before sharing a room with us at Groton, he'd grown up in Connecticut. But now he was living in Chile and it had become quite rare for the three of us to be together. I had no idea who the girl was. "Who's Evelyn?"

Chuckling, "Evelyn's is a bar."

And it wasn't far—Columbus & 78th. When we walked in, Benji spotted us right away and rushed on over. After a round of hugs we just stood there for a moment, smiling and basking in our love. Then someone came to get Oliver's attention—someone was always getting Oliver's attention. So Benji gave me the news from Chile as I surveyed the scene. Evidently we'd pushed most of the tables in the room together to create one long super-table.

"Where's Maya?" Benji pointed to his Chilean girlfriend, and I waved. Then I waved to Oliver's girlfriend Alexis, who didn't see me, and then she did and waved back.

Down at the far end I could see Benji's and Oliver's younger sisters, Fiona (Middlesex '93), and Sara (Groton '93), respectively, sitting across from each other. In an incredible, all-too-perfect twist of fate they also happened to be best friends and had even roomed together at Brown. Separated by just two years these two brother-sister combos provided the nucleus for everyone at this long table—Manhattan, Black Point, Groton, Harvard, and Brown all revolved around that benevolent tetrarchy, forever intersecting and intertwining our wining & dining into the infinite.

I can't say I was never jealous that I couldn't add a sister to the mix, but my parents never loved each near enough to warrant another birth. So I'd adopted Fiona as my own. Benji was happy to share and she was thrilled to have me and so it was. This was my family.

It musta taken a full thirty minutes to work my way down the table—saying all those hellos and squeezing all those hugs—but I made sure to save the best for last. The lovely Vanessa. By far the finest girl in the room, and the most single, she was part uber-prep and part princess. Born and bred in Newport, she'd also roomed with Sara and Fiona at Brown, where she graduated Phi Beta Kappa. Now she was living in Rome, working at the American Art Institute, and studying some combination of art and the classics. Fluent in both Italian and Latin, Vanessa was brainy, beautiful, and unusually chic for this conservatively coutured crowd. And she'd been my obsession ever since I first met her exactly one year ago in a Providence flower shop...

...It was a nice flower shop—lush and lavish, the kind of place where you didn't mind loitering while you waited for more friends to arrive before heading into the city to celebrate the millennium. So there I was, literally taking some time to smell the roses, half-listening to Sara and Fiona catching up with the lesbian owner, when suddenly the door flew open and jingled the tiny bell attached overhead. Before I turned I could already feel the icy cold New England air against the back of my neck.

And then I saw her. Beautiful blonde hair falling against a super-stylish purple coat that was cut just above her knee-high black stiletto boots, and a soft, delicate nose, and chilled rosy cheeks that I instantly wanted to warm with the palms of my hands. I swear this first sight played just like a movie—slow motion, smiling, eyes beaming, so happy to see Sara and Fiona at the far end of the shop. Then she must have caught me out of the corner of her eye—a stranger among familiar flowers—because she looked my way and our eyes met for a long fleeting second and surely something flashed between us. At least I felt it because my mind sure swooned. Trying my best to keep my balance and not knock anything over, I held her gaze as long as possible. And then she looked away, resumed her normal speed, and went to greet her friends.

After giving them a moment together I made my way over to introduce myself. As I smiled my best possible hello I wondered if she could tell that I'd already fallen in love with her. Then we both removed our black leather gloves so we could shake hands flesh on flesh—and what wonderful warm, smooth, lotion-loving flesh it was. And what a face. It beamed with all the things a young gentleman yearned for—warmth, beauty, grace, intelligence—and I could feel them all radiate against me like heat from a cracklin' bonfire on a cool night, and her eyes were just as mesmerizing as that single glowing ember floating upward into the dark, star-sprinkled sky.

Throughout the next evening, the big Y2K, I fell harder and harder for this dazzling principessa. She moved like a dancer, spoke like a royal, and looked like the finest piece of porcelain. And she was friends with my friends, part of the family, which perhaps made my desire damn near incestuous. But I hoped to hell it was a desire she shared as we flashed smiles and knowing looks that seemed to become more and more longing as the evening wore on—all the ingredients of a budding romance. Or perhaps just a whole lot of nothing, the drunken projections of a man way outta his league. In the end, I was too chicken to find out. Making a move woulda risked spoiling a wonderful evening. It was much more pleasant not to know for sure and allow myself to marinate in the hope that this was perhaps the beginning of something...

...Which was all well and good in a white gloved, *Remains of the Day* kinda way, but that was then. This was now. As I pulled over a nearby chair and squeezed in next to her I knew this year things were gonna be different. Of course, I couldn't promise myself I was gonna win her hand, but I sure as hell was gonna play mine.

I even had a conversational ace up my sleeve. By happy coincidence I'd interviewed a close friend of her family (a big-time Newport socialite) for my Claus von Bulow show. At the time I had no idea of the connection between Vanessa and the "Grande Dame of Bellevue Avenue." But I did now, and I was damn glad, too, because I couldn't have a better icebreaker than, "I interviewed your friend, Gertie, for my TV show."

"Wow, what a small world. I hope she didn't say anything offensive. Gertie occasionally likes to stir up trouble."

"No. No trouble at all. She was extremely well behaved. A pussycat."

"I find that hard to believe."

"I swear."

"So what was your verdict—guilty or not guilty?"

"Oh, we were pretty sure Gertie had nothing to do with it." I smiled.

"Don't be too sure," she kidded.

"I guess I pretty much agreed with Dersh. Claus was definitely guilty of something, being a bad husband at the very least, but not murder. But that was the boring part. Did Gertie ever tell you about all the necrophilia?"

"No, I think I would have remembered that."

I was actually surprised she'd never heard the rumors about Claus's penchant for the pleasures of recently deceased human flesh, especially since she'd grown up so close to Clarendon Court. Personally I'd never really believed them. I figured the stories were just cocktail party gibberish, which Claus had probably encouraged to add to his icy-cold mystique. But true or not, the stories were fun, so I treated her to one of my favorites—the one where Claus, Roy Cohn, and Truman Capote all walk into a necrophilia bar. But not together. It wasn't one of those jokes. No, the way I heard it Cohn and Bulow were already there skulking about in the corner while Capote had brought along an unwitting young writer to whom he delivers the punchline, which of course must be retold in Truman's trademark lilt, "What's so disgusting? They change the body every other day."

And I got just the right note of naughty laughter outta her, which led me to believe I was doing a decent job of steering the conversation clear of my Playboy gig. But just when I was about to ask her about Rome she hit me with an uppercut. "So tell me about your new job. I hear you're a pornographer." *Fuck.* Well, at least she'd been talking about me. No such thing as bad press, right?

"Well, technically I'm not *exactly* a pornographer. I'm more of a journalist."

"A journalist?" She smirked.

"Yes, a journalist whose beat happens to be, ah, on occasion, pornography."

"Oh really?"

"There is a difference, you know."

"I'm sure there is."

I could see this was gonna be a tough sell, so I tried a different line. "You know what the best part of the job is?"

"You want me to guess?"

"No, I definitely don't." A little self-deprecating laugh to keep things light, then, "It's the travel." And I served up a thumbnail sketch of my European adventure, wisely omitting all the extracurricular sex and focusing instead on the Van Gogh museum and my love for the Charles Bridge. "You've never been? Oh, you gotta go, you'd love it."

"I bet you just missed my mother in Amsterdam." Vanessa was not nearly as impressed with my travel as I'd hoped. "She was there last month for a gallery opening that was showing some of her paintings. I can't remember the name of it, though." I didn't say that unless her mother had painted an odalisque hanging in the parlor of a brothel, I probably missed it.

Instead I tried to appeal to her intellect—risky business since she was a helluva lot smarter than I was, but it was worth a shot. "Listen, I don't want you to get the wrong idea. It's not like I just hang out on porn sets all day. We do stories on all sorts of things—swingers, artists, photographers, parties, oddball fetishes. The oddball fetishes are actually my favorite because it's fun to get lost in the whole psychology of it. And the crazy thing is I get to ask people about their sexuality, I ask them things I wouldn't even ask most of our friends here tonight. And because I work for Playboy, and because I'm producing a television show, and because for some reason they trust me, I get to ask them anything I want and they'll actually answer me. It's really quite incredible."

"But you do go to porn sets, right?"

Fuck. Alright, here goes. "Yes, sometimes I have to go to porn sets, but it's really not that big a deal. In fact, it's pretty damn boring. Just a lot of waiting around and everyone thinks they're Martin Scorsese, you know, like they're making a real film or something."

"And I'm sure you hate being around all those naked girls." *Youch.*

"Fair question. Yeah, sure, I'll admit it. I'm a red-blooded American male. I don't hate being around naked women, but truth is they're actually not all that hot." Was this working? "At least not to me. They're all plastic looking, you know, big hair and makeup, fake breasts—that's not sexy." No, this was definitely not working. Her eyes were tagging me out all over the place. So I took a chance, "The best way to describe it is that it's like food photography. You know the Big Mac or Whopper you see in the picture at the drive-in? It looks good, right? But you'd never want to eat the actual burger that was shot for that picture because it's coated with glycerin and chemicals and all sorts of stuff to make it look good on-camera. Not that these girls are pieces of meat, of course."

"No, of course not." And she actually laughed.

"The thing about porn is it's selling a fantasy. All the pictures and videos, they're not actual girls. They're representations of girls, like Magritte's pipe, right? *'Ceci n'est pas une pipe.'*" I knew she'd love the art reference—it was even worth revealing my terrible French. "They're images designed to elicit an emotional response—or more specifically an erotic response. It's a fantasy, and in real life you can't fuck a fantasy because it'll just disappear like smoke." Wow, this was a colossal load of horseshit. But I think she was buying it because she kept nodding with a real pensive look. Or perhaps she was trying not to laugh. At me. "Are you buying any of this?"

"Ah, I think so. I'm not sure. I'm gonna have to think about it a bit more." But she was smiling, so I knew she believed it enough. "I do have to say I'm intrigued. I'd love to see one of your stories."

"And I'd love to show you. Anytime." That was a lie. There was no way I was gonna expose her to the reality of what I actually did. However, the fact that she wanted to see it, now that was progress. It meant that, at least for now, my current occupation was not going to stand in the way of my ongoing campaign.

Finally we moved the conversation to Rome and how much she loved living there, and although I admit I wasn't listening all that closely I absolutely adored watching her talk about it. My eyes were glued to her, but they sure did roam—wide warm eyes, flawless candlelit skin, straight no-nonsense hair, full lips effortlessly turning Italian phrases, sensible breasts bulging just enough under a wool sweater. I wanted to touch her so bad, so much more than I had a year ago, but of course I couldn't. Not now. Not tonight. Tomorrow. This was just groundwork. My prelude to a kiss. And by last call I knew I'd played it as well as I could.

I've heard a lot of folks say they hate News Year's Eve parties because they never live up to expectations, but obviously those poor bastards have never been invited to throw down at the Dakota. With its sprawling floor plan, super high ceilings, and eight foot windows that overlooked the snow covered Park, Oliver's apartment was the ideal venue for a night like this—a legitimate work of art—the kinda place you'd see as a backdrop in a *Vanity Fair* layout or on the cover of any leading house and home magazine. Although perhaps tonight we'd have a better chance at making it into *Debaucherous Prep Monthly* thanks to the Noah's Ark-like bar—two of every liquor imaginable—that we'd staged at one end of the cavernous living room. And as I stood by, spinning up a crisp Tanqueray & Tonic and surveying the swelling crowd, I didn't bother to suppress my smile. For sure there were high hopes and dreams attached to this evening, but with forty to fifty of our closest friends nestled within this pocket of perfection, plus enough booze to bathe a small whale, how could we possibly fail?

I'd already spotted Vanessa, super svelte in a low-cut black gown, and I hoped she'd seen me in my checkered hipster slacks and wild patterned shirt, boldly accessorized with a pair of Bono shades and a burgundy feathered boa. Surely all this plumage had caught her eye, just as her cleavage had caught mine, but for now I wasn't about to go find out. Instead I was deliberately avoiding her.

My master plan called for me to give her a wide berth during this initial phase of the evening so that I didn't seem to be draped all over her. Not yet. The way I saw it, everything was riding on sitting next to her at dinner. If I had her ear for the entire meal then I'd have plenty of time to pick up where I'd left off last night and seal my seduction. But if I somehow missed that window of opportunity I'd have a lot of ground to make up during the potentially sloppy post-dinner phase. Not impossible, but not likely either. So I bided my time, drank my gin, and enjoyed the company of everyone that wasn't nearly as lovely as Vanessa. Until finally the word was passed that dinner was ready and waiting—my call to arms and I sprang into action.

As Vanessa slowly made her way to the buffet table I converged perfectly like a lion on the prairie intercepting a gazelle. She turned and I was upon her, not tearing into her neck like I woulda liked, but with my best coincidental smile, "Oh, hi there."

"Hi." It was a long hi and a longer smile that bounced around her eyes, shining through a slight Vodka-Cranberry glaze, and I knew she was glad I was close.

"I love your dress." Then, dropping my voice to make it sound like it was our little secret, "You look fabulous."

"So do you. I adore the boa. Not many men can pull that off."

"Not many men would even try, my dear." And we flirted ourselves on down the buffet line and into the dining room where four large round tables had been set up so we could all sit and eat like civilized folks. But at the moment there was a bit of a bottleneck because so many of us were coming and going—some with plates, some without, some looking to sit, some already sitting, some looking to recruit for their table, some looking to be recruited, and many others just standing and talking. To me it was like the most dangerous game of musical chairs. I was petrified she'd get whisked away by any number of well meaning friends to a table with one too few seats and the music would stop and I'd be left standing with a plate of food and no Vanessa. So I made sure I stayed on her shoulder until finally we found ourselves standing over two empty place settings, "Should we sit here?"

"Yes, I think we should," she said. And as we sat I knew mine was the catbird seat. All I had to do was give a reasonable imitation of myself, listen to what she had to say, and ix-nay on the orn-pay and I was home free. So that's exactly what I did.

After dinner, dessert, and several rounds of toasts it was sneaking up on midnight so everyone hurried to fill a champagne glass and move back into the living room. Unfortunately, in the confusion Vanessa and I got separated, but there was nothing I could really do short of scurrying about like a hysterical mother searching for a lost child. So, hoping she'd come to me, I staked some ground by one of the big picture windows where I wound up toasting and talking with Benji & Maya.

Then someone turned off all the lights so we could better enjoy the upcoming fireworks while someone else put on Sinatra's "New York, New York." *Start spreading the news...* And then a few of the girls began counting down, "10... 9... 8..." *I'm leaving today...* I looked around for Vanessa but couldn't see her anywhere. "7... 6... 5..." *I want to be a part of it...* I knew this was a nice moment we were gonna miss, but even if I did go looking for her what would I say when I found her? "4... 3... 2..." *New York...* Though I was kicking myself for letting her slip away. "1..." *New York...* And all at once the noisemakers were blown, Benji kissed Maya beside me, and the first fireworks exploded brilliant red over Central Park. Then another one. And another.

Just then I felt something brush against my left arm and it was Vanessa looking up at me and the fireworks were exploding in her eyes and I leaned down and kissed her. I kissed her with everything I had and she kissed me back and if this wasn't the most romantic moment I've ever experienced then I don't know what was. And if this wasn't the best first kiss I've ever had, then it certainly was the most cinematic. Like a Woody Allen movie that never was but shoulda been. Then we kissed again to make sure we weren't dreaming. And I held her close and we watched the fireworks continue so huge over Central Park, dwarfed only by the fireworks reverberating through every inch of my body—pop-pop-pop-pop-pop. *It's up to you, New York, New York...* And then I understood that this was indeed heaven—one of those rare, other-worldly moments where everything I loved in life aligned, where longing became reality, where Perfection finally let me catch her.

"Does it get any better than this?" I whispered in her ear.

"No," she whispered back. "How can we be this lucky?" And we kissed again and again and again.

Neither one of us wanted the night to end, but eventually it had to. Around five in the morning Vanessa and I said our last good-nights and then retired together to the guest room. There are few things more delicious than taking a girl's clothes off for the first time—especially a girl you've been lusting after for an entire year.

And as I helped her out of her dress I was amazed by her perfect champagne glass breasts, her skinny little waist, her luscious long legs. All this time Vanessa had been hiding the body of a runway model but she'd never let on like she knew it. And now I got to know it.

Although after some exploratory fondling I started to get a little confused. What exactly was expected here? We were both naked, in bed, and naturally very much into each other. But it was also nearly dawn. I was exhausted and running on fumes. Surely she was too. And I certainly didn't want our first sex to be sloppy. But I also didn't want her to think I wasn't thoroughly attracted to her, that I was somehow rejecting her. At this late hour it's easy to become muddled about such things. So I took my best guess. "We're not supposed to have sex, right?"

"Oh no. Let's not. Sometime though, for sure."

"Oh good." I sighed and spooned in for one final kiss of her creamy shoulder blade, and as I finally drifted off to sleep all I could hear was the promise of her refrain. *How can we be this lucky... How can we be this lucky... How can we be this lucky...*

X

I Wanna Be Your Target

*O*f course, she lived in Rome. And no matter which road you took from LA, it was gonna be over 6000 miles away, so really, how lucky was that? A tough circumstance, for sure, and it shoulda torn my heart in two, or at least teared an eye on the flight home. But it didn't. Instead I sipped my Tanqueray & OJ and allowed my mind to wallow and wander through all the wonderful moments. And maybe it was the gin or the pressure in the cabin, but I swear I could feel Vanessa in my blood—swelling my veins from head to toe, turning my entire body into one big throbbing erection.

So many memories for so few minutes together...

How we stole away after the fireworks into the empty parlor and, leaving the lights off, snuggled together on the wide wooden window sill, and how we kept watch on the deserted, snow covered street corner below so as not to miss the occasional taxi test the icy road, only to spin slowly into a drift, then right itself and drive on like a drunken puppy on a waxed kitchen floor, and how we delighted in that...

And in us...

And how we confessed how long we'd been dreaming of each other...

And how we'd awoken to find the spell wasn't broken...

And how even cleaning the apartment was a pleasure with U2's "Beautiful Day" in the background and more and more laughter every time we found another one of my burgundy boa feathers lying on the hardwood floor...

And how we took that slow walk into Central Park with the afternoon sun beating down, setting to the impossible task of melting all that snow, and how cold it was, but not too cold, just enough to appreciate the hot breath inside our mouths as we kissed, and just enough to take off my gloves and finally warm her rose-colored cheeks with the palms of my hands, and how we smiled at her wearing the same purple coat and black stiletto boots as the day we met, and how we loved the geometry of coming full circle in one calendar year...

And, perhaps most of all, how we stood in front of the Dakota, bags at our feet, waiting for separate cabs to separate airports, and only then finally spoke of the unspeakable. "So my ticket says Los Angeles. What's yours say?"

"Rome."

"Maybe we could change it. I'm sure Oliver has some white-out. And, as I remember, back at Groton Benji took an elective on Document Forgery, or maybe it was Creative Writing, I can't be sure but we could find out." We smiled and almost laughed. But then we agreed, until our circumstances changed, our only play was a revival of *Abelard & Heloise*, and we pledged to see each other whenever she returned to the States or if my job ever sent me to back to Europe. Then we kissed one last time with her cab idling by, and that's when she told me the secret she'd been saving for this very moment—that she was coming to Los Angeles for a friend's wedding in just two short months so I'd be seeing her a lot sooner than I thought. And as she drove away I loved her for that hopeful farewell.

Because now, flying home, I could focus on the time instead of the distance. Eight weeks seemed a lot closer than Rome. Of course in *nine* weeks she'd be gone again and what then? But the heart doesn't think that way. It hopes well beyond its means, which is probably why I couldn't shake this overwhelming hunch that we were gonna find a way to make it work. We just needed a little patience and plenty of sappy emails to fan the flames and, in the end, all would be good. Besides, what was love without an obstacle? Wasn't love strongest when it was a little inconvenient? And c'mon, this was 2001—geography wasn't half the hurdle it used to be.

A week or so later I was in my office rereading her latest missive. *"I still can't help thinking of anything but the magical time we shared and when I'm going to see you next. Rationally, this all seems a bit crazy, but somehow it just feels really right."* Then, just as I was beginning to think how best to agree with her, there was a knock on my door. It was Kira, looking sexy as always, this time in a pair of painted-on jeans and a snug, low-cut tee. She'd just recorded a voiceover for our Amsterdam story and wanted to say hello.

"Come on in, but shut the door." Maggie was just down the hall.

"How was New York?"

"Amazing. I think I fell in love." This to deflect another "kiss me" moment, but also because she was a friend and I wanted to share my good fortune. So I told her a fast and furious version of Vanessa and me.

"Are you gonna tell Maggie?" Ever since I'd taken the job, Maggie and I had tried to keep our past history and current present a secret from everyone that worked on the show. But somehow Kira was well aware of it—probably because I'd told her.

"We're not really talking these days."

"Oh. I see." And then she spoke about her own New Year's Eve at the Playboy Mansion, where she was something of a regular, and how she'd partied with a few celebrities that I admired and even smoked a joint with Bill Maher. Then she went on to tell me how she and Doug had just gotten back from Las Vegas and the AVN Awards—the porn industry's answer to the Oscars. Although she wasn't actually a porn star she'd gotten a freelance gig interviewing nominees on the red carpet. But of course the real reason she was there was because it was one helluva party.

After giving me a few of the highlights, she asked to use my computer for a second. "I want to show you something we shot in Vegas." I started to give up my chair but she was already sitting in my lap, and as she pulled up her site I was prepared for some humorous outtakes from her interviews. But then she explained that Doug had shot her having sex with a porn star named Billy Glide. *What?* Her husband actually *filmed* her having sex with another guy? Well, evidently the answer was a big fat yes, because there she was sucking his big fat cock.

"He's huge."

"Uh-huh," she said with obvious pleasure. She was proud of this? As they slid into a 69, I noticed the garish bedspread of their cheap-looking hotel room and I couldn't help remembering the similar bed we'd shared in Prague. Of course, that wasn't what Kira was thinking. How could it be? Watching him turn her over and plunge himself so deep inside of her, I was certain this giant cock of a man had flushed me from her system, erasing me off the face of her memory—or at the very least her *muscle* memory.

"Listen, I don't need to see this."

She laughed. "Isn't it fun?" But she didn't turn it off. She was playing with me again—*Make the preppie blush.*

And her sitting on my lap didn't make it any easier. "I guess, but really I'd rather not see it."

Finally, mercifully, she clicked off her site. Of course I had a million questions bouncing round my mind—mostly variations of "How could you do *that* in front of your husband?" "How could your husband *film* you doing that?" and "Why exactly are you showing that to *me*?"—but I didn't ask any of them. Because I didn't really want to know. I was disgusted. Didn't she have better taste than that? And what was the point? Money? Excitement? Pleasure? And what was Doug getting out of the deal? *This was a marriage?*

Later, however, it dawned on me that maybe she'd shown me the video because she honestly wanted to know what I thought. Perhaps she'd wanted me, as a friend, to somehow validate what she'd done. I was pretty sure having hardcore sex on-camera with a man other than her husband was a first for her, which meant she'd crossed over yet another line in her life, and she had to wonder if she'd made the right decision. And if this would be something she'd continue to do. Or would it be just a one-time thing? Unfortunately these were questions I wasn't qualified to answer, and although I still considered her very much a friend, at that moment I couldn't have felt farther from her.

Maybe two weeks later I was standing in Ken Marcus's parking lot. It was 10:00 a.m. and Max pulled up right on the nose. Inside, he threw up some lights and we sat Ken down for his interview. Once again he was wearing what I now surmised to be his signature look—black on black, jeans and a t-shirt—but, because he was gonna be on-camera, today's tee said www.KenMarcus.com across the chest. Shameless or shrewd, it was a smart move and sure to win him a few more members, and a few more members was what his business was all about.

But first I got him talking about his life before the Internet, back when he shot on film and actually used a darkroom. These were his halcyon days. At the age of thirteen Ken had begun a thirteen-year stint studying with the legendary Ansel Adams. Then, in 1972, he'd been hired by Bob Guccione and had developed *Penthouse*'s signature soft glossy style by stretching a piece of French pantyhose between his lens and the body of the camera. Two years later he'd signed on with Hef and, over the next decade, gone on to shoot forty-three centerfolds. In those days it would have been hard to argue that he didn't have the world's most glamorous job. "My instructions were, 'Travel first-class, stay only in the best hotels, eat in the best restaurants, get lots of publicity so everybody knows who you are and where you are, tip big so that nobody steals your stuff, and whatever else you do, always try and look like you're having a good time.' So, you know, that was my life for over a decade."

Now his life was all about shooting fetish and bondage for his website—a website I'd naturally spent plenty of time researching. The first thing I'd noticed was that every single model was absolutely gorgeous. They were mostly web-girls and porn stars with a few former Playmates and Penthouse Pets mixed in. Of course, being a bondage site, a lotta them were tied up, which in theory I could enjoy, but in practice I found the bindings to be so intricate and tightly woven that they tended to distort the body in an unnatural and unappealing way. Particularly I disliked the way they could misshape a girl's breasts, squeezing them like a half filled water balloon.

I also didn't care for the extreme and often bizarre things being done to them. Although I gotta say, from what I saw Ken could be wickedly creative. The girls were red and raw from flogging, mummified in saran wrap, pinched with clothes pins, hung upside down, dripping with candle wax, and there was even one who was drinking her own urine.

And upon closer inspection of that particular photoset I realized it was Kira. It was hard to believe, or maybe it wasn't, but there she was, naked, peeing into a wine glass, and then gulping it down so deeply some of it overflowed off the corners of her mouth and onto her breasts. I guess I'd expected to find Kira on the site—since she and Ken were so close, of course he would have shot her—but what really surprised me was how turned off I was. Surely this was fake, some sort of bait and switch or Photoshop trickery. Who was really gonna drink their own piss?

During Ken's interview I meant to ask how they got the shot, but we were running late and it probably wasn't gonna make it into the final cut anyway so I decided to skip it. Besides, in a way he addressed the issue with his final soundbite. "I'm not a photo-journalist, you know. I don't shoot the truth. I create lies, I create fantasies. I see them as stories. If a photograph is worth a thou-sand words, *my* photographs start off with, 'Once upon a time.'"

"Perfect, Ken. Thanks. That's all we need."

As soon as the words were out of my mouth I heard Kira's voice. "Ken!" She came running around the corner like an excited little girl about to hug her daddy, and I wondered how long she'd been waiting quietly in the hallway.

And then I realized she wasn't alone. A man emerged from the shadows shooting a small one chip DV camera, and as he stepped into our bright lights I could see it wasn't just a man, it was *her husband.* "Hey, Ken."

While Doug said hello, Kira came my way. "I hope you don't mind. Doug's gonna shoot some behind-the-scenes stuff for MarriedCouple."

"You don't mind, do you Ross?" Now Doug was walking toward me and rolling tape on what musta been my bewildered face. This was the first time I'd seen him since fucking his wife. But then I remembered she'd also just fucked Billy Glide, ergo, coming after me at this point would be selective prosecution—a big no-no in this country—so I caught my breath and even managed to shake his hand without stuttering, "No worries, whatever you need. The more the merrier."

Soon we were shooting the first girl, a former Penthouse Pet named Julie Strain. Although physically she wasn't my type—six-one, brunette, with huge fake breasts—I was incredibly impressed with her as a model. Not only was she on time, she was *early*, which was virtually unheard of in the adult biz. And once she and Ken got going it was like they were connected—pose, click, pose, click, pose, click. Julie didn't need to be told a thing. Each and every vogue was different from the last. Wearing only a few thin strips of pleather, she worked a black leather bench like it was a pommel horse while simultaneously hamming it up with an over-sized glass dildo—gripping, licking, worshipping—a dynamic, high energy dance that went straight through a good fifteen to twenty minutes. And then she was gone as fast as she came. A total pro.

The second model was another Penthouse Pet, the adorable redheaded Aimee Sweet. Ken put her in a gold pony girl costume—shoes that looked like hoofs, tiny stirrups that dangled like a garter belt near her slim tuft of red hair, a corset that exposed her beautiful breasts and those rosy nipples that redheads so often have, and a bridle complete with a bit that framed her super cute freckly face. Kinda odd, yet kinda hot.

Next up was Mika, the Asian contortionist, and Ken decided to keep things simple. He had her get completely naked, then put her atop a wooden table where she went through a myriad of impossible maneuvers. Didn't do a damn thing for me sexually, but it was impressive to watch.

The last model was Skye, a central-casting buxom blonde bimbo—big curled hair, huge fake tits, long skinny legs, and a dynamite ass that was dying to be fucked. She seemed to be all curves and no depth, d'oh-eyed instead of doe-eyed, and although I couldn't be exactly sure how slow Skye was upstairs, down below

I knew she'd be lighting fast. Ken decided to drape her in a tiny chain-mail top that exposed every inch of her heavenly body. As I watched her twist and turn and do her best to steam Ken's lens I found myself feeling guilty for being so aroused by this cartoon of a woman. Was this a sign of my sexual immaturity or perhaps my lowbrow taste? But then I figured there had to be something instinctual about her look that sent my blood running south. Surely this was nature at work, an innate reaction to a visual cue that was way outta my hands. I had no more control over this than I had over my need to breathe, or eat, or piss. This was just about being alive. Yes, that had to be it.

When we were done shooting her, Kira went ahead and did what I should have done myself—she asked Skye to stick around and join us all for dinner. And after Skye said yes, I swear Kira flashed me a look that said *she's all yours.*

We only had one shot left, but it was also the most difficult—a stand-up that involved hanging Kira upside down. Ken had an industrial strength winch attached to his ceiling, so that part was relatively easy. What made it difficult was that Max also had to turn the camera upside down and zoom in so it appeared Kira was right-side up. To complete the effect we'd even put her hair in a ponytail and tied it down so it wouldn't fall "upwards" and give us away. As Kira began, "Once the proper environment is achieved the artist is ready to turn fantasy into reality..." the idea was for Max to pull out while simultaneously spinning the camera and thus revealing her predicament just as she was finishing her line, "...because in the world of Ken Marcus, things aren't always what they seem."

As if all that wasn't hard enough, Max had to remove the eyepiece because it was in the way, and he couldn't exactly look through it anyway as he was spinning the camera. This meant the only way for him to actually see what he was shooting was to hook up a monitor and use that as his viewfinder, which was an incredibly unnatural way to shoot. On top of that, Kira was only good for two takes at a time before the blood rushed to her head so badly it looked like she was about to explode like a tick. So Doug had to lower her down every other take and then we'd wait for her to recover. Finally, after almost an hour on this one shot—way more time than it was worth—Kira and Max both nailed their parts and we all burst into applause. And no one clapped louder than me because I was damn proud of both of them.

Within 30 minutes, Ken, Kira, Doug, Max, Skye and I were all cramming into a booth down the block at Swingers, one of Ken's favorite diners. I made sure I was sitting next to Skye, then ordered a Sam Adams with another on its heels. There's nothing thirstier than a long day's shoot, and as we toasted everyone's hard work it hit me how much fun I'd had today. It was a great group and we had a lot of laughs. All the girls had been wonderful—especially Skye—and I was even fine with having Doug around. He was a helluva nice guy, and Kira and I were just friends so it was no big deal. If anything, having her husband around cemented our status as "just friends"—maybe that was why she brought him. Not sure, but either way, we'd all worked well together and it was a good day.

Now, as I watched Kira sip her glass of white wine, I was suddenly reminded of the question I meant to ask Ken earlier. "Hey Ken, how did you fake those shots of Kira drinking her own pee?"

"I didn't." I couldn't tell if he was kidding.

"C'mon. She didn't really—"

"She did."

Turning to Kira, "You did?"

"Yep." And she smiled and took an extra long pull of her wine, either to add an exclamation point or to help erase the memory.

Then Doug chimed in. "I think she had a harder time hitting

the glass than she did drinking it."

We all laughed, but Max had heard enough. "Can we change the subject please?"

As our group conversation crumbled into smaller ones I drew Skye in by asking about how she and Ken first met. Turned out it was just a few months ago at a fetish and bondage convention. She'd been going from booth to booth in search of a dog collar because, as she said, "I was feeling a little naughty." Ken, spotting this damsel in distress, offered to escort her to the proper booth, whereupon he decided a dog collar was only the beginning. "And this sweet man fully dressed me, from dog collar to corset to ankle cuffs to wrist cuffs and about a month later I was shooting with him." *Bet he didn't learn that from Ansel Adams!*

By the time our food came I was asking Skye where she lived and hoping she'd say someplace nearby. But the answer I got was even better—San Diego. She'd driven up just for the shoot and was gonna go home after dinner. By then it'd be pushing 10:00 p.m. and it was nearly a three-hour trek. So, chivalrous gentlemen that I was, I discretely whispered an alternative plan. "You know, you're more than welcome to stay with me. It's the least I can do after all your hard work today."

"Where do you live?"

"Beachwood Canyon."

"Where's that?"

"Hollywood. It's close."

"Oh." Then her attention was called to another part of table before I could get a read on what *"Oh"* meant. A lot of my conversation with her went like that. Her delivery was so vacuous it was beyond deadpan and almost devoid of meaning. Was she blowing me off, considering it, or saying *Okay, sure, let's go fuck like wild banshees*? Who knew? I certainly didn't. And it seemed rude to press. Surely she'd understood the offer set before her and if she wanted me, she'd say so. If she didn't, she wouldn't. Before long I was picking up the tab on the company dime—not quite the Playboy of Ken's day, but at least it was something.

When we were all outside and saying our goodbyes Skye came over and hugged me and I could feel her breasts on my chest as she whispered, "I'll follow you home." *Nice! No confusion there.*

Quarter of an hour later I was leading her into my apartment. I was like a Christmas morning kid staring at a brand new bicycle awkwardly wrapped in paper and a bow. There was no disguising what was underneath. And I couldn't wait to tear into it and take it for out for a spin. But first I had to show some patience.

So I broke out a couple of Sierra Nevada Pale Ales and we smoked a little pot. Then she said, "I'd like to see you wet." Although I had a couple ideas, once again, I wasn't quite sure what she meant. She explained that her fetish was for a guy to get dripping wet as if just stepping out of a shower or a pool. I couldn't tell if she was seriously turned on by this or if she just wanted me to get the stench of the shoot off my body before she fucked my brains out. Probably the latter, because I sure did stink.

I was beginning to wonder if Skye was actually smarter than I'd thought. Maybe she'd planned all along to spend the night at my place. Had it really been Kira's idea to ask her to dinner, or did she invite herself? Had I sat next to her, or did she sit next to me? For sure, she'd been the tactful one, waiting until the final and most opportune moment to accept my invitation so no one else would know. And now here she was politely, and rather sexily, getting me to wash my balls before she licked them.

So naturally I took off all my clothes and got into the shower. Mine was the kind with a swinging door so I left it open for her to watch in case wet guys really did turn her on. I certainly didn't give a damn that water was spraying all over the bathroom, not with this leggy bombshell sitting on my oversized sink sipping her beer and watching me lather up my undercarriage. And for some reason the fact that I was the only one naked—that she was still wearing her jeans and super tight t-shirt—made the experience all the more arousing.

When I got out I brought her back to the living room and sat her down on the couch where I finally got to unwrap my bicycle. Even though I'd seen her naked just a few hours earlier it was nothing like putting my eyes and hands all over her in my own apartment. Inevitably I went for her breasts, which were the first fakes I'd ever felt, and although my public stance on silicone was that it was a big mistake, privately I had to smile at how nice these were. Then, making my way down her unbelievable body, past her taut tummy to her wisp of a landing strip, I noticed for the first time she had a pierced pussy—a tiny metal ring right through the tops of her outer lips—and I marveled that not only was she built for sex, she was groomed for it too. As I felt the cold steel click and clack against my front teeth, I wondered how much of her life was spent preparing for moments just like this? I found her clit with my tongue and so on and so on until I felt her pelvis pulse and thrust into orgasm.

Later, lying in bed her cell phone started ringing, and after a look at the caller ID she said it was her boyfriend. *She had a boyfriend?!?* Yes, she did, and in fact she was supposed to see him tomorrow. But she didn't pick up. "He's just calling to see if I made it home okay."

"Makes sense. He's worried about his girl."

"I should probably call him back and let him know I'm alright."

"You want me to go in the other room so you can have some privacy?"

"No, it's okay. I'll be quick." And I couldn't believe it. She actually called her boyfriend while lying naked in my bed! Then she proceeded to tell him that she was at Ken's studio, that he'd let her crash on the couch, which to me sounded like plenty enough to make a boyfriend jealous. Not nearly as bad as the truth, of course, but still, if I heard that alibi I'd be imagining her in bed with Ken for sure. But I guess it worked. "I love you too. See you *mañana*, babe. Kisses." *Incredible.*

Now I *knew* she was a lot smarter than I'd thought. So I told her so, or at least something similar, "You're way too smart for him, aren't you?"

She smiled. "You better fuck me again right now because you can't in the morning."

"Why not?"

"'Cuz I'm gonna be seeing my boyfriend and I can't fuck you both in the same day." Made sense. Doing us both under the same sun woulda been horribly insensitive. So I gave her what she wanted and we drifted off to sleep.

The next morning when I awoke I was rubbing up against her and I thought I heard her say, "I wanna be your target."

My *target?* What the hell did that mean? "Huh?"

A little bit louder now, "I wanna be your target."

"I don't understand?"

"I want you to cum on me!"

Oh right, of course. I can't fuck you today because you're gonna see your boyfriend. But I *can* blow a load on your ass. So I did.

After Skye left I was glad she was gone because remorse was already seeping in. My thoughts were running back to Vanessa. And when I sat down to check my emails, of course I found her name—bold and unread—in my mailbox. *Fuck.* I never shoulda opened it so soon, but I did. A reflex perhaps. And reading her sweet, oblivious words—how she missed me so much and hoped I was having fun—my stomach hollowed out and sank to my knees. The only way out of it was to flee, so I ran like hell to the movies and forgot about my absentee morality in the comfort of the cool, dark theater.

But later on it got better. I'd just needed a little time to rationalize my way through. And to realize how silly it was to keep kicking myself. After all, what was the point of working for Playboy if I couldn't revel in the perks? Wouldn't these be the days I remembered on my deathbed—tired, toothless, and terribly medicated, wouldn't I be thanking myself for stomping on the terra? And besides, what if things didn't work out with Vanessa?

Of course, I didn't put all that in my next email. Instead I sent off another sap-packed installment of my enduring love, which I hoped didn't read too guilty, like getting flowers for no good reason. Nothing like guilty flowers to get a girl's mind rumbling. Deciding it was probably fine I pressed "Send" and grabbed my hockey gear and headed down to the garage. I was looking forward to a hard skate. But I never made it to the game.

XI

You're Not in the Porn Business!

$\mathscr{I}$ was on the 405 North about to get off on Roscoe—just minutes away from the rink—when my cell started ringing. The caller ID told me it was Maggie, so there was no way I was gonna answer. We'd barely spoken since our falling out and now I half expected her to be screaming *"I know what you did to that blonde girl—I know you came on her ass!"* When she called again I just turned up the music to drown out the ring tone. But by the third time I started to get worried she was in some sort of trouble. So on the fifth call, I had to pick up.

My hello was met with hysteria, "Lucy's hurt! Lucy's hurt! She's hurt bad, baby—You gotta get over there—She can't move her back legs!" And I felt the same hysteria surge through every bone in my body. I'd just pulled onto the off-ramp, but instead of turning right toward my game I made a left and then a left again and got right back on the way I came.

Meanwhile, Maggie calmed herself long enough to tell me what was going so terribly wrong. She was in Ft. Lauderdale shooting that *Lesbian Cheerleader* story while an old boyfriend was house sitting and taking care of the dogs. They'd gone to the park to play Frisbee and Lucy had landed funny, and then an hour later she'd lost control of her back legs. He'd taken her to the emergency vet, but he didn't have a credit card so they couldn't start the procedure. I wasn't exactly sure why they couldn't take Maggie's over the phone, but they couldn't, so I was hightailing it over to the Glendale vet clinic.

When I walked in I saw the old boyfriend hanging his head— sad for Lucy I'm sure, but also a bit embarrassed that Maggie had to call another ex to take care of the bill. But I didn't care about all that. And I certainly didn't care if they were fucking again. I just cared about Lucy. I gave the vet my Visa and told him to do whatever needed to be done. Then I listened to him explain that he thought Lucy had some kind of embolism—like a blood clot but not quite—that was pinching a nerve or not letting something flow or somehow messing her up real bad. I didn't totally understand, but the bottom line was she couldn't move her back legs.

I was led into a huge, overly lit treatment room with a bunch of cold steel tables and a hard tiled floor. Lucy was lying on a blanket about fifteen feet away. When she saw me, she yelped and tried to get up, but her legs weren't gonna cooperate. Poor thing didn't know what was going on. And neither did I. All I could do was stay with her until it was time for the knife. So I did.

Later, when I finally got home, I poured five fingers of scotch, cranked up Clapton's "Bell Bottom Blues," and opened the floodgates. Like a schoolgirl with a skinned knee. Strange how life is— one minute I'm balling a web model, the next minute I'm bawling my eyes out because my favorite dog in the world is paralyzed. The high-highs and the low-lows and so it goes.

In fact, I was so broken I even did the math and realized that nine hours and 6,732 miles away it was 8:00 a.m. in Rome. And then I did the unthinkable—I called her. We'd agreed never to telephone because we didn't want to be in the habit of long international phone calls, not only because of the bills, but because emails were infinitely more romantic. But this wasn't about romance. This was about solace. I needed her voice.

Vanessa picked up on the third ring and she sounded so close she coulda been on the couch with me. After some initial surprise, I could tell she was thrilled I'd called. Then I told her about what had happened in the few hours since I'd sent my last email, which she'd read just minutes earlier over breakfast. Only later did I wonder if it was wrong or weird to share my desolation over an ex-girlfriend's dog, but maybe that was because I didn't see Maggie as an ex-girlfriend. I saw her as a friend. Even sometimes as a sister. Sure we'd fought like hell and we'd hurt each other bad—like an Ike & Tina limo ride—but in the end I knew Maggie wasn't going away. And if Vanessa was indeed going to be in my life as my lover and my wife she needed to get to know Maggie sooner or later. And Lucy. And even Lola.

So yes, I called Vanessa and once again she was perfect, absolutely amazing, saying all the right things with no shred of jealousy, just complete comfort and understanding. It took nearly two hours, but finally I was in bed with the lights off, and she reminded me that in just five weeks she'd be lying there with me. But I told her she already was. And then she whispered, *"Ti mando un bacione grosso come una casa."*

I had no idea what those gorgeous words meant, but I knew I loved them and I loved her and I almost told her so, but I stopped just short. Instead I said, "Thank you," and after hanging up I repeated it aloud, "Thank you, thank you so much, my dear Vanessa," because I hadn't been lying. She really was there with me. And then I was asleep.

In the morning I went to see Maggie. She'd left Hoyt & Frank in Florida to finish the *Lesbian Cheerleader* story by themselves and hopped the first flight back to LA. She'd gone straight to the vet but Lucy was still sleeping from the surgery, so now she was waiting it out at home.

When she opened the door I could tell she'd been crying for quite a while. We hugged long and silent and then she took me inside. Sitting down on her vintage Victorian couch, she showed me a photo of the dogs she'd been clutching the entire plane ride home. Once again we shared a mournful hug, and when she kissed me her lips tasted of salt from so many tears, and I kissed her back. And then we had sex. Nothing like the last time we'd fucked—full of gin, power, and control with nubile lesbians licking at our heels. No, this was about solace and sharing and bringing each other through.

As I was buckling up my pants the phone rang. Maggie answered it. And then she turned to me. "Lucy's ready."

"I'll go with you."

Soon we were listening to the vet explain that they did what they could but they weren't able to reach the embolism, so nature was just gonna have to take its course. Lucy was paralyzed below the waist. With time, she might regain some use of her legs. Or she might not.

I spent the rest of the weekend at Maggie's. And it wasn't easy. I don't know who had it rougher, Lucy or Maggie. I tried to be with them as much as I could, but all that really meant was dropping by after work. Meanwhile, Maggie told Bruce she had to work from home, so day and night she was nursing her girl back to health—making her pee, picking up her poo, massaging her legs, but mainly just letting her know she'd never give up on her. As long as Lucy wasn't in any pain and could still smile and knew how loved she was, Maggie would be there for her.

She even went online and found a doggie wheelchair. She'd hook Lucy up to this strange contraption that held her back legs in a sling in between the wheels and we'd take her for the usual hike in the hills. At first it was hard for her to pull all her weight with just her two front legs, but she managed and the exercise did her good, and every once in a while we saw her back left leg move—whether it was voluntary or just a reflex we couldn't be sure.

No doubt, a lotta folks woulda just put her down—I know because that's what I was told by plenty of other dog owners—but not Maggie. Not a chance. She'd sooner put herself down. I wasn't sure if it was her maternal instinct emerging or just a general fortitude of character, but whatever it was she certainly rose to the occasion and earned a whole new level of my respect. Not once did I ever hear her complain—instead she stayed positive, rolled up her sleeves, and dealt like the champion she was. And how could I not love her for that? How could I not want somebody like that on my side?

February was winding down, which meant Vanessa was on the horizon. First, however, I had to survive a trip to Houston—a sweaty, sprawling excuse of a town with all of the provincial negativity of the Lone Star State but none of the good stuff. Even though Kira was hosting I'd been dreading this shoot ever since I found out about it. But seriously, has anyone ever looked forward to a trip to Houston?

By the time we got to our hotel it was after eleven and we learned that it wasn't a hotel at all. It was a classic fleabag—sandpaper sheets, cigarette burns on the bedside tables, gaping holes in the blankets, cats drinking from the muddy pool, whole families huddled in the coin-op laundry room, plus-sized prostitutes loitering in the halls—and I cursed myself for, just this once, not checking the place out online after our budget conscious production coordinator had booked the rooms. Bad move, and a direct result of my head not being in my work. One look at Kira and I knew she was plenty pissed. Dexter, my cameraman, wasn't too thrilled either. I suppose I coulda found us another place, but it was late and we were tired so I did what I could, which was to grab a six pack of Lone Star from the store across the street and sit in my dirty room, on my dirty bed, flipping dirty channels, and sipping dirty beer 'til I was dizzy enough to fall asleep.

The next morning we had some eggs at Denny's and then headed over to the shoot which was at a house in one of the endless Houston suburbs. The story, of which I also wasn't a big fan, was about a website called CU-Central.com. They'd taken high-end video conferencing software and created a series of chat rooms designed as a kind of online swing club where you never actually met or physically touched another human being. To log in you had to be sending live video of yourself, so everyone on the site was able to see everyone else. The idea was for men, women, and couples to sit safely in the comfort of their own homes typing flirty messages and basically getting off on each other. This was cyber-swinging.

Because my budget wouldn't allow me to go door-to-door visiting with their eight thousand members the company's founder, Marc, had arranged a party for some of the local CU-Central users who were willing to go on television. The plan was to make it look like I went to three different homes by shooting the house's three different bedrooms. A computer would be set up in each one so we could film three types of users—a single girl, a girl-girl couple, and a boy-girl couple. The living room would serve as the location for the party, which I'd use as a way to interview more members to round out the piece. Meanwhile, the members would get to do some "real" swinging. Which wasn't a complete fabrication because sometimes members would, in fact, get together to fuck each other in real life, or "IRL" as they say.

When we arrived around ten, I found Marc in the open garage tapping a keg. From our previous phone conversations I knew Marc was just a businessman. He didn't use the site himself so this venture wasn't about realizing his own kinky dreams or getting himself laid, it was about making a buck.

Inside, we introduced ourselves to the twenty-odd members, and I could tell by the way they were looking at us that we were in trouble. "Oh, I can't wait to play with them," I heard one woman say, and I had a hunch she wasn't kidding. I coulda guessed Kira was gonna be the hottest of the lot, but never in a million years would I have thought Dexter and myself would be placing and showing. But we had a job to do, and no matter what happened it'd all be over by the end of the day, and this time tomorrow we'd be on a plane back to LA. So we broke out the gear and got to work.

And I should say, I did appreciate how outgoing everyone was. They were all so damn horny and gung-ho to be on Playboy TV that they were up for just about anything. Within minutes every reasonably comfortable surface in the house seemed to be supporting some sort of sex act, whether we happened to be shooting it or not. But it was all pretty damn grotesque. At one point I barged into a room I thought was empty and found, spread out on the middle of the floor, a heavy-set man on top of his heavier wife. He had a vibrator pressed firmly against her clit and his other hand was wrist deep inside her. "Oh, pardon me." He looked up like a kid caught with his hand in the cookie jar—and I suppose in a way he was. "Don't let me interrupt. Please continue." Although I meant to say, *Please stop and never, ever do that again.*

Unfortunately all that hot sweaty sex was making them thirsty, and it didn't take long for them to get deep into the keg. And predictably, the closer they got to the bottom the more obnoxious they became. Soon every trip through the crowded living room was like a gauntlet run up the middle of a goal-line defense playing grab-ass for keeps. And it got worse. Around mid-afternoon their communal drunkenness peaked and I could feel their primal energy surge through the house, and suddenly I knew the fear & loathing poor Piggy musta felt, stranded on that island watching all his fly classmates paint their faces.

It got so bad Kira refused to leave the bedroom we'd staked out. Which was just as well, because by that point I knew I had the best footage I was gonna get out of them. The only way to save the story was to have Kira put on another of her little shows. Brave soul she was, she agreed to log on to one of the chat rooms and pretend to masturbate. Before she got nakee butts I made sure to lock the door, just in case. A good thing too, because once she got going, word spread fast. Judging by the hoots & hollers it sounded like everyone had flocked to watch on the other two computers. But as Kira got good and into it I began to hear whispering in the hallway, followed by someone trying to turn the knob, and then more voices, and then they were pounding on the door—the barbarians were at the gate!

Kira looked a little scared, then a lot pissed. And I couldn't blame her. Here she was using *her* body to sell *their* product, and how were they repaying her? By damn near threatening her. So I spoke up before she could shout something probably none too nice. "Sorry, but you're gonna have to watch the show from one of the other computers."

More pounding.

"We don't want Marc to have to suspend your membership, do we?"

Still more pounding.

"Or revoke your beer privileges!"

Then silence as the drunken savages slouched off to Gomorrah.

After Kira was through we waited a good thirty minutes for their excitement to subside before we dared open the door. I went out first to do a little recon, and sure enough most of the members seemed to be tuckering out. As far as I could tell there was just one final sex act still flickering—a woman lying naked across her husband's lap while he absentmindedly fingered her. Normally this wouldn't have fazed me, but on my second pass after hitting the kitchen for a few bottled waters I noticed that the woman wasn't moving. At all. And her eyes were shut. Yet the guy kept rubbing away. So I had to ask, "Ah, is she okay?"

He was an older guy—late forties, glasses, with a schoolteacher vibe. His answer was so deadpan that I actually almost believed him. "Sometimes when I'm pleasuring her she has such an intense orgasm that she actually falls asleep." *Riiiiiight.*

Back at the hotel the three of us sat in Kira's room, drained, smoking one of her joints and washing the taste of the shoot out of our mouths with a bottle of Jack Daniels. Me, I had a lotta disgust built up—more than any story I'd done so far—as well as a lotta sadness. I couldn't stop thinking about all the members and how they seemed so lonely and lost. One woman had told me she'd joined the site because, in essence, she was just looking for a friend. "We talk about our jobs, we talk about our kids, and you get to know the person behind the image on the camera. You go into a swing club and it's people looking for notches on the bedpost."

Another woman had explained she was there because she was afraid of what she'd encounter on a real date. "In a chat room we don't feel obligated, we don't feel pressured, especially as females, you know. We set our own pace, we do what we want, or we *don't* do what we want, you know, it's up to us what we do." *Damn.* Why wasn't it always up to her what she did? What kind of animals had she been dating IRL that made her believe the only way not to be raped was to play it safe online?

Then there was that guy who'd laughed as he said, "All's I tells the guys at work is there's this place to go see some good looking pussy." I didn't know which was worse, that *on-camera* he'd actually referred to women as "pussy," or that to him these ladies were attractive.

It seemed to me CU-Central represented what was both good and bad about the Internet. Taking like-minded folks out of the dark corners of the country and bringing them together in an online community had to be a positive thing, but wasn't it also just another step on society's trail of tears where people have become afraid to actually get out there and meet someone? The net was like a pair of X-ray specs through which we could finally see the loneliness that lurks inside the heart of man. And this not-so-quiet desperation was measured no longer in coffee spoons, but in so many memberships to meaningless websites filled with plain looking people, meekly serving up their sexuality, hoping not to be rejected even in this anonymous world where they were known simply as MissLonelyhearts1973.

I gotta say, getting a glimpse into their collective sadness was a tremendous downer, and I was ready to let it all out. "I tell ya, the worst thing about being in the porn business is—"

"*You're* not in the porn business!" Kira was glaring at me with drunken scorn. "*I'm* in the porn business."

Wow. I'd never seen her look at me like that. Dexter laughed and the conversation moved on, but I didn't. I sat on that moment because I knew she was right. I wasn't in the porn business. I wasn't getting nakee butts and pretending to masturbate for a bunch of strangers. I didn't have simulated sex with low-rent actors, and I didn't fuck my spouse and the occasional porn star for money on the World Wide Web. No, I was just a television producer for a seldom watched program on a premium channel that few people actually got.

And this was still on my mind when I noticed Dexter was standing to say goodnight, and I wondered how long I'd been silent. Then I made sure to say my own goodnight before he left, because the last time Kira and I were drunk, stoned, and alone together we'd hooked up, and although I was pretty sure we were just friends I didn't want to test that theory—especially with Vanessa coming to town in less than a week. So I left.

Two days after Houston and three months after New Years, Vanessa finally arrived in Los Angeles. She was spending tonight, a Thursday, at the Beverly Wilshire Hotel with her mother, Friday and Saturday in Palm Springs for the wedding, and then Sunday and Monday back in LA with me. So as I drove across town to pick her up for dinner I knew this evening was just an appetizer. But still, I was hungry as hell to see her.

Although, I gotta say, as I walked into the five-star lobby I did wish she was staying at a different hotel in a different part of town because the Beverly Wilshire kinda gave me the creeps. Situated at the foot of Rodeo Drive and recognized around the country from so many *Pretty Woman* scenes, this was hardcore Beverly Hills. And Beverly Hills was a living wax museum—home to zombie women with their faraway eyes and their skin drawn tight and their monster, Louis Vuitton "fuck you" handbags. And their oily men, imposing their will all over the room like a scattergun, spending and pretending they were the last surviving member of the Rat Pack. Not my favorite part of town.

Luckily, I was only staying for a minute. Once Vanessa came downstairs I was gonna whisk her away to Sushi Roku because I remembered an email where she lamented the poor quality of raw fish in Rome. And because it was my favorite restaurant in town. When she stepped off the elevator we locked eyes and she strode full and radiant in her straight leg denim and cute black top. We hugged tight and tighter, then I kissed her long and longer, like it had been three months since the last time. But when we started talking it was like we'd never been apart.

Later, as we were sitting side by side at the sushi bar, I felt like I was part of one of those real couples I'd heard so much about, and as I pressed her hand in between mouthfuls of spicy tuna and salmon sashimi I tried to remember the last time I'd felt so good. Since moving to LA Maggie was the only woman I'd been halfway serious about, but given our decade gap we'd probably been doomed from the start. Before that I was in Jackson Hole where I'd had an affair with a girl dying to dabble outside her five-year relationship, and although I'd slipped and loved her way too much it was another doomed romance because ultimately she went back to her banker boyfriend. So that pretty much leaves me with my Wesleyan girlfriend as the last—and only?—time I felt like I was in an honest, healthy, fully reciprocated, two-to-tango relationship. And that was six years ago. And it was college. So I guess I could understand why I was so ready for Vanessa, and why, as we spooned our way into the infamous Roku chocolate lava cake, I wanted to ask her to marry me right then and there. But of course I didn't. I still hadn't even told her I loved her.

After dinner, as much as I hated to drive her back to the hotel, it was pushing midnight and mother was waiting, so that's what I did. Although I couldn't resist pulling over and parking on Wilshire where we kissed and groped, and I took off my seat belt and then hers and I climbed into her seat so we could grope some more and I wanted her so bad. But all we could do was steam up the windows like a couple teenagers trying not to tangle our braces.

And at the Beverly Wilshire I kissed her one final time with the doorman watching and waiting to do his thing. Walking back to my Chevy Blazer with a chubba pressed heavy against my Diesels, I was glad I hadn't worn slacks.

Time is an odd thing—so rigidly measured, yet so subjective. How else could you explain why the next two days seemed so much longer than the last three months? Perhaps it was because the thought of having the love of my life and future wife in my apartment and all to myself for a full 48 hours was just too good to be true. I imagined us spending 46 of those hours in bed, exploring and mapping every inch of each other's bodies, and planting our tiny little flags in all the hard to reach places. And when Sunday finally came I was ready to devour her as soon as she walked through the door. Her suitcase had barely hit the floor when I was upon her, hugging, kissing, pulling off her shirt and then mine and then, "Wait."

"What is it?"

"I just got here. Let's get something to eat."

To be honest, I hadn't given dinner much thought. I figured we'd just order in some Chinese and wind up eating in bed. But I could see she wanted to go out so I put my shirt back on and led her down the block to Prizzi's. It was Italian and probably not a great choice for someone who just flew in from Rome, but it was easily the best restaurant in walking distance. And I wanted to stay close because the quicker we ate and got back home the quicker we'd be naked and enjoying our dessert.

So exactly one hour, eleven minutes and seventeen seconds later we were back in my apartment for take two. This time I put on Sade's *Lovers Rock*, lit some candles, poured a couple glasses of red, and anted up a string of soulful, slow-tongued kisses before removing our shirts. Yet still, despite all my cliché overtures, I was sensing some hesitation. Or maybe I wasn't. So I had to ask.

"Are we gonna have sex?"

"No. Not yet."

And my whole body went into shock. Everything seemed so perfect—the music, the lighting, the wine, the me—how could she possibly resist? There had to be a reasonable explanation. "Is it the woman sickness?"

"Huh?"

"You know, your—"

"No. No, I just, I dunno..."

"Hey, it's okay, there's no rush, we got plenty of time for that." Although really we didn't. After tonight we only had one more evening together, and then who knew when we'd get to see each other again? But maybe that was precisely the reason she was holding back. *I knew* I loved her and would move heaven and earth to see her again and again until we were wearing each others' rings and sleeping under the same roof for the next hundred years, but how could *she know* that? I hadn't told her yet. So I did.

"Listen, this may sound outta the blue, but you know I love you right? I mean this—us—it's gonna work out. We're for real. You know that right?" Even as I was saying it, I had a hunch it was probably a mistake, and then, watching her face fall, I couldn't have been more certain. The only thing worse than the timing was the delivery. It sounded like a lot of pressure—the desperate, eleventh hour lie of a drunken frat boy willing to say anything to get laid. But it wasn't a line. And it wasn't about getting laid. Still,

I never shoulda told her. Not like this. It woulda been better saved for a candlelit dinner instead of spilled on the floor next to her discarded shirt and bra, even if Sade was singing backup.

So before she could deflect my stammerings I bid a hasty retreat. "But you're right, we shouldn't. Not now. We're gonna have plenty of time together." And she managed to smile at this. Then I suggested we throw on a movie to change the subject. She hadn't seen *The Big Lebowski,* and I could never see it enough, so that's what we watched.

But I just couldn't get it outta my head. And later, lying in bed—together, yet not—it felt so wrong and unnecessary. How could she come all the way from Rome and not want to make love? I didn't get it.

And yet, part of me sort of agreed with her. It *was* best not to rush, far better to ease into our sex like a warm bath. I even believed sex on a first date could jinx a relationship. I remember I'd liked Maggie so much I was trying to excuse myself at the end of our initial night together, but she just wouldn't let me leave. "Relax," she'd said, "You wouldn't be over here if I didn't like you." And so I stayed and the jinx was on. But if sex on the first date was off limits, the question was *when*? I also believed it was wrong to wait too long because then it grew to be an issue, and that warm bath turned cold and who wants to take a cold bath? The second date, then? I'm fine with that, but three always seemed like the perfect number, and if New York was our first, Sushi Roku our second, then tonight was our third, and I gotta say it seemed like the right time to me. But for some reason, not to her.

The next morning I found myself being overly polite and deferring to her on everything. And when she said she wanted to visit a classmate from Brown that worked over at LACMA, I drove us there. Her friend met us in the lobby and brought us back into the bowels of the museum to her tiny office, where we stood making small talk.

"So what do you do?" she asked.

"I'm in television."

"Anything I would have seen?"

"Do you get Playboy TV?"

"No."

"How bout E!?"

"No."

"You do have a TV though, right?" I teased, but I knew she wasn't gonna be teasing me back.

"Yes, but I rarely watch pornography."

"E! isn't pornography."

She flashed a look that said she begged to differ. "Ever do anything for HBO?"

"No. Not yet." And now I pretty much felt like shit, so I excused myself to walk the halls under the pretext of letting them have some space to catch up, but really I just wanted to get outta there. As I went looking for Picasso, I smiled at the thought of trying to convince Vanessa and her friend that someone like Ken Marcus was an actual artist. *But look at how he captures the skin tone of her aureole.* By the time I found what I was looking for, *Weeping Woman With Handkerchief,* I realized what I should have known already—that Vanessa was more cerebral than physical. Despite her slender good looks, she wasn't what you'd call athletic. She'd never played sports to win, and maybe she was even a little afraid of sex, like she'd probably been a little afraid of the ball on the JV soccer field back at St. George's. Not that there was anything wrong with that. Me, I'd always considered myself 50-50 mental and physical, though lately I'd been feeling more the latter. And I wasn't just talking about sex. To me physical just meant being attuned to the pleasures of the body, which also included playing a hockey game or getting a back rub.

That night, however, she was gonna get a good long look at something physical because I was taking her to see the Kings play. To avoid the deadly rush hour traffic we hopped the recently finished subway downtown. And we wound up seeing a helluva game, a 4–3 victory over Montreal. And maybe it was because we were so safe on my turf, or because we drank so many beers, or because Ziggy Palffy scored the winner so late in the third, or because her slightly glazed eyes reminded me so much of New Year's, but whatever it was I could tell this evening had somehow put us back on track.

On the train ride home our car was empty after the Wilshire & Vermont stop, so we drunkenly pawed each other all the way back to Hollywood & Vine. Somewhere along the line I rambled a long, all too honest apology for how I must have come across the previous night. "I'm so sorry, I didn't mean to make you uncomfortable, and I know that wasn't the best way to tell you how I felt, but I want you to know—I *need* you to know—that it was the truth. I do love you. So much. I've never felt like this about anyone before. And I know it's been fast, but that's what I feel. So there it is. I love you." And she smiled that she understood and kissed me and all was forgiven. But she did not say she loved me. Instead she slid her hand down my pants, and although it wasn't quite as hot as the *Risky Business* train scene she was touching me for the very first time and once again I was glad I was wearing jeans.

Back in my apartment she unbuttoned my shirt and I pulled hers up and over her beautiful blond hair and once again unhooked her sexy black bra and we held each other tight to feel our flesh on flesh and breast on breast. Then she started unbuckling my pants.

"Yeah?"

"Yeah."

"You sure?"

"Yeah."

"You know, we don't—"

"Shhh. I love you too."

XII

I've Seen Things You
People Wouldn't Believe

hree weeks later I was in a Tokyo bar going beer for beer with an Australian stripper named Hannah. After another tiresome dinner with my crew I'd stopped at the first watering hole I'd seen with the singular purpose of throwing back three double Johnnie Walkers. I figured that might be just enough scotch to fool my jet-lagged mind into thinking it was, in fact, time for bed. And maybe then I could finally get a decent night's sleep. But before I'd sipped my second I was already trading eyes with this Aussie lassie sitting at a nearby table with two friends. The four of us were the only gringos in the dive and with me all by myself, no doubt looking as lonely as I felt, it wasn't long before she asked me to join them.

And by the time I was finishing my third and switching to beer her friends were saying goodnight, and then Hannah and I settled in for a serious drunk. I couldn't believe my luck. Besides being surprisingly well read—at least she knew the Beats and the Losts, who were all I really cared about—she was blonde, curly-haired, and deeply tanned from the Australian beaches, with modest natural breasts beneath a white cotton jersey and the kindest, warmest eyes. Not quite what I'd expect from a traveling stripper.

But exactly what I needed because, so far, I'd been having a terrible time in Tokyo.

At the risk of sounding xenophobic, I just wasn't a big fan of this town. Of course it didn't help that I couldn't speak the language—or anything close—and that most of the locals didn't know a lick of English. While I did have an interpreter, he was only around when we were shooting. So after we wrapped I was on my own and suddenly communication became something akin to acting in a Charlie Chaplin film.

But visually Tokyo wasn't anything like a silent movie. This town was sci-fi all the way. Especially Shibuya Station which, according to my interpreter, was the busiest pedestrian crossing in the entire world. With its tall buildings, flashing neon, and gigantic television screens, it was Times Square times a thousand. Besides its gargantuan size, what made it so unique was its design. Shibuya was a scramble crossing, which meant the traffic lights were set so every ten minutes all cars were stopped from passing through the intersection. This allowed thousands of people to cross at once, going every which way, even diagonally, flooding the area for about 60 seconds before emptying as if someone had pulled the stopper out of the drain. Then, one at a time, the waiting lines of cars got their green lights and were allowed to cross while a fresh batch of people began to swell at the curbside until it was done all over again. I've never seen so many people in all my life.

Shibuya epitomized Tokyo's futuristic *Blade Runner* vibe, and combined with the impossible language barrier and the crippling jet-lag I couldn't escape the surreal feeling that I was so much farther away than another town in another country. It was more like another time on another planet—a sensation that was only reinforced during my first day of shooting.

I was supposed to be doing a few interviews for one of the two stories I was here to produce. The subject was something called *hentai anime*, which meant *bizarre* or *perverted animation*. Back home I'd watched a few tapes and found that basically they were feature length hardcore erotic cartoons in that classic Japanese *Speed Racer* style. But what was surprising was they rarely featured your standard guy-girl or girl-girl sex scenes. Instead hentai anime tended to depict strange alien monsters with masses of tentacles which they used to capture and restrain a human female, who was usually wearing some sort of schoolgirl uniform. With their free tentacles the aliens would then penetrate the girl via her three major orifices while she squealed her feverish delight.

And it got stranger. Before leaving LA I'd spoken with the owner of Bonzai Anime, a Culver City store that specialized in this kind of stuff as well as mainstream anime. He'd explained that in the original Japanese scripts these girls wore short-skirted uniforms because they were in *middle school*. They were intended to be *twelve or thirteen years old*! But when the subtitles were added for American distribution, suddenly the girls became college freshmen. Wow. *Hentai* was a polite word for what this was.

Playboy TV didn't have many rules, but underage sex was a definite no-no, so while I couldn't go near it I was glad to know what was lurking below the surface. And now I couldn't wait to talk to someone who actually got off on this stuff because I just didn't understand the appeal. I mean, even after the crazy aliens, extreme storylines, and the underage sex, it was still just a cartoon, and how could anyone actually masturbate to a *cartoon*?

My lead interview was with a Japanese gentleman who worked for one of the major hentai anime producers. He was in charge of distribution to America and his English was decent, albeit heavily accented, so I didn't need to speak through the interpreter. Right away I asked if he personally used what he was pushing, and I was thrilled to hear him say that yes, as a matter of fact he did. "So why do you like *hentai anime*? What's the turn on?"

He answered immediately, almost as if he knew the question was coming. "I like the *lupe* of the *charldren* in the *charges*." I had to ask him to repeat this several times before I understood that his reply was the single most deviant sentence I'd ever heard during my entire tenure with *Sexcetera*. Incredibly, he had admitted on the record, on-camera, and with a smile that he liked "the *rape* of the *children* in the *churches*." With that one line he had touched on the only three things I was forbidden to mention on Playboy TV—forced sex, underage sex, and religious desecration. Impressive. So badly I wanted to end the interview right then and there with that classic Alvy Singer line, *Right, well, I have to go now Duane, because I'm due back on the planet Earth.* But I didn't. Instead I chuckled as politely as I possibly could and changed the subject.

Later, tossing and turning through another sleepless night, I kept asking myself the same two questions over and over—Where was I? And when could I go home? Worse, and what made this trip so damn frustrating, was that I knew it didn't have to be this way. I woulda been having a much better time had I been traveling with Kira and Max instead of Scott and Ryan, the two new guys whom I was shepherding through their first *Sexcetera* shoot. Scott Potasnik, the host, was a funny little fuck from Indiana. A couple years younger than me, he'd come over from MTV and was still a little green, but a nice enough guy. Then there was Ryan, the fifty year old married-with-children cameraman, who was, as they say, way too old for this shit.

And way, way, way too old to fight his way through a Tokyo fetish party, which is exactly what our second story was about. It was thrown by the notorious London-based Torture Garden, which had been around since 1990 when it was started by a couple blokes named David and Allen. They were a pair of glorified DJs-turned-party-promoters, and, although they had their own club in England, they routinely exported their kinky brand of revelry to various cities around the world.

This one was held at an enormous seven-level club with a myriad of playrooms as well as endless nooks & crannies—perfect for stealing off for a quick flogging or spanking or perhaps just an old fashioned blowjob. Naturally there was a constant throbbing of techno music drowning out all but the most persistent of thoughts. And the place was packed wall-to-wall with the kinkiest of Tokyo's kinky, all sweating profusely in their skin-tight leather and latex.

Oh, and they weren't just sweaty—most were almost naked. Like the guy with the sumo wrestler build wearing only a gimp hood and a leash led by a wisp of a woman dressed in latex. And if only I had a nickel for every dime-bag of male Japanese genitalia I saw, and I wished I could say I was always able to avoid the back-swing of every flogger I passed by, and I'm not exactly sure why I was so disturbed by that bald woman with so many lit candles attached to her head, dripping pools of wax onto her stubbly cranium, but I was.

Supposedly no Torture Garden party was complete without a wildly erotic stage show, and for this gig David and Allen had brought along two of their favorite performance artists from London. Lucifire was a punk-looking chick with her hair dyed bright red. Her specialty was, as her name suggested, playing with fire. She used a special power tool called a grinder, which had a tiny metal wheel that spun around real fast and shot a trail of sparks whenever pressed against a metal plate she wore on each forearm. She also played with a pair of fire sticks that she traced suggestively all over her nearly naked body. This daring routine culminated with a bit she dubbed "Fire in the Hole," which involved bravely extinguishing each flame with her cooze.

Meanwhile Empress Stah, another punker, wore her short, bleached blonde dreadlocks all akimbo. Her signature act was choreographed to the Queen song "Flash Gordon" and involved swinging and climbing on a cloth trapeze while wearing nothing but a strap-on dildo, with which she made all sorts of lewd gestures.

For the grand finale they came on stage together, each wearing a costume modeled after a man's pinstriped business suit complete with matching fedora. To the tune of Pink Floyd's "Money" they began to remove each other's outfits, revealing Yen stapled to their skin. Then they proceeded to rip the currency off one another's bodies, leaving tiny trails of blood, before throwing the cash into the audience. And the crowd loved it. I guess it was hard to beat the winning combination of nudity, bloodletting, and free money.

After this last performance, we wrapped and stumbled out into the Tokyo dawn. Incredibly, we'd worked sixteen hours straight. Back at the hotel it was pushing seven local time and I shoulda been plenty ready for bed. But still it took two hours of bourbon to close my eyes, and even then they wouldn't stay shut for a stretch of more than three hours.

And all that time, strung out, staring up at the ceiling or over at the samurai prints on the wall, I wished Vanessa was lying next to me—sipping my whiskey, stroking my hair, and singing my lullaby. I had no idea if she could actually carry a tune, but surely she could get through a verse or two of "Sewanee River" or "Lay Lady Lay." It was strange, but I'd been so crazed since dropping her off at the airport these hazed, jet-lagged moments were the first chance I really had to process how much I missed her. Literally the very next day after saying goodbye I'd been assigned these two Tokyo stories and told I only had fifteen days before the flight to get them together. So yeah, only tossing in my room did I realize I'd much rather be home in bed with her instead of fighting my disoriented mind and this oriented mattress.

The next day, which was earlier this afternoon, I'd gone for a walk to find something I could pass off as a souvenir for my mother before hooking up with Scott and Ryan for dinner. And then, which was now, I was damn happy to be here with Hannah, my Australian savior, because, hey, if you can't be with the one you love, love the one you're with. What a welcome relief it was to be talking—actually communicating without an interpreter—with a flesh and blood woman. Someone who was within months of my own age. Someone who was just as strange in this strange land as I was. Someone I hoped would be coming back to my hotel room within the hour to join me in the battle for Fort Slumber.

And I thought my chances with her had to be good when she told me what she was doing in Japan. Turned out she was on a three-month work visa because as a blonde, blue-eyed dancin' babe she could make a helluva lot more money in the Land of the Rising Sun than she could in the Land Down Under, where her kind was about as common as a koala bear. "It's my fourth trip in five years, so I've got it down. I spend half my days dancing in a g-string and the rest dolled up in an evening gown at a hostess bar."

"What's a hostess bar?" It sounded a lot like a euphemism for a brothel.

"It's like a nightclub where rich businessmen come to hang out with cute, young girls. Usually very young. I'm getting a little old for it."

"C'mon, I bet you're the best looker in the whole place."

"Aw, you're a legend." I figured that must be some kind of Australian expression, and I liked hearing her say it.

"So what goes on there?"

"Not much," she laughed. "Buncha blokes blowin' a buncha money just to talk."

"Talk?"

"Yeah, and dance and maybe sing a little karaoke."

"No sex?"

"No. We keep our dress on the whole time."

"C'mon, you don't even get naked?"

"Nope." *How could this be?* According to Hannah the men actually dropped more yen at a hostess bar than they would at a strip club or even a brothel. I guess in a way it was sorta sweet. The poor bastards just wanted a moment or two of solace in between the daily hardships of their jobs and marriages. And afterwards they could go home and honestly say under cross-examination that they had not, in fact, cheated on their wives. Hannah said she made about $20 an hour before tips, but, again, she was a rare breed around here so she was tipped plenty and usually made about twice as much as a hostess as she did as a dancer—which was about ten times as much as she made back home.

"You must be a helluva talker."

"What can I say, I give good conversation."

When I told her what I was doing in Tokyo and what I did for a living, we laughed at what a small world it was. But then she confessed it was a world she would be soon leaving. She'd had enough. Making money from her sexuality and from exploiting the weakness of men had gotten to be too much for her. "I'm quitting. This is my last trip, and when I get home I'm telling the boys at the club I'm through."

"One final score before you get out, huh?"

"You got it."

"What are you gonna do?"

"I'm gonna open a little corner coffee shop." Hannah also said she wanted to get back into her painting and, in general, try to pursue a simpler, more zen existence. I told her how happy I was for her and how much I admired her exit strategy, although really I thought her plan sounded kinda dull.

When bar was ready to close I paid our tab and she called me a legend once again. Then she said she needed a taxi to take her home to her rented apartment. And I was just about to ask her to walk back to my nearby hotel when we stepped outside and found ourselves in a torrential downpour. Now I knew we'd both be needing a taxi no matter where we were going, so I ran to grab one and she followed. As we slid drenched into the back seat I was dumbstruck by her bra-less breasts, now fully visible through her wet blouse. So much so that for a moment I forgot about getting her back to my place and was barely listening as she gave the driver her address. By the time I came to realize where we were going and that it was a good deal farther than my hotel, it was too late. But still, I was curious about where she lived and knew it had to be cozier than my stale little hotel room.

When we pulled up to her building, I reached for my wallet to pay the driver and asked what I assumed she wanted me to ask. "Can I come up for a drink or something?"

"No, you're a legend, but I think we better not."

Deep down I knew she was right. It was late and I was pretty damn drunk and I'd probably just wind up falling through her rice paper walls and making sloppy love to her and really, who wanted that? We'd already given each other what we'd needed—a little contact, a little attention. And we hadn't even cheated on anyone.

So we kissed goodnight. And then I kissed her once more for my Lil' Guy, who was still hoping we could change her mind, but we couldn't, and as I watched her hurry off into the rain I understood why hostess bars were so popular.

Then I showed the driver a business card from my hotel—something I always put in my wallet upon check-in for just such an occasion. As we hurtled back across town to Roppongi Square, I slunk down into the backseat and looked up out the window and marveled at all the towering heights and dazzling lights dancing with the raindrops on the glass. And then Rutger Hauer's Roy Batty was in my ear, *I've seen things you people wouldn't believe... Attack-ships on fire off the shoulder of Orion... I watched C-beams glitter in the dark near the Tannhauser gate... All those moments... will be lost in time... like... tears in rain... Time... to die.* And finally, mercifully, I knew it was time... to sleep.

Ten days after Tokyo I was on another plane, this time to Montreal. The story was kinda lame—a sex tour of the city with a French Canadian stripper as our guide. She was a sweetheart and, Montreal being Montreal, I was able to talk hockey with just about everybody I met. But other than that it was pretty much standard *Sexcetera* fare—strip clubs, nude female oil wrestling, and some strange sex machine made out of Plexiglass that somewhat resembled a woman, but really it looked, and probably felt, more like you were fucking the frozen Han Solo from the end of *Empire Strikes Back.*

After we wrapped I caught a flight down to New York to see Vanessa. She was back in the States for another wedding—this one was in Newport—and she'd arranged to stay on a couple extra days so we could be together. I arrived first and headed over to the Dakota to hang out with Oliver and say hello to his super sweet mother.

When she asked about my plans, I explained that I was taking Vanessa to see the Devils play way out in the Meadowlands, and while I was well aware that a cab ride to exit 16-W on the New Jersey Turnpike wasn't the most convenient of evening activities, the Rangers and Islanders weren't in town so it was the only game around. And besides, I'd never been to the Continental Arena and I loved going to new rinks.

Oliver's mother smiled that fabulous warm smile of hers and said the perfect thing. "Does Vanessa like hockey?" Pithy, yet subtle and full of tact.

To rejoin, all I had was, "I'm sorry, I don't believe I understand the question." And I laughed and then she laughed, but I took her point with me as I cabbed it down to the Hudson Hotel to meet Vanessa.

I'd barely made it up to the room and gotten into the mini-bar when I heard a knock at the door. I jumped over the bed to open it and there she was, Vanessa, looking radiant as always. As I hugged her it was hard to believe it'd only been a month since I'd dropped her off at LAX. After she freshened up we went downstairs and caught our cab, and I hoped we were about to be thoroughly entertained. And we were.

The Devils and Blackhawks skated a hard, fast paced game that was tied 3–3 late in the third. And when the end-to-end action stopped for the final TV timeout I put my arm around her and gave her a kiss. "This is fun, huh?"

"Are we really gonna do this?" I knew she wasn't talking about whether or not we were gonna watch the final five minutes of the game.

"Yes-yes-yes we're doing this." I was exuberant about it. And not just because I was on my fourth beer. "It's gonna be great!"

Recently we'd decided over emails that she should spend the summer in LA. Her classes at the American Art Institute would be over and she was planning on applying to another high-powered school, but that wouldn't start until the fall so why not use the summer months as a trial run to see how we got along in the same town? One of her Brown classmates even lived a few blocks away in a good-sized house with a guestroom, so she could base her operations outta there since my place was on the small side. It was perfect and I'd been begging for it, and now that she'd made all the arrangements I couldn't believe how lucky I was. I'd been worried this day wouldn't come for at least another year—and that maybe I'd have to be the one who did the moving—but now she was coming to me. And in less than a month! "I can't wait!"

"Are you sure?" She was smiling, because she knew how sure I was. She just liked hearing me say it, and I liked saying it, so I did.

"Yeah, I'm sure—sure as a peacock in a funny hat shitting in the woods." Okay, that might have been because I was on my fourth beer. But this wasn't, "I love you so much."

"I love you too." And Vanessa smiled so warm and vulnerable. I kissed her again, and then the linesman dropped the puck and I watched the play flow up and down the ice until Randy McKay scored, giving the Devils a 4–3 lead, which they held long enough to win the game.

Afterwards we hightailed it back to the city where we met Oliver & his girlfriend, Alexis, at a restaurant called Isabella's. They were just finishing their dinner, but we were in time for drinks and dessert.

As I reached across the table and held Vanessa's hand while her other hand cracked into the crème brûlée that I'd promised to split but only had a bite of because I really didn't care for crème brûlée—preferring instead to sip my Tanqueray—I dreamed that she was my Future. We would get married and have a little boy named Bob and a little girl named Dylan and we'd always dress stylishly and be the talk of the town and our sex would only get better and she'd teach me about art, although sparingly about the classics because I knew I could never learn Latin because I'd failed so miserably to learn Latin back at Groton, but language would never stand between us, especially not a dead one, and we'd be so alive together! Hard to believe, but at that moment I'd never felt so warm and fuzzy, finishing my drink, loving her eyes so furrowed to burrow into the brûlée, and listening to Oliver & Alexis laugh over the latest misadventure of their Labrador.

And the night only got dreamier as we retired back to the Hudson—and what an adorably hip little closet of a room we had. After getting each other naked, I insisted she put back on her black stiletto boots, something I'd wanted her to do for some time. A minor touch that inspired some particularly dynamite sex despite her spiked heels narrowly missing my Balzac on several occasions, and yes, yes, yes, it was so good and I was so happy we had this little life raft of love that she just might puncture at any moment with those deliciously scary shoes—but wasn't that the delight of living dangerously?

Back in LA, I knew I had to tell Maggie that Vanessa was moving to town. But first, of course, I'd have to tell her that there was, in fact, a woman in my life named Vanessa with whom I was very much in love. Thus far I hadn't seen the need to mention her existence. Sure, Maggie and I had spent a lot of time together the past twelve weeks since Lucy got hurt, and yes we'd even made love a few times, but it wasn't like we'd been dating. However, now that Vanessa was on her way, it was time to fess up.

So as soon as I could I headed over for a hike, and that's when I was gonna tell her. But after Maggie put Lucy in her little doggie wheelchair she said she had a surprise for me. She gave Lucy a quick hug and told her to show me what she could do. Then, with a bit of a sputter, she suddenly started tooling around with a big smile and her back left leg was pumping like a piston and I knew that had to be more than a reflex. She was moving it on her own! Finally, a real, indisputable sign that Lucy was making progress, and I ran to catch up with her and gave her a big kiss and she kissed me back and I was so happy for her. And naturally I couldn't introduce Vanessa at a time like this. So I didn't.

But sooner or later I had to, so the next day I went straight over after work and told her. "Listen, I—there's something I got to tell you—last New Year's I met someone. And I've seen her a few times since and, well, she's moving to LA this summer to see what we're like together and, well, I guess I just—"

"Are you saying we can't have sex anymore?"

"Yeah, I guess that's what I'm saying."

"Lucy can hear you, you know."

"It's not like I'm seeing another dog. There'll never be another dog in my life."

"Oh honey." And she hugged me and then locked my eyes with a long, wistful smile. "Just shut up and take your pants off."

I did and we had our final sex. Good clean closure sex. And as I was leaving, she said, "I hope you find what you're looking for."

For some reason I felt like I had to reply. "Baby, I have *no idea* what I'm looking for." I guess I thought hearing that would make it easier for her. But then as I was climbing into my Blazer I realized how true it actually was.

XIII

My Mother Always Warned Me about Gangbangs

*V*anessa's first week in town was absolutely perfect. She arrived on Friday and we spent the weekend exploring the neighborhood, eating out, and making love. And then on Monday I took her to Game Six of the Kings-Red Wings playoff series. The hometown team had been on an amazing run and they had a chance to upset the more talented Red Wings thanks to an incredible, momentum swinging comeback in Game Four, which I'd also attended, where the Kings, down 3–0 with only three minutes left to play, wound up winning 4–3 in overtime. By far the craziest ending to a playoff game I'd ever been to. In fact, they were already calling it the Frenzy on Figueroa.

As excited as I was for tonight's game, I was doubly excited to show Vanessa what playoff intensity was all about, and from what I could tell she was excited too. Once again the Kings gave us a helluva game, winning yet another overtime thriller thanks to a goal by Red Wing-killer Adam Deadmarsh. And as we watched the two teams shake hands, I explained this great hockey tradition. Then, driving out of the arena with everyone honking and hollering and generally going nuts the way only a drunken mob can, I told her it was all because she'd just moved here and that this was the city voicing their overwhelming support and approval of their newest fellow Angelino. She smiled at this, but I preferred to pretend I wasn't kidding and I was damn glad everyone was so happy we were finally together.

Vanessa spent the next few days catching up with her Brown friend who'd just started med school at UCLA. I appreciated, nay, *needed* the space because I was scrambling to get ready for my next shoot at the end of the week. The story was proving to be a tough one because, to tell you the truth, I was scared as hell of the subject.

The West Coast Gangbangers was a gentlemen's club with one simple mission—to provide safe and reliable gangbangs to women looking to add some excitement to their sex life. At first it was hard for me to believe that such a thing existed. Why would any organization want to be associated with such a loaded word? Gangbang. At best it seemed to imply some kind of sexual degradation, and at worst a vicious group rape. Yet after chatting with John, the group's founder, I realized it *sorta* made sense, *in theory*. If you were a woman and you really wanted to have sex with five or more guys at once, where were you gonna go to find them?

Or, as my new gangbang guru explained, "It's taboo, so you can't really talk to your friends about it, and you're not gonna go to your boyfriend and say, 'Hey honey, can you get five or ten of your buddies to come over here and have a sex party with me?' And you definitely don't want to be picking up a bunch of strangers at a bar because who knows what winds up happening. So when you think about it like that it's not an easy thing to accomplish, and that's exactly why what we do really is a service."

According to John, the West Coast Gangbangers' greatest asset was their professionalism—they showed up on time, they gave the woman what she wanted, they never overstayed their welcome, and best of all their services were absolutely free of charge. John liked to stress the service angle. At one point, while discussing the importance of communicating with the client to make sure all her gangbang needs are met, he actually said, "They tell us beforehand what they're interested in doing, what their particular fetishes are, and then we will pretty much work within that. Maybe the girl is interested in something like facial cum shots and we say, 'We can do that.'"

Usually these gangbangs went down in hotel rooms, and although the number seemed unbelievably high John swore he attended between six and eight every month. And where was he finding all these women? Well, incredibly they were finding him through his website. John claimed he was contacted by women from all walks of life, even high-class professional types like doctors and lawyers. Supposedly one client held a high powered position in LA's municipal government, while another was some kind of minister or diplomat from the Czech Republic who'd flown all the way to Los Angeles just to be banged by John and his gang.

So yes, I suppose *in theory* the purpose of the club made sense, but of course that *theory* was based on the far-fetched axiom that a woman indeed wanted to be fucked by five or more men at once. And, if you asked me, a hefty assumption like that required a leap of faith that would daunt even the likes of Carl Lewis. When I confessed to John the difficulty I was having, he told me it was a completely normal reaction—naïve but normal—and then he cloaked himself in the indignant shroud of feminism. "I think there's a double standard. I mean, a guy getting together with a group of five girls would be considered a stud and a real player, so it's okay for a guy to fantasize about being with a bunch of girls. But if a girl wants to be with a lot of guys then it's kinda like, 'Oh, well, she's a slut and she's a whore,' when, fact is, it's just group sex, so why should we burn her at the stake for having that fantasy? Who are we to cast the first stone?" Once again *in theory* he was making a lot of sense—for sure I'd love to jump in bed with five swimsuit models, so I guess there was a double standard.

The shoot was happening that Saturday at a house in Riverside, which was about 60 miles east of Hollywood. When the day came I picked up the host, Susannah Breslin, and we headed out. Although I hadn't worked with her yet, I knew her reputation as a sexual pundit of sorts because I'd seen her as a guest on Bill Maher's *Politically Incorrect* and we'd even interviewed her for my *E! True Hollywood Story* on Larry Flynt.

I was glad Susannah was onboard. In fact, I'd requested her because she was the funniest of all the reporters. Far from sexy in any conventional sense, she was tall and kinda awkward, but her blasé, seen-it-all-before, deadpan delivery could be fucking hilarious. And for this story, humor was especially important. The only way I could deal with my fear & loathing of the subject matter was to laugh at it, and I knew Susannah was the only reporter we had that could pull off my opening line, *"I don't know about you, but when I was a little girl my mother always warned me about gangbangs. 'You know,' she said, 'there's just no way all five guys will respect you in the morning.'"*

When we arrived around 10:00 a.m. our cameraman, Dexter, was waiting outside. Right away we knocked out John's interview, which was just a rehash of everything we'd discussed over the telephone.

Then we moved upstairs to the bedroom to shoot the first gangbang. The guys were mostly in their late thirties and at least one was in his forties. The overall vibe I got was that they were all porn star wannabes, a ragtag bunch of weekend warriors who came to play because of their passion for the game. Or maybe they were just sex addicts. When they strolled in they barely said a word as they routinely removed their clothes. Although none of them got completely naked. John never bothered to take off his white undershirt, possibly to hide his beer belly. A thinner gentleman also refused to remove his Fruit of the Loom tee, deciding instead to tie the shirt tail in a knot, presumably so it wouldn't hang down and get in the way of all the fucking. And for some reason not a single gangbanger took his socks off. I doubt the client had requested *that*.

Then the bathroom door opened and there she was—the first girl. Jane. She lived and worked in Bakersfield as a secretary. And this was recreation for her. Like going skiing or skydiving, but a lot less expensive. She'd been changing into her lingerie, which was really just a ratty old teddy and a pair of thigh high stockings. I'd assumed she'd also been putting on some makeup or fixing her hair or something, but no, she looked as plain as her name. Late twenties, maybe early thirties, with long, dirty blond hair, flat and straight and not a puff of powder on her face. She was even wearing her glasses, big and thick with clumsy frames. I wouldn't have been surprised if she'd put in her retainer. She looked like she was ready for bed, as in sleep, not as in getting fucked by five strangers.

Once she was on the bed I told Dexter to start rolling, and I got down on the floor, low enough to hide behind the mattress. I needed to keep an eye on what was going on, but I also needed to stay outta the camera lines. Dexter was gonna have a hard enough time as it was trying to shoot this scene without putting any of the five feeding sharks in the frame. While Playboy TV was cool with broadcasting an erection, we still couldn't show it being pleasured, which meant no insertion and no vigorous stroking. *Good luck Dex!*

It began with the guys fanning out around Jane, who was now on her hands and knees, facing her bangers so she could greet them blow by blow. I could hear some mighty fierce slurping going on, and sneaking a peak I saw she was still wearing her dork glasses. *Why?* The only thing she needed to see was literally right under her nose. She couldn't possibly be that blind. And the whole image was absurd, like some kinda *Carrie* inspired revenge where the poor dateless math geek finally gets a year's worth all at once. When she moved on to devour the next cock I ducked back down. But then I decided I better say something. "Ah, do you think we can lose the glasses?"

The slurping stopped just long enough for, "Oh yeah, sorry, I forgot," followed by a chortle of a laugh and the sound of hard plastic landing on the Formica bedside table. Then more slurping.

After Jane had given them each a couple turns she lay back across the bed and spread herself wide open as one of the guys rolled on a condom and saddled up. This first gentleman had a chipped tooth and terrible hair plugs that he just might've done himself with a bag of yarn and a stapler. How she could even glance at him without giggling I had no idea. Although with her glasses safely on the table she might've been seeing Brad Pitt. Soon, however, it didn't matter what he looked like because another cock was in her mouth, and that's when I realized at a gangbang it *never* mattered what the guy looked like—it was all about the dick. Lots and lots of dick.

Meanwhile, from the floor I watched as all the socked feet inched closer and closer to the bed. Whenever I took a peek above the mattress I could see all the guys stroking their erections like so many on-deck batters taking practice swings, waiting for their turn at the plate. And I could see their faces, not smiling with delight at the task at hand, but concentrating—intensely—as if they were studying the pitcher's delivery, trying to discern the difference between his slider and his curve.

Within a few minutes the bed got to shaking so hard I had to move a foot or two away so it wouldn't bounce against my head. And it didn't take long to realize I could get a pretty good idea what was happening above by what was going on below. When I thought the bed was about to collapse, I knew the guy was really pumping away. But when it slowed to a gentle rocking that meant he was finding his rhythm in a new position. And when it stopped entirely, that meant they were switching batters.

By the fourth or fifth turn the tiny bedroom was getting pretty damn hot under our bright lights, and I could smell their sweat and their sex and I decided it was time to flee my not-so cozy position on the floor. Making eye contact with Dexter, I flashed a thumbs up and then a thumbs down to ask how it was looking—or rather, if he was able to frame out all the stroked and inserted erections. He responded with a thumbs up, so I figured I could go ahead and leave.

But I couldn't just walk out. I was on the far side of the bed from the door and standing would put me in the shot. And even if Dexter wasn't shooting my way at that particular moment everyone would probably turn to look at me and thus ruin the scene even if I wasn't in the frame—not to mention disturb their all-important concentration. So I crawled out. Like a soldier wriggling through the trenches, staying low so enemy fire didn't graze my backside, I made my way through the forest of legs and out into the cool safety of the hall.

I knew we still had a long way to go. The guys weren't supposed to cum until they'd batted around the order a couple times. From what I could tell, during these early rounds the goal was to bring themselves to the brink, then pull out, remove their condom, and stroke as needed while waiting in line to do it all over again.

So for now I shut my eyes and just listened. To the sounds of well lubricated sex. But mostly to Jane's moans and shrieks of pleasure. And I wondered if the various decibel levels corre-sponded in any way to the size of the different cocks inside her. Probably not.

Around 45 minutes later they were finally winding down. For today, I made John and his bangers promise there'd be no facial cum shots because I couldn't show it, and because it was already hard enough to shoot this clusterfuck. I'd also insisted they wear condoms because I didn't want to be sending the wrong message. Reality was, sometimes they wore 'em, and sometimes—like when they all had their test results handy—they didn't. Of course, when they did wear condoms they went through a ton of them. Three or four apiece, easy. John, cagey veteran that he was, always kept a fresh one unwrapped behind his ear like a pencil. So I sat in the hallway and watched as, one by one, they all came safely inside their condoms, which were safely inside of Jane. And when the last man climaxed, gangbang number one was complete.

After cleaning themselves up, they headed downstairs to the kitchen to refuel with a light snack and plenty of water. Then it was on to the living room to do it all over again. With a brand new girl. And three hours after that we were in the den, beginning to shoot the third and final gangbang. With the third and final girl. Who, interestingly, turned out to be a squirter, so I got to watch her hose down a couch like it was on fire.

And there was no doubt about it—she, like the two before her, had thoroughly enjoyed herself. So yeah, despite my puritanical inhibitions and bourgeois societal blues which had kept me from believing a woman could, in fact, *want* to fuck five strangers, I'd now seen it with my own eyes. And smelt it with my own nose. And heard it with my own ears. A woman could most definitely want it.

Yet still I couldn't help thinking that these women had just been degraded. Was it possible for someone to be degraded if they themselves didn't feel degraded? Certainly you could be an alcoholic without realizing you're an alcoholic. Was degradation—like beauty—in the eye of the beholder? Or, to bastardize Grace Slick, were you only as degraded as you feel?

Well, by the time we were wrapping up it was pushing 10:00 p.m. and I was caring less and less. I'd spent the past twelve hours shooting three consecutive gangbangs. And although the camera was packed away my mind's eye was still going strong. So many body parts—mouths, tongues, hands, arms, legs, backs, buttocks, cocks, so, so many cocks—continued to rub, suck, and fuck their way through my head. Bizarre broken images, an endless gallery of gangbanging *Guernica*s burning themselves into my consciousness. Like how you keep hearing the music long after the concert is over. I needed to stop. But I still had a 60 mile drive ahead of me.

When I finally got back to my apartment I knew I needed a long, hot shower—*Silkwood* style—the kind you got at the power plant after you tripped the Geiger counter. So right away I stripped off all my clothes and threw them in the hamper, then got the water going as hard as it could go. While it warmed up I threw on some music and fetched the Jack Daniels from my bar. There, naked in my living room with a not-so-thin coat of shoot-grime covering my body and Dylan's "It's Alright Ma" blaring, I brought the bottle to my lips and took the healthiest pull I could stand. And then another. And another.

Then, just as I was beginning to feel the bourbon in my blood, the phone rang. I could barely hear it above the music and it took me five rings to turn down the stereo and pick up. It was Vanessa.

She was going out with her Brown friend and some other folks and wanted me to join them. And I wanted to. I woulda loved to have her arms wrapped around me. But I couldn't. Not tonight. Not after seeing what I'd seen. No way.

So I told her I was too tired, which wasn't a lie. I was exhausted. But she could tell that wasn't the real reason.

"It's Saturday night, you know?"

"I know, I'm sorry."

"And we haven't seen each other since Monday."

"I know, I know. I just can't. I need to sleep." How could I tell her the truth? And even if I could, how could she understand?

"Well... I guess I'll talk to you tomorrow, then." And we hung up.

XIV

What the Fuck, Ross?

Come Monday, I still had visions of gangbangs bouncin' around my head. And I knew I needed to talk it out. So I went to see Maggie—the same way soldiers sought soldiers to confess their atrocities and admire their arrow wounds.

But when I showed up she told me to go sit in the hammock and wait. She had another surprise. Then Lucy came out the front door and scurried the ten yards between us. She was dragging her back right foot, but three of the four were moving just fine. I couldn't believe it! It'd been just three months since the accident and she was already walking. And even Lola was happy, barking her love and licking her sis all over and what a nice, warm feeling we all had.

Then Maggie and I sat in the hammock and we talked. And then I talked and she listened. I told her about the shoot—how I'd razed villages and raped women and ridiculed orphans and then lost myself in the reeds along the riverbed—and she said she knew. She'd done the same things a few clicks down river in another part of the valley, laid her own waste, been wounded herself, and before long we were scoffing at the horror and I was feeling better. Much better.

"What does Vanessa think about all this?"

"I haven't told her. In fact, I haven't told her much about any of it. I mean, not really. No details. Mostly just lies."

"That's healthy."

"C'mon, you can't unload this kind of madness on a civilian."

"She might surprise you."

"I don't know... But it wasn't always like this. What happened to all the good assignments?"

"Whaddaya mean?"

"What happened to the Amsterdams and the Pragues?"

"Oh, you mean the ones where you get to go to brothels and fuck hookers?"

"You know what I mean."

"Listen, I've been doing this longer than you, and trust me, sometimes the stories are good, sometimes they're bad, and sometimes it rains."

"*Bull Durham*?"

"It was on HBO last night."

Now, a lot less preoccupied, I could smell the grass and dirt underfoot, and the waves of fresh jasmine rolling in with each new breeze, and the moistness of my sunbathed skin approaching the tipping point that would send the first bead of sweat inching down my forehead. And then I could smell *her* skin—her temples, her cheeks, her neck, her arms—all the flesh left bare from her super tight t-shirt emblazoned with the phrase, Running With Scissors. Impulsively, I was moved to touch her forearm, where I lingered before letting my fingertips slide down her wrist to squeeze her hand. Intertwining our fingers, I gripped her tight and breathed in, like a junkie, desperate to inhale as many of these vernal pheromones as I could. Slowly, I felt my now swollen Lil' Guy lifting away from my thigh, rising up against my linen pants, and because I wasn't wearing any underwear I could feel the cool air tickling my Balzac through the lightweight fabric.

Maggie noticed this, and then checked to be sure as we kissed and kissed again. And then she was leading me into her bedroom.

When I got back to my place, I had just enough time to shower before meeting Vanessa. And I probably shoulda been feeling a whole lotta guilt, but sex was just sex, and sex meant so many things—love, recreation, friendship, sport—and sex with Maggie didn't mean the same thing as sex with Vanessa, just as going to the movies with Maggie didn't mean the same thing as going to the movies with Vanessa. *Yeah, right.* As I soaped Maggie off my undercarriage, I realized that even I wasn't buying this piss-poor rationalization. However, I also knew it was the best I could do in the time allotted, and one way or another I needed to get guilt-free by the time Vanessa showed.

Once again I was taking her to see the Kings—this time it was Game Three against Colorado—and I didn't want my poor manners to spoil the evening. And they didn't. There's nothing quite like playoff hockey, and even though we lost 4–3 it was still a helluva good time. When we got home we were feeling plenty frisky from all the cheering and beering, so we clawed our way through each other's clothes and made love and love and love until rolling over with a smile.

Only later, when I crept out into the living room to smoke a bowl, did I recollect my earlier roll with Maggie and realize that I'd just slept with both girls in the same day. *What the fuck was wrong with me?* The only thing I could really hide behind was the fact that it hadn't been premeditated. But c'mon, even Skye had shown enough discipline and decency not to fuck me and her boyfriend in the same day.

By the time I went back to join Vanessa in bed I was good and stoned. And as I spooned in behind her I felt certain my body was trying to send me a message, so I lay awake at least another hour, maybe two, trying to figure out what exactly that message might be. Besides of course the obvious—that I was a complete and utter asshole.

But I didn't unravel it that night, nor the next morning over breakfast, and as I went off to work leaving her to spend the day hanging out at her friend's place I was already thinking of excuses not to see her later that evening. *Crazy.* So far, she'd been here ten days, and I'd only seen her one night outta the last seven. Yet I still dug her. And she dug me. So what was the problem?

I wasn't sure, but I had a hunch all I needed was a mulligan. If only I could reconnect with her somehow and begin all over again. And I hoped I had just the thing—my next shoot was in Las Vegas at the end of the week so I decided to invite Vanessa to join me when I was finished. A little hotel time, a couple dinners, and maybe a show might give me just the jumpstart I needed. I even loaded the dice by asking Fiona to drive down from Jackson Hole with her boyfriend Luke. I figured having some family around might rekindle the magic of New Year's Eve. It was worth a shot.

A little before six Friday morning I headed out for Vegas. I'd decided to drive because some time alone on the road might do me good. So around fours hours later I picked up my crew at McCarran Airport. Aaron, who'd been with me on the Montreal trip, was hosting, and Max was shooting.

As we drove I filled them in on what we were doing. The story was on an Asian porn star named Mimi Miyagi and a magazine originally called *Oriental Dolls* but recently renamed *Asian Hotties*, because, as Mimi had explained, the new title made the girls sound younger. The masthead claimed she was the editor, but really she was a figurehead whose primary responsibility, besides posing occasionally, was writing a regular column that tackled hard-hitting issues like how hot and wet she happened to be that particular month.

Our first location was a photo studio that belonged to Justice Howard, a fairly well known female erotic photographer. She was the perfect advertisement of a Harley riding, leather pant wearing rock 'n roller. Helluva nice gal, too. Mimi also turned out to be a sweetheart. A super-fit, fake-titted, twenty-seven year old Filipino, she wore a permanent smile and was one of those odd folks that ended every sentence with a nervous laugh, like *The Simpsons'* Dr. Hibbert. But she was easy to work with and I knew she was damn glad for the promotion on Playboy TV.

The plan was for us to film Justice snapping off a fast photoshoot with Mimi and another Asian model named Keiko. As things got underway and I watched them move from pose to pose—untying each others bikinis, feigning lust through a half-assed medley of kissing, fondling, and licking—I couldn't help lamenting how silly and perhaps even vaguely racist this story was.

My assignment wasn't just to profile Mimi and the magazine. It was to use them as a vehicle to explore the so called Asian fetish, or, as it's known on the street, "Yellow Fever." Me, I've never been so afflicted. But luckily my boss Bruce had a bad case, so with his help I was able to cobble together a script. The set up was, *"Ever since Marco Polo returned from the East, Western man has been fascinated by Asian women. The mysteries of the Orient have always suggested exotic pleasures, which the blonde, blue-eyed girl-next-door simply can't deliver. And nobody understands the power of these 'Asian Hotties' better than Mimi Miyagi."* Then I'd planned to drop in a soundbite from Mimi—some pearl of Eastern wisdom that explained why The White Man was so obsessed with her kind.

But later that afternoon, when I was interviewing her in the bedroom of her Henderson home, she had trouble explaining the appeal. I asked her what exactly *were* the mysteries of the Orient, and she didn't have a clue. "The mystery is there is no mystery," and then she gave her customary laugh. But I guess I was partly to blame, or at least my assignment was, because, as they say, ask a stupid question, get a stupid answer. Eventually I was able to get her talking about all the physical characteristics that men found so desirous—diminutive stature, almond eyes, straight black hair, ageless skin, etc.

Before long we'd settled upon the most famous Asian stereotype of all—that the women were always subservient to their men. Of course, she said the stereotype wasn't completely true. "We are not all submissive, you know. We are human. Just like everybody else." However, she did feel it was based on truth and that her culture was to blame. "Asian society is very submissive. The generation that I grew up in, it was, you know, you submit to your husband or to your boyfriend. We were taught to be very submissive, very quiet, very peaceful. We're not used to any kind of violence, or yelling, or screaming in the household. That's why we take our shoes off, to show respect in the house, and peace. Everything is all about peace, so no matter what a man does, whether it be cheating or violence or gambling we're supposed to let it go. So, basically, that's the culture we grew up in and I think a lot of men are attracted to that."

I guess that was about what I expected to hear, and it certainly jibed with my long-standing personal theory that an overzealous yen for Asian women could be, on occasion, a sign of male chauvinism. Personally I found the whole submissive thing a big turn-off. Sure, it could make for some fun role-playing in the bedroom, but I'd never want absolute power as my reality. What was the fun in having a woman bending to your every whim, bringing you your slippers and scotch the moment you came home from work? I mean, if that's all you wanted from a relationship why not just get a dog and a jar of peanut butter? Shouldn't relationships be partnerships? Or challenging ships unafraid to send the occasional warning shot across one another's bow?

After the interview we went downstairs to the living room where several more Asian women were waiting patiently in their lingerie. We'd staged a little slumber party for Mimi and some of her girlfriends, one of whom had the largest set of breasts I'd ever seen. Her name was Suki, and I swear her tits were the size of watermelons—no joke. It musta taken a hundred and fifty separate surgeries to stretch her skin that much. I didn't understand why anyone would do that to herself. But then I was introduced to her husband and I got it. He was a gringo, a lot older, and evidently dying of some disease because he stayed off in the corner connected to an oxygen tank the entire time. Later I was told he was the one who had insisted on all the breast jobs and he, being the meal ticket, got what he wanted.

And speaking of showing respect for women... the point of this slumber party was to put on a good ol' fashioned pillow fight, which I instigated by asking Suki to hit Aaron in the head with one of her enormous tits. This was done with a quick twist of the torso, so Aaron wound up catching a watermelon right in the jaw—poor guy said it was like getting hit with a sack of potatoes—and as soon as he fell backwards everyone grabbed the nearest pillow and started swinging away, while simultaneously removing each other's lingerie. I should admit, I'm a huge fan of pillow fights for their giggly, jiggly fun. But of course the true poetry of the pillow fight lies in the backswing—the moment when all the force is drawn back like an archer's twine and then, unleashed like a lion, it lands like a lamb with a poof of feathers and who could not smile at that?

The next morning we went back to Mimi's to shoot some sex scenes with a couple of new Asian girls and their gringo boyfriends, and after three or four uninspiring hours we wrapped. I dropped Aaron and Max off at the airport, then drove to the MGM Grand where Vanessa was already checked in along with Fiona & Luke.

As I valeted my Blazer and rolled my suitcase onto the casino floor, I felt a sudden wave of dread cascade over me along with the cranked up Vegas air-conditioning. Then, making my way through the endless maze of ringing and blinging slot machines I felt a sharp pain pierce both my temples—*fucking slots*—until I finally escaped into the elevator, where my flash headache began to recede as fast as it came. But the dread was still there. *Why?* And it was only getting worse as the elevator went up and up, slowly, stopping at almost every floor to let some poor tired gamer get to their room. Getting off at the 27th floor, I rolled my suit-case onto the landing and looked down the endless hallway with its ridiculous, meticulously patterned carpet and I felt a surge of horizontal vertigo. *Did such a thing exist?* Maybe it did, maybe it didn't, but for some reason my legs were literally shaking from baby step to baby step as I walked to our adjoining rooms. What was happening to me? When did I become Bill Murray in *What About Bob?*

Room 2784. I knocked. And knocked again. But no one answered. So I moved to the next room. Room 2786. And I knocked again. A moment and the door swung open and Fiona was there with a big smile across her face and a Budweiser in her hand. Behind her, Luke had a similar smile and another Budweiser. And there was Vanessa, beautiful as ever, with the biggest smile of all. And a bottled water. Hugs and kisses all around, then I got the key card from Vanessa and hurried back to the other room to get the decompression I needed—a Tanqueray & Tonic and a shower and then another Tanqueray & Tonic as I changed into a pair of jeans and a dress shirt.

Then we all headed down for dinner. It was a good dinner. Pumpkin ravioli and plenty more Tanqueray—and it was great to catch up with Fiona and hear all about her life in Jackson Hole. Funny, she'd moved there about a year after I'd left and she loved it as much as I did. And, like I did, she knew she'd have to move on at some point. Unfortunately, I could see that Luke wasn't going anywhere, so although they hadn't figured it out yet I knew they weren't going to wind up together. Too bad, too, because I liked Luke. Nice guy—a huge hockey fan and a helluva player. He was even drafted outta high school, so yeah, I was sad they weren't gonna make it.

And the whole time Vanessa was sipping her white wine and smiling at all the right things, laughing at all the right places, and being so damn polite. *Had she always been this polite?* Then Luke asked me what Fiona knew enough not to. "So what were you shooting this morning?"

Maybe it was the gin, or the fact that Vanessa seemed so far across the table, or that Luke actually wanted to know, but I decided to tell him. And thus them. "Two different Japanese girls having sex with their gringo boyfriends."

"Were they hot?"

"I don't know. You might have thought so, but they didn't really do anything for me. Maybe 'cuz I was there. Not sure."

"What were they doing?"

"Luke, I don't think he wants to—" Fiona was jumping in for Vanessa's sake.

"No, it's okay, I don't mind. They were just having sex, you know, three or four different positions apiece. Nothing outta the ordinary. Although one of the girls," and I couldn't help chuckling at the memory, "she suddenly got her period right in the middle of her reverse cowgirl."

"Aw, no way."

"Oh yeah, blood everywhere." I was keeping an eye on Vanessa and I noticed the penne at the end of her fork was now wavering considerably. "I was actually in the next room dozing on the couch, but all of sudden I hear my cameraman yell, 'Ross! Got a problem!' So I had to go in there and calm the poor girl down— that is, *after* she came back from the bathroom—and tell her not to worry, our show was just softcore anyway so she could just simulate the rest of the scene and we'd be fine." Luke thought this was pretty damn hilarious, and even Fiona was laughing. But not Vanessa. "So yeah, just another day at the office."

When we were done eating, we all walked over to the sports book to see how the Kings were doing in their Game Six against Colorado. It was tied 0–0, so we watched and drank and talked and made each other laugh and when it was time for Vanessa and me to catch a cab to Treasure Island, where we had tickets to see *Mystere*, the game was about to go to overtime. Part of me wanted to stay and watch because it was hockey. And because if Colorado scored the Kings would lose the series, and if the Kings scored they'd force a Game Seven. But I'd never seen Cirque du Soliel and even I wasn't about to miss a live show for a televised hockey game.

So Vanessa and I were on our own for the fifteen-minute cab ride and, for the first time in our relationship, I didn't have a damn thing to say. Nothing. Nada. Zip. Truth was, I was kicking myself for not throwing down one last Tanqueray before we left, while simultaneously wondering if they'd be serving drinks inside the show. And then I was asking the driver's opinion of the traffic, and how it was being a cabbie in Las Vegas compared to other cities, to which he replied he couldn't be sure because he hadn't driven a cab anywhere else. Meanwhile Vanessa was sitting silent, and I had the overwhelming sensation that she was upset with me because I hadn't said something I should've—I hadn't complimented her on something, or thanked her for something, or asked her about something. An error of omission of some kind, but I couldn't think of what it could possibly be, so by the time we were walking into Treasure Island I'd decided it had to be some sort of trick of the mind, like déjà vu or something, so I let it go.

Two Tanquerays later we were sitting in our front row seats, and I gotta say the Cirque was one of the coolest things I'd ever seen. I absolutely adored it, and at one point I leaned over and whispered this to Vanessa and she nodded and smiled and I was glad she was having a good time.

But then I couldn't help noticing there was another woman to my right who also seemed to be enjoying herself. A brunette—quite pretty, well dressed, perhaps a few years older—and as I watched the alternately hypnotic and breathtaking ballet of these superhuman performers I found myself wondering what it'd be like to date this stranger on my right. Did she like Bob Dylan? Could I turn her on to hockey? What did her face look like when she made love? Would I be just as happy sitting next to her as I was sitting next to Vanessa? Then I wondered if I'd be just as happy if I was sitting here alone, next to no one.

Afterwards we spilled out into the casino with the rest of the crowd. Vanessa needed to go to the bathroom so I waited nearby, checking my messages because I'd asked Luke to let me know who won the game. Just as I was listening to his recorded voice tell me that Glen Murray had scored for the Kings two minutes into the second overtime I saw what I knew had to be a sign from a supernatural power.

Ron Jeremy, the Clown Prince of Porn, arguably the most famous face in adult entertainment, walked right past me. *He just happened to be in Vegas? At Cirque Du Soliel? Tonight?* I know I've said before that I don't go in for any kind of cosmic kookiness—I don't believe in Beatles, I just believe in me, so no tarot cards, no fortune cookies, no astrology, no divine intervention, and certainly no *signs*. But when the Hedgehog himself crosses your path, close enough to see the twinkle in his eye, then it has to mean something.

Although it was a hard harbinger to swallow, I took it to mean that my job would always be with me. And even more than that, *my job was me*—and *always* had been me. Or at least a part of me. Quitting or getting fired or just moving on wasn't gonna change who I was. Long after *Sexcetera* was off the air I'd still be Ross. So it wasn't so much a choice as much as a recognition.

That night the four of us stayed up drinking until almost 5:00 a.m. Then, in bed I played possum, pretending I was too tired for sex, but before long she was rubbing up against me and suddenly the possum was wide awake. Poor possum. Never was a very good actor. Which of course only gave me more guilt. It just didn't seem right to still be making love when you weren't feeling it all that much.

The next day around noon we all checked out and had one final meal together, and I tell ya, I couldn't eat fast enough. So badly I wanted to be outta town and back home. And I was not looking forward to spending four hours in the car with Vanessa. Although I still couldn't understand why four hours alone with a beautiful, intelligent woman seemed like such a bad thing. Watching her pick at her spinach omelette, cutting the tiniest of bites to place into her sweet, wonderful little mouth, I realized there was probably a lot I didn't understand—about her, about us, about omelettes.

But then she asked the waitresses for a refill. "May I please have some more water? Thank you." And suddenly it dawned on me. While the words themselves weren't anything out of the ordinary, there was just something about the way she said them. Especially the "may I" and the "please" and the "thank you," like somehow she didn't deserve any more water, like she was being a nuisance, like she was asking for the world, like getting a little more water was such a big fucking deal. And I knew right then that she was just too nice for me. Way too nice. Too polite, too respectful, too kind, too considerate, too humble, and you could give it a name and call it grace if it wasn't so damn awkward and excessive. I could see she was never gonna stomp on the terra and there was no way she'd ever bust my balls the way they needed to be busted and even if she tried, how could I ever take her seriously? And that was it.

The funny thing was, driving outta town I found *myself* trying to be polite, the way I'd be around a coworker I was carpooling with. And that's exactly how she seemed to me at that moment. Someone I knew only from what I'd gleaned from the pictures and tchotchke in her cubicle—she'd been to Paris, she liked dolphins, and she had an older brother with a nice smile who at least once in his life had gone skiing. But who was she? What a strange empty feeling to have as the big bad city faded away, leaving only the desert around us.

What made it worse was I still didn't know why I'd turned on her so fast. Vanessa had been in LA for less than twenty days and maybe, just maybe, I was overreacting. And maybe, just maybe what we needed was some time. A little patience.

As I glanced at her staring out her own window, thinking her own thoughts, I couldn't help seeing the end of *The Graduate*. Could it be that we were just like Benjamin & Elaine catching our breath in the back of the bus? Now that Vanessa and I were finally together in Los Angeles, perhaps it was perfectly normal to be staring out our own separate windows, to be feeling an enormous letdown and an overwhelming swell of *now what?* How could our day-to-day life possibly compete with the fireworks of our first kiss?

Of course I knew it couldn't. But I also knew it wasn't even close. The sad truth was I just didn't love her quite as much as I thought I did. We didn't work. And an hour later we still didn't work. And it was the same an hour after that, and an hour after that.

"Why?"

"I don't know." It was exactly three and half hours into the four-hour drive back to LA and I was breaking up with her.

"What the fuck, Ross? You waited until now to say something? You knew all afternoon? The whole time we were driving?!?" Seemed to me it was the best play for the both of us. I mean, who breaks up at the beginning of a four-hour drive? Besides, there was a part of me that didn't want her to have the chance to talk me out of it. Because I wasn't all that certain. "I didn't know you were such a fucking asshole!"

Well, we wanted to find out how we were together and I guess we found out. And hey, the good news was it took less than three weeks to do it. Sometimes a transplanted organ—no matter how healthy, perfectly matched, and well meaning—just doesn't take. The body rejects it. And the body doesn't lie.

"Then why'd we make love last night?"

"I dunno. I didn't mean to. Would it have made a difference if we hadn't?"

Sure, falling in love was easy and wonderful, like slipping into a warm bath, but falling outta love was like sitting in that same tub as it drains and you're left all pruney and tepid against the hard porcelain, with only the sound of your dirty water retching its way down through the pipes.

I guess the only good thing about it all was that she didn't cry. And that she hadn't been in town long enough to leave anything at my place. Not even a toothbrush. So I could just drop her off at her friend's house and that was it. As soon as she shut the door— a door she sure as shit should've slammed but didn't—I couldn't help thinking that maybe I'd made a terrible mistake. Maybe under different circumstances things would work out. Maybe if I just gave it more time things would work out.

And I even had an urge to go get her, to take it all back and tell her I was sorry. But I didn't. Instead I merged into traffic and called a hockey buddy to get the latest scores. Pittsburgh and Buffalo were tied after regulation, and I hoped I'd get home before the start of overtime.

XV

Your Debutante Just Knows What You Need, but I Know What You Want

en days later I was at LAX trying to get on the next plane to JFK. Missing my original flight was gonna cost me $100—roughly a dollar for each minute I'd overslept—but I didn't care. I was just thankful I'd found another seat without having to involve my office. With the savage hangover I was sporting, there was no way I could've handled getting on the phone with my boss and telling him the truth—that I'd slept right through my flight because I'd been up all night drinking and fucking his other producer.

It had all started innocently enough. Last night I'd dropped by Maggie's to say a quick hello to her and the dogs. But before long we were on our way to Sushi Roku, and I guess I'd known where we'd be going from there. I just hadn't suspected how hungry we'd be for each other. Gin, sushi, shamps, porn, and sex—Maggie knew how to push all my party buttons. In fact, she really was heaven in a lot ways. If only she wasn't ten years older. Five, I probably woulda married her. I woulda even considered seven. But ten, ten was almost eleven and another generation.

Although you sure couldn't tell it from looking at her. And certainly not from making love to her. Her stamina was Kenyan, and by the time I was slouching home it was well past five in the morning which meant I only had two hours to sleep before leaving for the airport. But I'd taken three and half, so now here I was, running on fumes with my brain swollen two sizes too big for my head, working through a pair of double cheeseburgers from the airport Burger King and waiting for my new flight to start boarding. Yeah, the office didn't need to know anything about this.

The next morning I was in Chelsea at 20th & 7th standing in front of a sex shop called Purple Passion. Waiting again. This time for a dominatrix named Mistress Claudia. We'd agreed to meet at 11:00 a.m., but at ten past there was still no sign of her. Although I can't say I was surprised. Because no one in the adult world ever seemed to be on time. Evidently deep-sixing your wristwatch came with the territory. At least she called to say she was running late—a full thirty-five minutes by the time she actually showed. And I probably woulda been more than a little annoyed if I didn't have such a crush on the good Mistress Claudia.

During our extensive phone conversations I'd become enamored with her sultry yet direct voice. And now that I was shaking her hand and could practically taste her last cigarette, I knew where she got her husky contralto. Brunette with a slim physique, she wore a leather jacket, jeans, and boots. And she carried a hell of an edge. She coulda been an hour late for all I cared. I was just happy to be shopping with her.

Inside, Purple Passion was about what I expected except there was just more of it—4,000 square feet of wall-to-wall fetish and bondage gear. The tightly packed racks of leather, latex, and lace gave way to rows and rows of various accessories and sex toys—ropes, whips, chains, dildos, vibrators, wrist cuffs, ankle cuffs, neck collars, nipple clamps, ball gags, cock rings, anal beads, butt plugs, gimp hoods, spanking paddles, riding crops. It was endless and I had no idea there'd be so much to play with. Perhaps BDSM was a little like camping—part of the fun was all the gear.

And I was lucky to have a guide like Mistress Claudia. For the past ten years she'd been working in town as a professional dominatrix, and recently she'd even written two books on the subject—two books that I'd enjoyed immensely, *The Art of Sensual Female Dominance* and *Erotic Surrender*. They were a re-introduction to BDSM, a new way in, aimed at readers who'd been scared off by the traditional images of whips and chains and yet, despite their fears, still remained curious about this mysterious sexual practice.

As I read them it slowly began to dawn on me that I was part of her target audience. Back at Club Kink I'd been both revolted and intrigued by what little I'd seen—fearful of the violence, yet seduced by the curious look of completion on the sub's face. Also, I came to realize I'd already been flirting with BDSM without even knowing it. I'd often enjoyed pinning a woman's arms up over her head during sex, and I'd imagined my own arms tied down, pretending to be powerless, as a much smaller woman had her way with me. So I seemed to be an ideal candidate. Still, I didn't believe sex should involve getting hurt and I especially didn't want to hurt anyone else—it was bad enough getting a leg cramp or a drunken elbow to the eye socket.

Also I liked the role-playing aspect of it. Not the dressing up like Cowboys & Indians kinda role-playing—although it could be that—but more the idea that you were becoming another version of yourself. A freer, sexier you—without your inhibitions, completely lost in your role of sub or dom. And wasn't sex already a form of role-playing? I mean, one minute you're having a polite dinner with someone you love, discussing politics and making humorous observations on popular culture, and the next minute she's got your cock in her mouth and her finger up your ass while you're pulling her hair and calling her a dirty whore. There's gotta be some kind of transformation happening between those two scenes—an unleashing of some kind.

So yeah, I was damn curious and it seemed like the more I learned the more I wanted to know. In fact, it was kinda arousing browsing through all these erotically charged items with this sexy, experienced woman standing so close I could smell her New York scents and sensibility. If I was a little bit bolder I woulda asked her to take me home and kick my ass and do whatever it was she did to bad boys like myself. She could be the unethical television producer while I played the innocent, unsuspecting interview subject. And even though I wasn't exactly sure what that meant, I craved it with the same desperate uncertainty that a virgin craves sex.

Kira and my cameraman Dexter got to the hotel late that night, and the next morning we all met downstairs for breakfast. I gotta say, it was good to see Kira. She was all smiles and brimming with energy—excited, perhaps to see me. But I think mostly because it was only her second time in New York so naturally she was thrilled to be here. And because, after hosting this story, she was staying on for a couple days to be a guest on *The Howard Stern Show*, which in the adult world was a huge deal. Like going on *Letterman*. Playboy PR had gotten her the booking so she could promote *Sexcetera,* but of course she was also planning on plugging her website, MarriedCouple.com.

Playboy PR was also able to get us a special rate at the Shoreham, so that's where we were staying. Located at 55th & Park, it was a hip, stylishly modern boutique hotel. But with its typical New York shoebox rooms it was way too small for my shoot, which is why I had to arrange a two-room suite at the Hotel Plaza Athenee up at 64th & Lex. The Athenee was a truly beautiful five-star, European-style luxury hotel with soft yellow walls and a light, airy décor—the perfect backdrop for our "kinder, gentler" storyline.

So around noon, after we'd had our coffee and eggs, we cabbed it over there. As planned, I did Claudia's interview first. Since the story had a BDSM for beginners angle I asked her to start off by translating the acronym. Not surprisingly, her answer ran a little deeper than the one I'd gotten from Bruce eight months earlier. Because, unlike my boss, she broke it down two letters at a time. The B & D, she said, stood for Bondage & Discipline, while the S & M stood for Sadism & Masochism. However, the middle initials, D & S, also had a second meaning, Domination & Submission. Then she explained this was an important distinction to make, especially for this story, because some practitioners believed the D & S subset didn't necessarily include the more physical side of B & D and S & M. Or, in other words, you could have Domination & Submission without the pain. And this was the way BDSM was— just when you thought you understood, another layer was peeled back, like yoga or religion or the songbook of Mr. Bob Dylan.

Then I got her talking about her books and how she'd set out to teach women that in BDSM, submission wasn't about weakness or meekness. In fact it was just the opposite—it was about strength. "What I wanted to do in the second book was empower women to be sexually submissive and not to be ashamed of it." For Claudia, the key concept to understand was that you were entering into a power exchange. "When you're a submissive, what you're doing is surrendering your power, surrendering your control to the top. And it's necessary for you to have a lot of confidence and self-esteem because if you don't have any power to begin with, then you don't have anything to surrender." So submitting was losing yourself in a temporary role, not living out a stifled life. And it didn't mean you were being taken advantage of or somehow degraded. According to Claudia, when done right, "Being sexually submissive is extremely sexy. It's like somebody turned on the faucet, forgot where it was, and just left it running." And I could tell by the weak-kneed sparkle in her eyes that she wasn't exaggerating. Not a bit.

For me the most liberating thing she had to say—the thing I think everyone could benefit from—was the notion that BDSM wasn't as goal oriented as a lot of straight sex was. "It's not all about the orgasm. 'Did you cum, did you cum? I'm not gonna be happy until I make you cum.' That's not it." Instead of a mad dash to climax, it was about enjoying the long, winding road. Delayed gratification. "When you actually go to have sex and be penetrated you are so free and so ready for it that it's just the most intense sex I've ever had in my life. It's like a full-body orgasm, where your whole body shakes in release, and you just feel limp but wonderful when you're done." And once again I knew she wasn't kidding.

Around two the couple showed up. Jim was a wholesome looking Midwestern kid in his early twenties, while Lacey was a curly haired cutie working her way through one of the local colleges. My office had booked them through an adult talent agency and although they weren't actually a couple they were pretending to be one for us. The conceit, as Kira explained to camera, was, "They want to bring a little adventure into their bedroom but they don't want to bleed to death in the process, so they've agreed to let Claudia show them the ropes."

We began the shoot by having them choose a "safe word," which was what you said when you wanted to stop a scene. Ideally it'd be something you'd never say unless you really meant it. For example *No* or *Don't* or *Stop* were terrible safe words because they might be something your damsel in distress character would say. On the other hand, *Cabbage* or *Flamingo* or *Pawtucket*, were all excellent safe words because it was highly doubtful you'd ever say something so incongruous unless you indeed wanted to stop the scene. I asked Jim & Lacey to use *Red*, which was the popular default because not only did it rarely come up on its own, it was also easily translated thanks to our traffic light system. For the same reason, *Yellow* could be used as a warning or caution flag, as in *I don't want you to stop what you're doing, but please slow down or tread a bit lighter because its getting to be a little uncomfortable.* Likewise *Green* was often used as encouragement, as in *Yeah, baby, harder, faster, I love it—green—green—green!*

Then I had Jim tie Lacey to the bed, but instead of using rope, which might've appeared "too scary," we used four different neckties. They were straight from my closet and because I didn't want to risk any of my favorites, I'd only brought the dusty leftover losers from my Groton days. So there Lacey was, naked and beautiful, bound to this wonderfully ornate bed, with silk ties I hadn't worn since Sunday Chapel snuggly gripping each of her luscious limbs. And how could I not smile at that?

Next I asked Jim to put the leather blindfold on his pretend girlfriend so we could illustrate sensory deprivation, the idea being that when you took away someone's sight all their other senses were increased. Especially touch, which is why we had Jim take the peacock feathers and lightly trace them over Lacey's body. Then he did the same thing with the bunny mitten before using his tongue to lick all her hot spots.

Soon we were introducing some of the everyday household items that, as Claudia liked to point out, could easily and quite effectively be brought into the bedroom—things like ice, flowers, strawberries, and candles. And as I watched Jim feeding a strawberry to the blindfolded Lacey with one hand while pressing an ice cube against her erect nipple with the other, it suddenly dawned on me that the film 9 ½ *Weeks* had been about a BDSM relationship and I hadn't even realized it.

Later, when we broke out the candle wax, I cringed as Jim poured the hot liquid all over Lacey's tits. But according to her it wasn't so bad. "At first I was really, really scared that the wax was gonna burn me. But once it went on it felt almost refreshing. And as soon as it started congealing, it was like a grip on my breasts. It was really cool."

So far, so good. Although I gotta admit, personally, I couldn't really imagine taking a time-out from the natural flow of a sexual encounter to break out a fistful of feathers or a bowl of strawberries. It just didn't seem like me. However, I *could* very easily see pulling a flogger from under the bed and taking a few swings against a young lady's exposed buttocks, or even letting that same young lady whip my own ass.

And so I was paying extra special attention when it came time for Mistress Claudia to give our couple a quick lesson with the $75 Cabretta leather flogger that she and I had purchased the day before. Of course I was well aware that such an item would push our fear envelope a bit, but when Claudia had handed it to me back at Purple Passion I'd instantly fallen in love. According to her the main thing was not to wrap the tips around the person you were hitting because that's when it really hurt. Instead you wanted the strips to land squarely on the target and without too much force. Much like swinging a golf club, you wanted a nice even stroke, allowing your instrument to do most of the work. Jim was a quick study and Lacey seemed to honestly enjoy the feeling of all that leather.

Now we were heading down the backstretch. After shooting Jim & Lacey having some simulated sex in a variety of positions we finished off with Kira's closing line. Hiking up her sexy, cream-colored teddy, Kira bent over a chair so Claudia could flog her beautiful derriere. "They say that love hurts, but now you know it doesn't have to. For *Sexcetera*, I'm Kira Reed. Mmm, a little harder please, mistress." *Thwap!*

About an hour later the suite was all cleared out—Claudia had thanked me with a signed copy of her latest book, Jim & Lacey had each been paid their $300, Dexter had packed up the gear, and then they'd all gone their separate ways. Only Kira and I remained. She was in the bathroom, showering and doing her Kegels or whatever it was she did to get ready for dinner, and I figured there was a damn good chance she was just as thirsty as I was. So after pouring myself a Jack on the rocks I spun her up a Jack & Coke and went a knockin'. "Hey, I made you a drink."

"What?"

I cracked the door so she could hear. "I made you a drink!"

"Come on in, silly."

Opening it, I saw her head peeking out from behind the shower curtain. The water was running hot and steamy. "Jack & Coke?"

"Yes, please." And as she reached out her hand, I went to give it to her, but instead she took hold of my wrist and pulled me in. "Kiss me." So I did. Nice and long. And wet from the spray of the shower and just the right amount of tongue. Then she took her drink and sipped. "Thank you."

I wasn't quite sure what to say, so I went with, "You were great today."

"So were you. We make a good team."

"Yes. Yes we do."

"When are your friends getting here?"

"Any minute. I better go wait for them."

"Okay." She was in a fun mood. And so was I.

Back in the living room I had to laugh at the mess I'd made. Over the course of the shoot I'd violently rearranged every single piece of furniture, some of which I'd even turned upside down. I hadn't bothered to put any of it back and I wasn't about to start now. I was much too busy drinking my whiskey and waiting for Oliver & Alexis and George & Helen to show up.

George was another one of our Groton buddies and Helen was his woman. They were both six-figured New York bankers and they both came from super loaded and super Republican families and, even though they weren't even engaged, they both acted like they'd been married for at least a decade.

When they all arrived I was puzzled to see George in a tuxedo and Helen wearing an evening gown until they explained they'd just come from a cocktail party for Mayor Giuliani. Meanwhile Oliver & Alexis, dressed casually as I was, had just come from taking their dog for a walk. They entered the suite first and started laughing right away.

"Love what you've done with the place, Ross," Alexis joked.

"Musta been some shoot," Oliver said.

George started to laugh, but stopped short to study Helen's reaction. She was surveying the room as if she was at the scene of a Manson murder. "What *happened* here?"

"Oh, you know, the usual. Just a little porn."

Then she looked like she was about to be sick. "I'll be downstairs." And she beelined for the door.

"Helen, I was only kidding," I called after her. "It was just softcore, very tasteful, very artistic, no bodily fluids were shared, or even produced." Then she was gone, but I continued on for the rest of the room. "Although I did sneeze once, but that was only because the peacock feathers were so damn ticklish. You know, I feel bad, she didn't even get to see the bedroom. Would any of you like to see the bedroom?"

Now George finished his laugh. But still, he knew what he had to do. "I better go with her." On his way out he rolled his eyes. "We'll be in the bar."

As the door swung shut behind him I turned to my two remaining friends. "So, what are we drinking?"

"I never listen to him. Oliver, do you ever listen to him?" Alexis asked.

After Kira had come out in a busty purple shirt and a snug pair of shiny black pants we'd gone down to join George & Helen for a drink. Then we'd piled into a couple cabs and crossed the park to Shun Lee at 65th & Columbus. By the time our food started to come out I was already bragging to the table about how Kira was going to be a guest on *Howard Stern* later that week.

"Sometimes," Oliver answered.

Me, I never listened to him. And we all knew Helen didn't. But George sure did. And he said so. "I love him. I have him on every day at the office. He's a riot." While George and Kira laughed about some bit from a recent show, I grinned through my latest whiskey. I gotta admit, I'd been a little nervous about bringing both my worlds together, and although they were light years apart, right now you could hardly tell as we orbited our way through dinner.

Sure, Helen was vaguely horrified by Kira's presence, but she seemed equally horrified by the fact that her Beijing prawns came with the heads still attached. And since George was so obviously enthralled by my new friend and by what she and I did for a living I figured he & Helen basically canceled each other out. As far as Oliver & Alexis were concerned, I think they were amused by this mildly fascinating chapter in the life of their dear friend. A chapter that made for some interesting dinner banter. Up to a point.

As soon as Helen excused herself to go to the bathroom, George turned and leaned into me. "So what were you shooting up there? Was it *dirty*? Don't leave anything out. It was dirty, wasn't it?" I was kinda surprised how curious George was. But I guess I shouldn't have been, because I knew he was on a short leash. So I gave him a quick rundown of what we'd done and made sure I was finishing up just as Helen was returning to the table. And poor George soaked up every vicarious word.

Meanwhile I noticed Kira and Alexis were getting into their own conversation.

"Really? You're both completely naked?"

"Uh huh."

"Wow. And it's a guy you just met?"

"Yep."

"So do you touch? I mean, your... does it touch his...? How do you keep from—"

"The guy's wearing a sling."

"A sling? What do you mean?" I knew Alexis was honestly curious. And that, in her mind, she was politely showing interest in Kira and her career.

But I could also tell that Kira was annoyed by the line of questioning. "It's like a sock, but it's got a string that goes around his waist."

"Oh my god."

"And the girl wears a pussy patch."

"A pussy patch?" Now Alexis laughed.

Yeah, Kira was definitely a little pissed. "It's a piece of fabric that covers you so there's no actual contact down there, so no fluids get swapped."

"I can't believe it. So how do you—"

But Kira'd had enough. "Excuse me. I have to go to the little girl's room."

As soon as she'd left the table, George leaned in again and tried to be as subtle as he possibly could. "You tap that?"

Wow. I suppose I kinda expected to hear that question at some point this evening, but not quite like that. Still, I wasn't gonna lie about it. Not to him. "Ah, yeah. Once. In Prague."

"How was it?"

Helen could hear him. "George!"

"It was good, wasn't it?" He just had to know.

But that didn't mean he deserved to know. "My friend, words couldn't possibly begin to describe it."

"I knew it! You're a lucky man. A very lucky man." And he reached out to toast my glass, despite a rather nasty glare from Helen.

By the time Kira got back, Oliver and George were debating some political article they'd read in *The Economist*, while Alexis and Helen were discussing the latest exhibit at MOMA. So finally Kira and I got the chance to chat, just the two of us. And I was so happy to be sitting next to her, sharing our steamed dumplings and sesame chicken and crispy duck and fried rice, and I was even happier that she was matching me whiskey for whiskey.

Afterwards George & Helen caught a cab back to their Upper East Side digs while the rest of us walked up the five or so blocks to have another drink near Oliver's place. But when we got close I threw out an audible—why not just have our drink up at the Dakota, because I was sure Kira would love to see it. Oliver agreed so we all went up, grabbed a beer, and walked out to the living room to show her the view from the big picture windows.

"Wow…"

"Not bad, huh?"

Then I asked if we could step out onto the mini-balcony and Oliver said go for it. This meant raising up the old window as far as we could, which wasn't very far, then squeezing underneath to a ledge that was maybe five feet long but only a couple feet wide, and with the railing only a few feet high, it was really more of a decorative balcony, not intended for hanging out or even standing up. So Kira and I knelt together, alone, on this 6th floor perch over Central Park, a pair of imposters enjoying a borrowed view.

And I gotta say, it gave me a lot of pleasure to share this with her. "Strawberry Fields is right down there. Yoko dedicated it to John as *'A place for quiet contemplation'*—at least that's what the sign says. And you can't see it, but the Meadow is over there. It's actually called the Sheep Meadow because I guess sheep grazed out there back in the day, but we used to go there to play Frisbee and drink tall boys. And then way down there is Tavern on the Green—" That's when I looked and saw the awe and wonder in her eyes, and I knew she wasn't listening.

So I shut up and imagined what might be going on inside that foxy head of hers. Bastard outta Kentucky, Cinderella of Circumstance, she'd stooped to conquer so many times and locked away so many secrets. And now she was poised to seduce Gotham. Or at least Howard. And wasn't Howard larger than Gotham? Yes, I think so. And I think with the cool night air flowing through her hair and Howard's national audience just days away and the sparkling city laid out before her like a silver sixteen-piece place setting and her so damn hungry, surely somewhere inside that wounded mind she musta shed a tear for how far she'd come.

And despite my lifelong fear of heights I was feeling pretty damn good too, sipping my beer with that same night air and that same borrowed view. Except I wasn't any place I hadn't been before. In fact, I'd been standing at this very same window last New Year's Eve when I'd watched the fireworks and kissed Vanessa. You'd think that memory mighta been nagging at me a bit more, but it wasn't. Because now that I was on the other side of the window, with my vertigo shivering up my legs and Kira so close, how could I think of anything else but her? Especially now that she'd turned her eyes on me.

"Thanks for bringing me up here."

And then I kissed her and she kissed me back because we both knew that was what the moment needed.

Twenty minutes later we were back at the Plaza Athenee opening another beer and sharing another kiss. Then I was unbuttoning her purple shirt, pulling back the curtains on her black satin bra. And although I remembered to find the clasp in front I'd forgotten how nice they were underneath and how much better they felt in my hands than in my mind.

I'd also forgotten the best part. That she never wore underwear. Because that was the perfection—the peeling away of her tight black pants, like taking the skin off a piece of fruit. Flawless and firm, so ripe and so juicy, this ass-fruit was indeed the greatest single thing I'd ever seen. And I'd seen things—Da Vinci's smirk, Rodin's pensive rock, The Great One behind the net, the Tetons towering over Jackson Hole, Jerry shaking down "Sugaree," Dylan blowing his harmonica, Ginsberg howling his poetry—and I wasn't exaggerating. This wasn't the booze or my Lil' Guy talking. This was the truth. None of them could compare to Kira's ass.

Then I too was undressed, rising to the occasion, and we were tearing up the room even more, fucking each other all over the place, hitting every inch of the sprawling suite like the big fistfight at the end of a movie. Eventually we settled onto the bed where I took her from behind with the windows wide open and the wind whipping through the white gauzy curtains and the streetlamps spilling into the room like moonlight, bathing her glorious body, as if somehow it wasn't enough that I was about to explode inside her. And then I finally understood the difference between a four-star and a five-star hotel room.

The next morning I awoke to the sound of Kira bustling about, getting dressed and packing up. There was a big plate of bacon, eggs, and toast lying on the bed next to me, and I was damn happy about it. I took a bite of bacon and it was crisp just like I like it.

"Good morning." Kira's voice was bright and full of life.

"Mornin'." Mine was groggy and full of cotton. "Where'd all this come from?"

"Room service. I thought you'd want some eggs. Did I do good?"

"You did perfect. This is exactly what I want." The eggs were scrambled light and fluffy and damn delicious.

"There's also juice and coffee on the table next to you." And there was. Amazing.

"You're the best."

"Have you seen my pants?"

"Huh?"

"My pants. I can't find them." She was looking under cushions, behind sofas, in closets, everywhere.

"Well, they're not under the eggs." I thought maybe I was being funny.

"Did you try under the toast?"

"I'll find them after I'm done eating. Can't go looking for pants on an empty stomach." But we never did find her pants, because after I'd finished breakfast we had sex instead.

And then it was time to check out, so we did, and cabbed it over to the Shoreham, where I had to check out once again before moving myself and my bags over to Kira's room. This was my last day in town and officially I'd planned on crashing at Oliver's, but I was enjoying my time with Kira, and since she wasn't trying to get rid of me and I was still pretty damn tired I lay down on her bed and shut my eyes.

But it was only for a moment because right away she was telling me she wanted to go to the movies, which seemed like a good idea, and that she wanted to see *Moulin Rouge*, which I wasn't opposed to. So she found a nearby showing and I got outta her bed and we went. Unfortunately though, tired and hungover as I was, I had a hard time enjoying the pitch and roll of Baz Luhrmann's frenetic style. In fact, the whole thing made me seasick. Kira, however, was thoroughly entertained, and afterwards told me how much she always enjoyed a good love story, while I tried my best not to vomit.

Then it was back to the hotel and back to her bed to shut my eyes once more. But again I wasn't allowed to sleep for long.

"Hey Taimie, it's Kira. I'm in New York, call me."

Kira was sitting next to me in bed making calls on her cell phone. She'd scribbled several pages on the hotel notepad, which was presumably her to-do list, and now she was taking care of business.

"Hi Jonathon, it's Kira. Just wanted you to know I made it to New York and the hotel's great, and I'm so excited for Howard. Thanks for all your hard work. I just had a couple last minute questions, so call me when you can."

"Yes, hi, this is Kira Reed. I was a guest in your hotel last night. I seem to have lost my pants, and I was wondering if anyone found them...? Black... Room 1329... Well, if they turn up please let me know. I'm staying at the Shoreham now."

"How many calls—"

"Shhh—Hi honey, it's me. How's everything at home? New York's great. I love it, the shoot went well, everyone was so nice, and Ross was great. He took me out with some of his friends last night and we had this great big Chinese meal—the food here is so good and..."

I was beginning to see I wasn't gonna be sleeping anytime soon. And I wasn't about to ask her to make her calls down in the lobby since it was her room, so I got up, put my shoes back on, and headed downstairs to the bar. It was the middle of the afternoon and the lobby was deserted, but the front desk clerk said he'd send someone over right away to mix me up a Tanqueray & OJ. In the meantime I made a couple calls of my own. The first was to my mother to let her know that all was well in New York, that Oliver sends his love, and that I just spent an amazing sex-filled evening with Kira.

"What does her husband think of that?"

"He doesn't seem to mind."

"Really?"

"Well, I'm not so sure he knows."

"Be careful."

"As long as it stays on the road, I'm fine."

"Be careful."

"Ma, this isn't a movie. And it's not some episode of *Jerry Springer*. Nothing's gonna happen."

"Be care—"

"Alright, alright. I'll be careful."

Next I left a message for George saying how great it was to see him, and then I got Oliver on the phone and we discussed plans for that night. He had a big day of work tomorrow and couldn't get too crazy, so because of that, and because I had a hunch he & Alexis might want a break from Kira—and vice versa—I suggested that just the two of us meet for an early drink.

Then I ordered another Tanqueray & OJ and called a hockey buddy back in LA to discuss the playoffs. This was a pleasant way to pass the time, and before long Kira was walking into the bar and ordering a mimosa, so I got off the phone.

"Taimie's flying out."

"Oh yeah?"

"Yeah, I need someone to run around with after you're gone. I'm gonna take her on Howard with me."

"It's only fair. Howard has a sidekick, you should have one too." Then I told her my plan for the evening—that I was meeting Oliver for an early drink, but afterwards wanted to have dinner with her. "That is, if you're not sick of me."

"No, I'm not sick of you." She smiled. "That sounds good."

Then I asked her something I probably had no business asking. But because of the chat I'd just had with my mother, and because I was curious, and because the security wasn't all that tight in my apartment building, I couldn't resist. "So Doug's cool with all this?"

"Sure."

"How? I mean, how does he—?"

"Honey, Doug doesn't know."

"He doesn't?"

"No. Why would I tell him?"

"I dunno. Is this a regular thing?"

"What do you mean?"

"Do you hang out with other people too? Do you have an open relationship? Does *he* hang out with other people?"

"And by 'hang out' I assume you mean 'fuck'?"

"Uh, yeah."

"You really want to talk about this?"

"No." I didn't.

"Cause we can if you want. I don't mind."

"No, no. You're right. Let's talk about something else."

"What about that girl you were so in love with?"

"Vanessa."

"Yeah, Vanessa. What happened to her?"

"I dunno. I guess she just didn't bust my balls enough. And the job didn't exactly help, either. I thought I could be like Hawkeye or Prince Hal, you know, run with the Indians and dance with the debutantes, but in the end I just couldn't."

"How was the sex?"

"Good. Fine. I mean, I don't think that was the problem, although it was never anything like last night, that's for sure. As much as I thought I loved her, and as much as I thought I was enjoying our sex, we never stayed up all night fucking like *that*." And now I inched closer to her and gave her my slow conspiratorial tone. "Nothing could compare to last night, because you, my dear, you are a Ferrari, and everybody else is just peddling their bicycle." I gave her a short kiss and she liked this compliment. And she liked it even more when I added, "And I can't wait to get back behind the wheel tonight."

"You wanna go for a ride, huh?"

"Uh-huh," and I kissed her again.

"Well, if you're good."

"Oh, I'll be good. I promise."

So a little later I had my drinks with Oliver, and that was fun, but the whole time I kept seeing Kira outta the corner of my mind. And on the way back, sitting in the cab, the numbers on the little green signs couldn't go down fast enough.

I met her at the hotel and we walked over to a nearby French bistro called Rue 57. I ordered the steak frites but substituted mashed potatoes because I found them comforting. She had the roast chicken and we traded bites and reminisced over all our past adventures. We laughed about Orlando and how naïve I'd been in the back of the truck-a-zine, and about Amsterdam and how naked she'd been in the back of the boat. And we remembered how much we both adored Prague and Richard Mailer, and I confessed how badly I wanted to kiss her that day on the Charles Bridge and we kicked ourselves for missing out on what woulda been a helluva first kiss. And then we shuddered at the mere mention of Houston and how horrible it'd been and how happy we were to have missed kissing there because that trip was bad all around. And it felt just like a spoonful of buttery mashed potatoes with the skins still on when I realized we'd known each other long enough and stomped on the terra hard enough that our history together could already carry us through an entire meal.

On the way back to the Shoreham we stopped off at a bar for a couple beers. Soon, a tired-looking businessman, drunk and ready for bed in his rumpled suit, got our attention from a few stools away. Or rather, he got Kira's attention. "Excuse me..." He was slurring his words in between pauses so pregnant they were in their third trimester. "Are you... the girl... in those movies..." And then I could tell he was unsure or perhaps embarrassed to describe the films he had in mind, but then he smiled as he thought of a way. "That I like... to watch?"

Kira laughed. "Yes."

"Cool." And he went back to his beer. Then we ordered another round and I moved us to an outta the way table in the back.

"Are you embarrassed to be seen with a softcore movie star?"

I guess I was kinda surprised she'd been recognized. Of course, I was well aware she'd made a ton of films, but who was so familiar with these movies that they could spot the girls out in public? I suppose the guy at the bar was my answer—and he didn't even look like a degenerate. He obviously had a job, a suit, a television set, and a subscription to several premium cable channels. And he just happened to be a huge fan of the girl sitting across from me. The girl I was about to fuck. "It actually got me kinda hot."

"Oh yeah?"

"Yeah. As a matter of fact, I've been thinking about getting you back to the hotel all evening. On the way down to see Oliver I almost turned the cab around."

"And we have all those toys..."

"No, we don't. I sent everything back with Dexter." And she flashed a disappointed look. "Everything, that is, except *the flogger*."

Now she smiled again. "Oh goodie. You wanna flog or get flogged?"

"Both."

"*Really*?" She was enjoying this. And so was I.

"Uh-huh." Then I dropped my voice to a whisper. "You know, I've never told anyone this before, but I've always had these rape fantasies."

"Raping or getting raped?" Then she added with another smile, "Or both?"

"No, not both," I laughed. "Raping—raping, definitely raping." Then I made sure to clarify. "Of course not *actually* raping. Roleplaying. Just 'cuz someone wants to dress up like a cop doesn't mean they want to carry a gun and arrest people."

"Don't worry. I get it."

"Good."

"You wanna rape me?"

"Kinda."

"Just kinda?"

"No, not just kinda. Much more than kinda. Very much so. I'd very much so like to rape you."

"And what exactly does that mean?"

"Well, for starters tying you up and fucking you."

"You can tie me up tonight if you want."

"Then fuck you?"

"Uh-huh." There was an inebriated electricity in her eyes. So I just stared at her, speechless, swept up in our current, riding the pulse as it passed through us, eye to eye, eye to eye, again and again, quickening the charge with each lap, building and building until she whispered, "Wanna go play?"

But of course all I could hear was Dylan's raspy translation, *Your debutante just knows what you need, but I know what you want.*

XVI

Use Your Mouth, Use Your Chin, Use Your Nose, Use Everything You Can

So the whole plane ride back to LA, I had this stupid grin on my face because I couldn't stop thinking about her. And our night at the Shoreham. I kept replaying it over and over and over again, and every time I felt my blood run south and stiffen, rising up against my white linen pants and pressing into my tray table, which I'd been forced to lower so as not to frighten the other passengers in my row. It's true, no one wanted to know that the unshaven stranger in the aisle seat, quietly sipping his Tanqueray, had a rock hard erection. But then there was nothing I could really do about it.

Because, as I said, there was no way I was gonna stop thinking about last night. About Kira. About how I'd tied her arms to the bed using the two terrycloth belts from the bathrobes. And about how because the modern, minimalist Shoreham headboard didn't have any suitable hitching posts I had to pull the whole bed away from the wall and then reach down to tie the first belt to the frame and the second belt to the first, and then, only then could I tie her wrists with that second belt—all of which wasn't made any easier with my Lil' Guy screaming for me to hurry up and Kira feeling about the same. But still, I took the time to retrieve my shirt from the floor to use as a makeshift blindfold before finally getting inside her mouth. And that was nice.

But not nearly as nice as trading places and having her tie me up and then getting on my hands and knees so she could flog my backside.

Thwap. Thwap. Thwap. "Am I doing it right?"

"I dunno. Just don't stop."

Thwap. Thwap. Thwap. "Do you want me to stick a finger up your ass or something?"

"No, no. Definitely not! Nothing up my ass. Who said anything about that?"

"Okay, okay." *Thwap. Thwap. Thwap.* "Does it feel good?"

"I think so. Maybe a little harder. And how 'bout some dirty talk."

Thwap. "You like that, don't you?"

"Oh yeah. Harder."

Thwap. "You're such a little slut, aren't you?"

"Harder."

Thwap.

"Yeah, just like that."

Thwap. "You want to fuck me, don't you?"

"Yeah, baby."

Thwap. "I'm so wet right now."

"Mmm."

Thwap. "I want you to fuck me." *Thwap.* "I want you to fuck me so fucking hard."

"Okay, not so hard."

Thwap.

"Hey!"

Thwap. "I'm dripping wet."

"Gretzky!"

Thwap.

"Gretzky!"

Thwap.

"Gretzky is our safe word! Gretzky! Wayne Fucking Gretzky!!!"

"Oh, sorry, I forgot." And she put the flogger down and rolled me onto my back so she could kiss me. But right away I missed it— I missed the weight of all that leather against my skin and the way it felt like soapy mops at a car wash.

"You were wrapping it right onto my Balzac," and I said this not accusingly or angrily, but slow, with the same satisfied drawl you might use to tell someone you loved them or that you wanted a double fudge ice cream cone. "You fuuucking whore... Mmm..." Then, with my hands still tied and my arms over my head, I leaned into another kiss. But she pulled back, teasing me.

"I wasn't playin' about being all wet." And she climbed up on my face, and how exciting it was to imagine that I was actually trapped and forced to eat my way outta the situation. For some reason being in this pretended predicament made me even hungrier and her even tastier—as if her sweet sweetness, the sweetest of all sweets could possibly be any sweeter—and as I felt her entire body build and build above me and then shudder and shake through each pulse of her pelvis, releasing all her power and intensity and pleasure into my mouth, I woulda sworn I was floating six feet above the bed like some kind of magic carpet.

But the best by far was when we switched places one more time and I bound her wrists all over again and she looked so damn gorgeous with her arms stretched above her head, elongating her torso, accentuating and exposing those sensational breasts and as I lifted and spread her finely toned legs I admired the shape and musculature of her inner thighs and the lines they made. And I thought she looked vaguely like the rarest and most breathtaking species of butterflies pinned under glass to the white board that was our white sheeted bed, and even more so when I went and pushed my own pin into her, mounting her all for myself, forever framing her on the mantle of my mind.

Leaning over to kiss her again and again, I took hold of her throat and squeezed just enough to feel the blood pulsing through her neck and I pressed my teeth against her cheek and so badly I wanted her. It wasn't enough we were attached down below—I wanted every inch of our bodies to be inside one another, I wanted to hold her so tight I actually passed through her, I wanted to wear her skin inside out, to devour her, to suck the marrow out of her bones, to chew the gristle off her soul, and fuck and fuck and fuck her again and again and again. And when the image of Picasso's *Dora and the Minotaur* flashed in my mind's eye, I wondered if perhaps I was the first man since Picasso himself to think of Picasso while pausing between thrusts.

Finally, inevitably, I turned her over, grabbed hold of her ass like I had the whole world in my hands, and this went on and on until I blew my mind into a billion tiny little pieces that would never fit back together in quite the same way ever again.

And now, beaded up as I musta been by her memory, slipping into my fourth Tanqueray & OJ, I couldn't help comparing this cross-continental flight with the one I'd taken just shy of five months ago. Back then I'd been in love. With Vanessa. Or at least so I thought. And my feelings had run deep enough to fool my soul with the promise of a mate and a vision of the future. But, c'mon, whaddaya expect after an entire year of pining is resolved with such pomp & circumstance? This, however, was different. An awakening of sorts. Perhaps even a revolution. But definitely not love. I wasn't that stupid. Not only was she married, she was MarriedCouple.com.

Although, I gotta say, I *was* crazy about her. And I couldn't help feeling that there was something between us. Something warm, something close. Something more than lust. But something that could just as easily have been a mirage. With her vast experience with men and her training as an actress and her fifty softcore films, she certainly could've been faking the whole thing. Or at least exaggerating. She was so uninhibited, so attentive, so damn good at everything she did, I bet she made every guy she fucked feel this way.

But didn't our connection *have* to be superficial? With no real attachments we could enjoy the good parts, and only the good parts, without the complications of everyday life. When it was time to go, all I had to do was wish her good luck on *Howard Stern* and I was gone. I walked outta that hotel room with no obligations, no promises to keep, no excuses to dream up down the road. The fantasy was still intact. If it was real, if we actually had a chance of falling in love, then it woulda been such a shame.

I arrived at the location around 9:30 a.m. I was early. About a half-hour ahead of my crew. Probably because I was a bit nervous. It was a sprawling Tudor mansion overlooking the ocean in the Pacific Palisades. Supposedly, it was once owned by the legendary actor Charles Laughton. He'd been nominated for an Oscar for the classics *Witness for the Prosecution* and *Mutiny on the Bounty,* and he'd won in 1934 for a film I'd never heard of called *The Private Life of Henry VIII.* So he was a heavy hitter for sure, but way dead, and definitely not the reason my panties were all in a bunch.

I was nervous because, as far as porn shoots went, this was about as big as they got. Squeezing past the production truck in the driveway I noticed the crew all wearing matching jumpsuits as they unloaded the gear. Inside, I walked into the kitchen and found a granite-topped island covered with various snacks, from the healthy to the not-so-healthy, and then I almost tripped over a pair of wide open coolers stocked full of waters and sodas.

Just off the kitchen a small room had been turned into a makeup area with two canvas chairs and several tackle boxes that were no doubt jam-packed with powders and pads and glosses and whatever else they used to clean up the girls. Backlit from the super-bright, sun-filled sliding glass doors behind them I could see two makeup artists chatting away in their dungarees. I figured I should go introduce myself and find out how far behind schedule things were running.

"Excuse me. Hi, I'm Ross with Playboy TV, and—" Right then was when I got close enough to realize one of the makeup artists, the one wearing a backwards baseball hat to keep her long blonde hair outta her face, was not, in fact, a makeup artist. It was her! "You're Jenna Jameson."

She laughed. "I am. Thanks so much for coming out today." And she held out her hand.

Which I shook, simultaneously blurting, "You're shorter than I expected."

"I know, right? That's what *everybody* says." She smiled. Jenna Jameson was *smiling* at me, and I was weak in the knees. Because she was also a lot better looking than I expected. After seeing so many super-stylized, glammed-out, hard-edged pictures of her over the last few weeks I never woulda imagined Jenna Jameson to be this natural, this down to earth, this damn cute. And nothing coulda prepared me for those eyes—those warm sparkling pools of blue like wading out into the Caribbean on a hot day with a cold beer.

She didn't seem like any other porn star I'd ever seen. Perhaps because I was looking at a woman in charge. A strong, confident, happy woman. This was her set. She owned it—or at least her new company, Club Jenna, had rented it for the day.

"By the way, I want to congratulate you on your company. Really, I can't tell you how nice it is to see a woman running the show."

"Thanks."

"And keeping all the money."

She laughed at this before adding, "I couldn't agree with you more."

This past year she'd started her own business and launched her own website, ClubJenna.com, and that was what my story was about—Jenna Jameson, CEO. Today she and her business partner, Jay, who also happened to be her director and her boyfriend, were filming the very first Club Jenna feature, *Briana Loves Jenna.*

It had been seven years since her first on-camera sex scene and six years since she'd signed her first contract with Wicked Pictures, famously telling her new boss, Steve Orenstein, "The most important thing to me right now is to become the biggest star the industry has ever seen." And, as the story goes, that's exactly what she did. That first contract had paid her $6,000 for each of her eight movies that year. Now she was supposedly making $60,000 per film and only doing five a year. She was also getting $8,000 a night as a feature dancer, usually touring two weeks out of every month. So yeah, you could say she was a pretty big star. But I think what amazed me the most was that she was only twenty-six—just one year younger than I was.

"Love the jumpsuit, by the way." Now that my breathing had returned to something resembling a normal pattern, I realized Jenna wasn't actually wearing dungarees as I'd previously thought. Instead she had on a blue jumpsuit, the same as the crew was wearing, with an orange racing stripe down the side and "Club Jenna" spelled out in big white letters over the chest and on the back.

"Thanks," she giggled. "They were Jay's idea. Pretty cool, huh?"

"Is he here?"

"Oh yeah, he's downstairs shooting a scene." *What?* They were already shooting? I couldn't believe it. Not only were they not running late, they were actually *ahead* of schedule.

"Well, I'm gonna give you some space and go wait for my crew."

"Okay. I'm here if you need anything."

A few minutes later I was outside meeting Aaron, the host, and Dexter, the shooter. After a round of hellos and how you beens we went straight downstairs to catch the tail end of whatever Jay was directing. Then, after a break for lunch, we reconvened on the enormous second floor balcony with its sweeping ocean view. A damn fine place to shoot Jenna's first scene of the day.

When she was ready she walked out stiffly, as if on stilts, because of her absurdly high-heeled platform shoes. For a second I didn't even think it was her. I could barely recognize the sweet girl next door I'd just met a few hours earlier. And although she was completely naked except for those crazy shoes, she somehow seemed more clothed now than when I'd first seen her in her jumpsuit and baseball cap. Or at least more protected. Like she was wearing a suit of armor, a medieval knight riding into battle— her super-glammed-out hair and heavy makeup were her helmet and visor, her Double Ds were her breast plate, her platform high heels were her iron plated boots. And her eyes, those beautiful blue eyes, were now icier, harder, and more focused. But I guess this makeover made sense. She couldn't be that girl next door anymore. When the cameras rolled she had to be Jenna Jameson, Super Star. She had to be in the zone.

I watched as she performed an extremely professional, well-executed masturbation scene, slowly working herself down to the floor, which musta been a nice shot with the ocean off in the distance. But it didn't really do anything for me. I guess I was feeling nostalgic for the girl I'd met earlier. I woulda loved to see her do a scene like that—adorable and giggling as she unzipped her jumpsuit, shimmied out of it, then pushed down her white cotton panties, and yeah, that woulda been nice. But it didn't happen.

After another break we went back down to the basement where Jenna was gonna do a girl-girl scene in the large, luxurious screening room. Jay put a Jenna DVD up on the widescreen to loop in the background. Then Jenna and her co-star—a sexy brunette named Isabella—came down, both looking kinda elegant in their black outfits, and pretty soon they were going at it on a bright red couch. I was feeling a little drowsy, so I closed my eyes in the back of the room. About a half-hour later the nearby shuffling of feet woke me up. The energy in the room had changed and I could tell something exciting was going down.

Both girls were naked and Jenna was wearing a black strap-on. And she was really giving it to Isabella. They were still on the couch, but Isabella was bent over and leaning against one of the arms while Jenna took her from behind. I was glad I hadn't slept through this because now, finally, Jenna was putting on a show. A lotta times I'd seen a girl don a strap-on and be totally lost, like, *What I am supposed to do with this thing?* But not Jenna. She knew exactly what she was doing. She was right in tune with Isabella, and as they moved together like a pair of dirty dancers it was good. Real good. I actually found myself getting aroused—rarely do I ever get stirred on set, but this was something. For me the best part was when Jenna reached around Isabella's waist and grabbed her with one arm and held her tight without breaking her rhythm. I could tell she was honestly into it. And if she wasn't honestly into it, then I was even more impressed because it sure as shit looked that way.

Later, right before her interview, I praised Jenna's performance and commented specifically on this reach-around maneuver. She said she liked it when guys did that to her, so that's why she did it to Isabella. And that's why she was such a good performer—she imagined how it felt to be on the other side. I remembered that's exactly what had impressed me eight months earlier when I'd watched her first blowjob scene with Maggie—her ability to know, or to sense, what her partner was feeling. Even more impressive was the fact that she didn't have to go that extra mile. It was plenty to just show up, do the scene, get her check, and go home. But Jenna wanted more than that, so she gave more. She insisted on making it special, like a singer who lives each song all over again every night instead of sleepwalking through the words.

As the scene wound down Jenna put her cock in Isabella's mouth and had her suck on it for a while. Then Jay gave Isabella a glass of milk, which she sipped without swallowing so when she continued the blowjob she drooled the creamy liquid out of the corners of her mouth. When they edited it later it would look like the strap-on had actually cum. Another sip of milk and they ended the scene with Isabella drooling into a silver bowl, then lapping it up. Very nice.

All we had left to shoot was her interview, and when Jenna walked into the office where we'd set up she was somewhere in between the woman I'd first met and the woman I'd watched masturbate—light makeup and gently tousled hair, dark pants, and a white collared long sleeve shirt. Damn beautiful, and the perfect look for her role as the sexy CEO.

And, in her case, it wasn't just a role. Far from a figurehead, she was actually running things, and to make sure my audience understood this point I let her explain right away how she and Jay worked together. "He works on the technical end and I work on the artsy end, and so when we come together it turns into what you saw here today."

Besides having a boatload of pix & videos, Jenna felt the success of her site would depend on her accessibility—after all, it was called Club Jenna—so she was giving her members various ways to get to know the "real" Jenna Jameson. Like hosting a weekly chat room. "It's funny because a lot of my fans, when they talk to me, they're like, 'Jenna, I cannot believe what a real person you are, I can't believe you're making dinner right now, I can't believe you have dogs.' They expect me to be, like, this sexual nymphomaniac freak. So this gives my fans a chance to talk to me like a normal person, and it feels good to just have normal interaction with people."

She also kept an online diary. "I make sure that I post twice a day telling them what I'm doing, whether it be mopping the floor or eating a girl out, or both." Jenna was known for her penchant for pussy, so that very well may have been an actual entry.

But of all the extras Jenna was offering the one that interested me the most was her sex advice. Members could email their questions and she would post her answer. *Brilliant!* Naturally I wanted to know what the most common topic was. "Guys always ask me about eating girls out. Because they're like, 'You know, I'm worried that I'm not pleasing my woman, I don't know if she's faking it. Jenna, what do you suggest?' My funny answer is, do your ABC's. That's funny, but it doesn't work. Trust me guys, it DOES NOT WORK. And don't just do that tongue thing that they do in pornos. That doesn't work either. You need to really get into it. Put your face in there, use your mouth, use your chin, use your nose, use everything you can. And if you keep a very, very steady motion she'll cum within two minutes." Then she paused and made sure she ended with a joke. "And it's funny, they actually listen to me. Too bad my man doesn't." And that's what I loved about her—she never took herself too seriously and always seemed to be having a good time.

As we wound down the interview I asked what kept her going, what was still driving her, because after already breaking through so many glass ceilings you could see she wasn't about to stop when she was ahead. "The cash is nice, but that takes a back seat to the feeling of actually being in control of my own destiny. For me it's not so much trying to accomplish something *out there*, I'm trying to accomplish something *within myself*. I think that it's really important that I succeed, and I've been that way in every aspect of my life. I want to conquer. And now the Internet is in my way and I want to climb that mountain."

She had that uber-drive that all great men and women have—that need to keep pushing, that insatiable lust, that feeling that someone or something was always licking at their heels and they couldn't rest or they'd lose it all. The dream would end and they'd have to slink back to where they came from. But there was no way Jenna was ever going back.

Afterwards—and I never do this—I asked her to sign one of her t-shirts for a guy on my hockey team who was way into porn and nearly pissed his cup when I told him I'd be spending the day with Jenna. She did it with a smile and then I thanked her, gave her a big hug, and left her to finish shooting her film in the once-upon-a-time home of the late, great Charles Laughton.

XVII

Darling, It's All about Adding a Zero

A week or so later I was at a campground in the middle of nowhere—Roselawn, Indiana, population 4,000 souls—watching a feeding frenzy of photographers snapping away at a bunch of strippers posing around a couple of motorcycles parked at the edge of a small lake. Dexter asked if I wanted him to start shooting and I shook my head no. This was ridiculous.

"Why aren't they naked?" Kira asked. Good question. The strippers hadn't stripped and were still wearing their bikinis.

"I dunno, maybe some of these guys are shooting for mainstream magazines."

"Now what are they doing?" Some silly bastard was actually giving the girls more clothes to put on! He was passing out identical t-shirts, and when they put them on, I could see they were emblazoned with the name of one of the event's sponsors.

"Sponsors' shots."

"What're you gonna do about it?"

I smiled, then gave her my best tough guy Clint Eastwood impersonation. "I'm gonna *wait* my *turn*." She laughed at this, just as that same guy began passing out yet another round of t-shirts.

"I'm gonna get some sun." Kira walked a few yards off to the side and took the pareo from around her waist and began spreading it out on the grass. She was also wearing a cute dark blue bikini with the Playboy logo on it. I called after her, "Don't be taking your top off or your tits will wind up in every girlie mag from here to Timbuktu."

As I watched yet another round of t-shirts being passed out, all I could do was chuckle. Normally I'd be getting frustrated by having to suffer though all this nonsense, but there were worse places to be than the Ponderosa Sun Club. This was my first time at a nudist camp, and I liked the fact that it was family owned and operated. And that there was a hearty, down home vibe about the place.

But Playboy hadn't sent me here for the hospitality. Or for the nudists. No, I was here for the Nudes-A-Poppin' Festival. Twice a year since 1973 the Ponderosa Sun Club hosted the world's largest and longest running outdoor beauty pageant for the country's top exotic dancers. Held primarily as a fundraising party to finance the camp, the contest also awarded forty different trophies for all kinds of titles like Miss Nude Galaxy, Miss Nude Go-Go, Miss Nude Up & Comer, Miss Nude Rising Star, and on and on and on. But by far the biggest and best and most coveted trophy was Miss Nude Showstopper.

Tomorrow more than a hundred strippers would be descending on this sleepy little town tucked halfway between Chicago and Indianapolis. But today only a select few of the bigger feature dancers were here. They'd been invited to come in a day early for photo-ops and, supposedly, any minute they'd be done and I'd get my promised half-hour with them. So for now I walked over and lay down next to Kira. Damn, she looked good today in the hot summer sun—a lot better than all these fake-titted strippers, that's for sure.

"Have you ever seen a girlie mag from Timbuktu?"

"Nope." She opened her eyes behind her pink shades and smiled, knowing a joke was coming.

"Awww," I went into my gravelly Larry Flynt imitation, which, by the way, was spot on, "it's some reeeaaally kiiinkeee stuuuff." This got her laughing and then I was laughing and we were feeling groovy on this beautiful afternoon, gently mocking the amateur photographers and their general waste of twelve willing & able young women.

"It's all the same shot."

"I know, I know. It's like they're too nervous to ask the girls to do anything fun. They got seventy-six acres of campgrounds here and they're tethered to the lake."

"Seventy-six?"

"Done my homework, babe."

"Well, at least it's a nice day." She closed her eyes again and listened as I rambled on about nothing in particular.

Until Scarlett, the super sweet owner of the nudist camp, came over. "Alright Ross, they're all yours." I guess normally Scarlett would have been naked as a jaybird, but for festival weekend the campers kept their clothes on because of all the "outsiders" wandering about.

"Thanks." So far I was big fan of Scarlett. Really cool, really down to earth, and really organized, which was about the best possible compliment I could give on a shoot day.

I told Dexter to get ready, then I went to address the girls. "Good afternoon, ladies. My name's Ross. I'm with Playboy TV's *Sexcetera*. This is my cameraman Dexter, and that young lady with the microphone is our host, the wonderfully talented Miss Kira Reed." Whenever I spoke in front of this many people I always thought back to my brief days as summer school teacher. "I want to thank you in advance for the next thirty minutes of your lives that I'm about to borrow." Of course, this class was a far cry from those inner city fifth graders I'd taught in D.C. "First of all, because this is for Playboy TV, I need everyone to get naked and then follow me."

Then I led them like a pied piper through the campgrounds while all the photographers followed along, suddenly extremely excited. In thirty minutes flat I shot naked tennis, naked volleyball, naked golf cart racing, naked shuffleboard, naked hot tubbing, and naked swimming. The key, of course, was to keep things moving, shooting only a few minutes at each station, just enough time for one of Kira's stand ups and a little b-roll.

But the final shot was by far the best. I got them all on this super long and super high swing-set. There musta been at least ten swings, all in a line, and with a naked girl in each seat, all swinging at different paces and heights it was a helluva nice image. Kind of a Rockettes thing going on. Especially when you stood on the side and shot down the line so you could see them all at once. Naturally that's where I placed Kira for her stand up.

When I had what I needed I figured it couldn't hurt to let Dexter roll a little longer. Besides, the girls seemed to be enjoying themselves, and I knew for sure the photographers were in heaven. Several of them even came over and thanked me profusely for the shots they'd been able to piggyback.

Of course, I didn't tell them the main reason I was moving so fast was that I needed to make an important phone call at precisely noon. By now, it was already 12:06, which meant I needed to get dialing. Struggling with one bar of service I was barely able to get through to my ticket broker who said he had, indeed, just received the Bob Dylan tickets I was waiting for. But before I could give him my credit card info, I lost the connection. This happened two more times so I started walking about in various directions searching for a second bar. Then I noticed Kira was nearby doing the exact same thing.

"Any luck?" I shouted over to her.

"No!" She shouted back. "I'm trying to get on a conference call with Doug and our accountant. I think I'm buying a house." After her appearance on *Howard Stern* her site had gone through the roof, and for the first time in her life she was making real money.

So while the girls were swinging and the photographers were shooting, we were zig-zagging our separate ways across the lawn until finally I found that elusive second bar. I called Kira over and we stood together, face to face, on this tiny island of reception. And then we hung up at the exact same time.

"I just bought Bob tickets."

"I just bought a house!"

"Where's the house?"

"Near Mulholland & Beverly Glen. Where's the show?"

"The Hard Rock in Vegas."

"I wanna go to Vegas."

"I wanna live in the house."

And we laughed.

But not for long, because it was time to interview Scarlett. We set up outside with a creek and a cute wooden bridge in the background. Naturally I had plenty of questions about how hard it was to judge so many girls and award so many trophies, but mostly we wound up talking about how the Ponderosa Sun Club was such a family oriented place. I listened as she talked lovingly about several of the families that had been members for generations and how she'd known so many of them since she was a little girl. And how important a role the camp had always played within her own family. How the camp *was* her family.

As emotionally involved as she obviously was, I was still surprised by her answer to my final question. I'd asked her about the future, which was pretty much the standard ending for all my interviews. "The Ponderosa Sun Club will eventually be passed

down to my children. I have an eight year old daughter and a two
year old son and one day..." Here she began to mist up and her
voice trembled a bit. "One day she'll be following in my footsteps
and he'll be here too, helping her run the business." Now there
was a full blown tear running down her cheek. "And it just keeps
going on and on from generation to generation." Wow. Things
sure ran deep around here.

By the time we were done for the day and making our way back
to the hotel it was a little after five. The closest decent place to
stay was the Merrillville Radisson, twenty miles away, so while we
drove I tested Kira and Dexter with my *Fargo* accent, "Ya know, it's
the Radisson, so it's pretty good." But they couldn't guess where
it was from and eventually I had to tell them.

Hard to believe, but Dexter actually had family nearby, and
after they came to pick him up for dinner Kira and I had the rest
of the evening all to ourselves. There was a place called the Lone
Star Steakhouse a couple doors down, so we walked over for an
early dinner. The food was a lot better than I was expecting. I had
a bunch of scotch and a filet and a baked potato and then a bunch
more scotch and it was a nice slow meal.

It was the first time we'd really gotten a chance to talk since
New York, and I was dying to hear about her *Howard Stern*
appearance. I knew she'd been a big hit, but I still hadn't gotten
the details.

"At first it sucked. I think maybe he expected the Playboy girl
to come out and be all bleach blonde and fake tits, you know, 'cuz
right away he was kind of a dick."

"Like how?"

"He was making fun of my feet."

"That's crazy. Your feet are perfect."

"I know, I've been a foot fetish model, for chrissakes. People
worship my feet."

"I love your feet and I'm not even a foot guy. What was he saying about them?"

"He said they looked weird."

"What?"

"And that my toes were stubby."

"Stubby? That's ridiculous." What was ridiculous was me having to make Kira feel better about her body. "What does he like—long curly monkey toes?"

"I dunno."

"So what did you do?"

"Well, I made sure he was looking and I hiked up my skirt and crossed and uncrossed my legs and—"

"You weren't wearing any underwear, were you?"

"Nope."

"You did the *Basic Instinct* move, didn't ya?"

"Uh huh."

"I love it!" And I did. The thing about going on *Howard Stern* was you could be on for five minutes or for a whole hour depending on how much he liked you. So when Kira sensed she was in trouble, she knew it was one of those crossroad moments that could make or break her. But she also knew she had an ace up her sleeve—or rather, up her skirt—and she'd played it, laid it down real slow and flat so everyone could see. And she'd won the hand.

"After that it was all good."

"I bet."

"We probably spent five minutes just talking about my trim job. And of course he wanted to see my tits."

"Of course."

"Then I got to bring out Taimie, and we played and put on a great show and it was so fun. We were on for almost an hour." Of course, she'd promoted the hell out of her site, and overnight her membership spiked from the hundreds to the thousands. "Since *Howard* I've made over a hundred grand." Kira was loving her windfall. "Darling, it's all about adding a zero. But you know what's crazy? If I didn't think to get extra bandwidth before I left for New York it woulda crashed the server and I wouldn't have made a dime."

"*And* you wouldn't have made a dime if you hadn't thought to wear a short dress with no underwear."

"That's right. And now I'm buying a house in the hills." She laughed and sipped her Jack & Coke.

When the check came Kira snatched it up and slapped down her brand new business AMEX, and I could tell she enjoyed paying for our dinner with her brand new money. And as I watched her over-tip and sign the slip I couldn't help thinking of my recent time with Jenna Jameson, CEO, and how much she and Kira seemed to have in common.

Like Jenna, Kira was ambitious as hell and had been savvy enough to keep her eye on the money. She'd learned how to build her own website from scratch, and then continued to run it herself instead of farming out the work along with half the profits. And like Jenna, Kira recognized a business opportunity when she saw one. After making a name for herself in softcore films she understood her fans would gladly pay to see her have real, hardcore sex. So she'd given them exactly what they wanted, but only on her own website where, once again, she got to keep all the money. And now they had another thing in common— they'd both flashed their tits on *Howard Stern*. But most of all Jenna and Kira both had a lot of balls.

After dinner we went back to the Radisson and smoked one of Kira's famous smuggled joints and then brought some drinks out to the indoor pool, which, like the restaurant, was a lot better than I woulda expected. It had this crazy waterfall that came down hard from about ten feet above, so hard that standing under it and letting it hit your neck and shoulders was like a really intense massage. And especially relaxing stoned with a head full of scotch.

Then we made another round of drinks and went outside to a second pool, and it was so nice floating with her under the Indiana moon, slowly twisting through the water, holding her in her teeny bikini. Her skin was wet and cool and I wished this was my own backyard pool so I could sit her on the edge and make love to her right there. We almost coulda, too, because there wasn't anyone around. It seemed like we had the whole hotel to ourselves—no screaming kids, no barking dogs, no NASCAR arguments. And when we moved over to the adjacent hot tub, I sipped my scotch and was so happy to be alone with her.

Back in my room I took off my wet bathing suit and threw it in the bathtub to dry. Somehow Kira's pareo had wound up with my stuff, so I wrapped it around my waist like a skirt. Then I fixed myself another scotch and headed on down the hall. Even though the hotel seemed deserted, for some reason Kira and I were on opposite ends of the building. Strange. But I was actually enjoying the walk. Her silky paisley patterned pareo felt cool against my bare skin. And my buzz was absolutely perfect and with Kira waiting in her room, I was in heaven, or at least on my way, and I knew it.

Walking down that Radisson hallway I understood precisely how happy I was. I was absolutely, acutely aware that I hadn't felt this good—this alive, this free, this free to be me—since, well... never. Right then I actually told myself that no matter what happened to me because of this ridiculous job, no matter how screwed up my mind got, it would all be worth it for this one single walk. And then I decided for this hypothetical bargain with myself I better throw in that walk I'd taken back in Prague across the Charles Bridge. Yes, for these two walks it was all worth it.

When I made it to Kira's room I found her swaying to a sultry blues station she'd found on the radio, naked and softly lit from all the candles she had burning. They were the kind in the metal screw top canisters that were made for travel. I kissed her and then again, and she showed me a bottle of almond scented massage oil that she'd brought along with all the candles. And I smiled at the thought of her packing her suitcase back in LA, preparing to blow my mind, imagining what she was gonna do to me and what I was gonna do to her.

We moved to the bed and I laid her down on her stomach and poured the oil over her back and slowly, for the next forty-five minutes or so, I worked every inch of her glistening, candlelit body. And it was so nice rubbing her legs—her thighs, her calves, her feet, yes, those cute little feet. Because I knew how much I loved having my own legs rubbed. Finally I ended my slow tour at her ass, which I kneaded as long as I could until I was about to burst and had to take her.

And then it was my turn. As I felt the slight chill of the oil dripping along my back I thought, *What a splendid idea—a rubdown after sex!* Previously I'd only known backrubs as foreplay. But soon she was working me so good and so thorough that I understood this massage was to be foreplay as well. There was more sex coming around the bend, and in my dreamy bliss I coulda sworn I actually heard the delta bluesman on the radio sing that very line—*There's more sex comin' 'round the bend.*

By the time we were blowing out the candles it was after midnight and I could safely say that my body had never felt this completely satisfied. And as I drifted off to sleep with Kira in my arms I felt like we were back floating together in the pool under the Indiana stars, and I thanked those lucky stars for the past six hours that she and I had shared out here in the middle of nowhere, halfway between Chicago and Indianapolis.

The next day we drove back to the Ponderosa in time to interview the emcee before the show got started. There was a clubhouse off the stage area with a few dressing rooms and that's were we were supposed to meet him. And that's where we found him—The Hedgehog himself, Ron Jeremy.

Although I'd already seen him up close & personal that night in Vegas, the first time we actually met was about a month ago at his apartment building. He lived in Hollywood about ten minutes from my place, so I'd agreed to stop by to hear his Nudes-A-Poppin' pitch. Of course I got there right on time and of course he didn't. Being a porn star, he showed up a full 45 minutes late. After a quick apology, he sat next to me on the couch and launched into a long litany about how *great* the festival was—the crowd was great, the girls were great, the performances were great. But the only thing I really heard was what he'd said about the Ponderosa Sun Club and how sweet and wonderful Scarlett and her whole family were. Ron said he'd been emcee-ing the event for the past 15 years and the reason he kept going back wasn't for the money or for the girls, but for the family.

Now that I was interviewing him on-camera he gave me the funny version of how his relationship with Nudes-A-Poppin' had begun. He'd first come as a performer. The festival has always had at least one male event, but even fifteen years earlier Ron didn't quite have the body to compete. But he had something else—a not-so-secret weapon. "The other guys were better looking than me, but I could do things that they couldn't do. So I would throw the old schmeckle clockwise, then counter-clockwise, and then kiss it goodbye. Top that, bodybuilder prick."

I was well aware of the Legend of Ron Jeremy and how he was one of the few lucky bastards that could actually suck his own dick—or as they say, perform auto-fellatio—so when he said he'd kissed it goodbye I knew he wasn't kidding. I couldn't help wondering how his unique ability had affected his outlook on life. No matter how bad his day went, he could always go home and give himself a blowjob.

It was tough not to like Ron. He seemed sharp and had a playful, self-deprecating sense of humor. "Back then I was doing spreads for *Playgirl* magazine. Now I'm lucky to get into *Field and Stream*." And while he certainly wore a sleeve-full of the frustration that he hadn't quite had the mainstream success he thought he deserved, he wasn't sad or depressing at all. He was a helluva guy, and I got the impression he put his heart & soul into everything he did. And did I mention he also happened to be able to suck his own cock?

When the time came, Ron ran down the long thin ramp from the clubhouse to the stage, high-fiving the crowd as he went. Incredibly, there were now six thousand people out there, pressed up against every inch of the fenced barrier that was keeping them away from the performers. After a little schtick Ron introduced the first category of girls, and it was on. Loud music blaring, hot sun glaring, and a small army of drunk, horny Americans tempted and teased with so much naked flesh, so near yet so far. I couldn't help thinking of *Apocalypse Now* when the Playboy Bunnies do their little dance number and the soldiers storm the stage—a scene I could certainly see happening this afternoon, and I was all too aware we were without a getaway chopper and Ron and his schmeckle could only hold them back for so long.

With one camera and so many strippers to shoot, plus interviews with the fans and the dancers, the four-hour event went by in a flash. And some of the performers were actually quite entertaining. A lot of them were the big-time feature dancers I'd heard about but never seen—the ones that brought props and actually spent some time choreographing their routines. One fake-titted brunette came out in a tuxedo outfit with a skirt and danced to Shania Twain's "Man I feel Like A Woman" with a bottle of champagne, a bunch of strawberries, and a canister of whipped cream. Messy, but sexy. Another girl—this one a fake-titted blonde—danced to the classic disco number "Car Wash," and she had a cute little car on stage along with a pair of working showers overhead.

When it came time for Ron to announce the big winner of the Miss Nude Showstopper trophy it wound up going to a fake-titted brunette, who worked outta Atlanta, and who, as I later learned, had won the same award the previous year as a fake-titted blonde. The girl was good.

Naturally, I made sure Kira was there to get her immediate reaction. "So you just won Miss Nude Showstopper—are you gonna go to Disneyland?"

She was all smiles. "Um, no. I think I'm gonna head back to the hotel and get laid."

As the six thousand slowly made their way outta the campgrounds, Kira and I were done and we took a walk. We wanted to see some more of the camp and we were curious about the living conditions, so we headed down the road where most of the trailers and mobile homes were hitched. As we passed by one of the campers we saw a middle-aged couple out front sitting on lawn chairs, drinking beer, and enjoying some quiet after the crazy loud day. They recognized us and invited us over to join them, which we gladly did.

It was so nice to be with this mellow couple, drinking their beer and telling our stories and just sitting and basking... In the Indiana summer. In the relief of each new breeze against my sunburnt skin. In Kira's closeness. In the peace of my satisfied mind a million miles from anything—from noise, from bosses, from bills, from husbands, from morning, from anything that wasn't here.

And as this kind couple told us all about their camper and how it gave them everything they could ever want, I let myself imagine that this was our camper—Kira's and mine—and that this was our little lawn, and our cooler full of Michelob, and our Golden Retriever panting in the afternoon heat. And as we shared a long look I wondered if Kira was thinking the same thing. But of course she wasn't. Because she didn't need a camper. She had a brand new house in the hills and a husband waiting for her back in Los Angeles. What a shame.

XVIII

You Taste Like Scotch

As July turned into August, things were kinda quiet. Season two of *Sexcetera* was coming to an end and production was winding down. I didn't have any more stories scheduled with Kira, so I didn't expect to be hearing from her for a while. And Maggie, having finished all her stories, had decided to spend her hiatus outta town. She'd taken the dogs and headed north to have some time with her family in Idaho before going camping in Jackson Hole. Like me, she was a big a fan of the place. In fact, back when we'd both worked at E! some of our earliest conversations were sparked by a framed picture of the Tetons she had on her desk.

Me, I was staying in LA to start pre-production for season three. When outta the blue I got a call from Kira. I was at home and it was after eleven. "You still want me to come see Bob Dylan with you?" In Indiana we'd joked about this, but I'd assumed it was just that—a joke.

"Uh, yeah, of course, but—" *What are you gonna tell Doug?* was what I was trying to ask, but, as usual, she was way ahead of me.

"A friend of mine is directing a movie in Vegas that week and I got myself a part." She was talking low and fast, and I bet Doug was close by. "The show's the 24th, right?"

"Yeah, Friday the 24th."

"Good, 'cuz I told my friend I had to have that day off."

"Awesome."

"And I made him put me up in the Venetian, so you don't need to get a room."

"Awes—"

"Can you come out Thursday in time for dinner so we can spend all Friday together?"

"Sure."

"So we're all set?"

"Yeah."

"You alright?"

"Yeah, I'm great. I'm stunned. I just didn't think—"

"I gotta go." And she was gone.

When the 23rd rolled around we were sitting across from each other at Prime, the Bellagio's kick-ass steakhouse. I had a Tanqueray & Tonic in my hand and a gorgeous cut of filet, medium rare, simmering next to three different kinds of mustards and a gigantic baked potato. For fun I'd thrown on my brand new black Prada suit, and she was wearing one of her delicious black dresses. I gotta say we looked damn good together.

Sooner or later the conversation settled on our last trips to Vegas. Mine had involved the Mimi Miyagi shoot and the folly of my final days with Vanessa. "Can you believe after chasing a fantasy for 18 months I could only stand the reality for 18 days?"

"Hey, sometimes the only way to tell if a dress fits is to try it on."

"And it never looks as good at home as it does in the dressing room mirror, right?"

"Right."

"Still, I probably coulda handled the breakup better. But it's never easy, right? I mean, who afterwards is like, 'Wow, we should really break up again sometime?' Who tells their friends, 'You know, you really should get him to break up with you. He does all the right things. Mmm, he gives such good breakup?' Any way you cut it, it's a losing proposition. So how bad should I feel?"

"Probably not that bad."

"That's correct." And I finally shut the fuck up.

Then Kira told me about her last trip to Vegas—when Doug had shot her fucking the horsecock Billy Glide—and how what had started out as a fun, envelope pushing evening had gone too far and ended with a fight. "Doug wanted to go back to the room but I wanted to run around and play. So I did. With Billy." And she gave a guilty little laugh. "And Doug went home all pissed off."

I shook my head, taking Doug's side. "That's rough, babe."

"He coulda stayed out." She didn't like to be wrong.

"And partied with you and the horsecock that just fucked the woman he loves? That doesn't sound like too much fun to me."

"I know." She sipped her Jack & Coke. "I was just following my heart."

"You saying you loved the horsecock?"

"You saying you're jealous?"

I started to say no, but then stopped. "Actually, yes. Yes I am. In fact, I'm more jealous of the horsecock than of your husband. Is that strange?"

"Why do you think that is?"

"I dunno. Maybe 'cuz he's got something I don't got."

"It *was* nice."

"Thanks, thanks a lot."

"But he's nothing like you."

"Too late," I teased.

"I didn't even get off."

"Now you're just lying."

"No seriously. I mean, it was great—really great—but I couldn't cum. He didn't know how to lick me. He was just all porn star tongue, ya know?"

"Aw, that's sweet of you to say." And we laughed and ordered another round of drinks, but really I wanted to ask why she'd felt the need to stay out and play with the horsecock. Had she been trying to make Doug jealous? And was that what she was doing here with me? Was this just her way of getting back at him for spending too much time with his golfing buddies, or for taking her to the same Mexican restaurant every week? She'd keep fucking me until he noticed, then they'd go back to how things used to be until he lost interest all over again, which would send her looking for another playmate. Was that how it went? Maybe. "Is this the best fucking steak you've ever had in your entire life, or what?"

The next morning we slept in and ordered up some eggs. But before they arrived, the phone rang. Kira was in the shower so I picked up.

"Good day, Mr. MacDonald." MacDonald was Kira's married name and evidently the name she'd used checking in. *Mister* MacDonald was Kira's husband. "Did you want coffee or tea with your order?"

"Uh, coffee."

Kira came in naked with a towel just as I was hanging up.

"Who was that?"

"Room service. They wanted to know if we wanted coffee or tea."

"Coffee," she chirped. Amazing how she could always be so cheery in the morning.

"Did you check in as Kira *MacDonald*?"

"Yeah."

"Why?"

"Because that's what it says on my driver's license."

"They called me *Mr.* MacDonald."

She smiled and kissed me. "Did that bother you?"

"I'm not sure."

"Well, it's probably not a good idea for you to be answering the phone anyway."

"Why?"

"Because it could be Doug calling to check up on me."

And I shuddered at my carelessness. *What if it had been Doug?* I wasn't supposed to be here. We weren't working. For the first time, we were together on the road without a cover story. "Good point."

"Alright, so here's the deal with me and Bob." We were already at the Hard Rock Hotel, having dinner at Nobu. And as I sucked down the Tanqueray and sushi I was feeling my usual pre-show jitters—Would he be *on* tonight? What would he play? Would my buzz be peaking at just the right time? But I was also nervous about what Kira was gonna think. Whenever I brought a girl to her first Bob show I was worried. Anyone who's seen *Diner* will understand this was my Colts Test. I could never take a girl seriously who didn't enjoy a Bob Dylan concert. "It's real simple. He speaks to me."

"*Speaks* to you?"

"Yeah. He gets me. I wouldn't deign to say that I get him, but I *know* he gets me. And it's so nice to have someone out there like that, someone walking above it all, just a step above and beyond. And his songbook, it's endless. You can really lose yourself in there. It's like the Bible. There're so many great lines you can find whatever you want—a direction, a way to live, or a validation for the way you're already living. Like from "Absolutely Sweet Marie," *To live outside the law, you must be honest.* I've been living on that for years. It's like you and me. We're breaking some rules here, certainly some laws of man."

Kira looked down at her sashimi. "I know."

"But as long as we're *honest* about it, as long as our heads and hearts are in the right place, then it's all good."

"You promise?"

"For sure. And even better, *Bob* promises."

"Oh good."

I went on and on for a while longer, quoting line after line and explaining what they all meant to me, and she listened like she was buying it. Or at least some of it. And as we paid our tab and made our way into The Joint, I just hoped what she was about to see didn't remind her of an animatronic Yoda on stilts speaking in tongues, sleepwalking through the forgotten songs of another generation. Because that was my biggest fear—that she'd see my Bob and laugh.

But she didn't. Not once. Instead, she said how cute he looked in his silver western suit and black string tie. And how surprisingly energetic he was—bouncing along with his electric guitar, doing his little duck walk, and even floating his way through a harp solo. And she was right, he was kinda cute. And energetic. But even more than that, Bob was *on.* With my buzz peaking into perfection, the set list was rolling out just right, especially the three-song, mid-show run, "Love Minus Zero," "Mama You Been On My Mind," and "I'll Be Your Baby Tonight." I made sure to lean into Kira's ear and tell her the name of each song right after the opening notes, and when he played "Absolutely Sweet Marie" I reminded her this was the song with the line, *To live outside the law, you must be honest,* and she seemed to like that.

After our two hours of Bob heaven I did my own duck walk over to the raised bar in the middle of the casino floor, and Kira followed, laughing right along. Over drinks she told me how much she loved it and asked me about a couple of the songs. And I delighted in answering her questions in all too much detail.

Later, back at the Venetian, I made love to her like it was the last time because I knew it might be. At least for a while. With no stories scheduled and her about to leave for Prague to shoot another movie, there was no telling when I'd see her again.

Which might have been why I couldn't sleep. Or maybe it was because I still had so much Bob on the brain. Whatever the reason, I guess my body just didn't want the night to end. So with Kira sleeping soundly next to me, I got outta bed, poured our last glass of red, and drew back the curtains so I could look out on the Vegas skyline. With so much bright light suddenly spilling into the room I was kinda surprised Kira didn't wake up. In fact, I wished she would wake up. But she didn't. She just lay there, breathing softly through her adorable little nose, a picture of peace. No makeup, no expression, just a vaguely childish visage. Nothing close to the angst of my wine stained lips and my scruffy, unshaven face. And nothing close to whatever madness was going on out there, down on The Strip.

Exactly two and a half weeks later—a Tuesday—Bob Dylan released his next album, "Love and Theft." It was his first since 1998, and naturally I'd had the date marked on my calendar all year. But I never made it down to the record store. Instead my phone started ringing a few minutes after 6:00 a.m. By the time I was awake enough to understand hitting the snooze bar wasn't doing a damn thing, the ringing had stopped on its own. But then right away it started all over again. There's never any good news this early in the morning so I didn't pick up. And I didn't pick up for the third call either. *Why was someone bugging me this friggin' early on a Tuesday?*

I figured I better check my messages, and immediately I heard my mother's recorded voice, a little shaky, almost not believing she was saying what she was saying. "We're under attack. They're flying planes into the World Trade Center. Both towers. Turn on CNN. And call me."

May sound strange, but I actually rolled over and fell back asleep. Then a half-hour later she was calling again. I had to answer. But it wasn't her. It was my friend James—we'd been roommates at Wesleyan and now he lived down the block. "Are you watching? It's so horrible... Both towers are in flames... People are jumping out of the buildings... I can't believe it..."

Then, for the first time, I started to think about all my friends in New York. "I'm coming down. You got any food?"

"Just cereal."

"I'll bring some bagels. You think record stores are open this early?" James was also a big Dylan fan and we'd been to our share of shows together.

"I already have it."

"You do?"

"I got an advance copy yesterday at work." He was an editor at CBS and perks like this came with the job.

"Is it good?"

"It's awesome. Just get down here."

So I was finally getting out of bed when my phone rang one more time. "Are you watching this?"

"No, Ma, not yet. I'm just getting up."

"Another plane just hit the Pentagon."

"What the fuck is going on?"

"They think it's terrorists. Are you near any possible targets?"

"It's LA. We don't have any possible targets."

"What about the Hollywood sign?"

I did live just down the hill from it, but I wasn't too worried. "Ma, no one's gonna blow up a bunch of letters."

When I got down to James's he was playing *"Love and Theft"* and I could tell he'd been crying. And not from one of Bob's love ballads. It was from all those poor people falling from the sky—like the Hindenburg but this time on TV. But as terrible as it was, and even though I couldn't think of a worse way to die, I just couldn't cry. Instead I toasted up a couple bagels and brewed us some coffee and tried to get through to Oliver and George on my cell phone, which of course wasn't gonna happen because the lines were overloaded.

Then, at 9:59 a.m., the unthinkable happened. The South Tower crumpled in on itself like a flower blooming in reverse. Easily the most horrifically spectacular thing I'd ever seen. You could live a hundred years and never see anything like it ever again. And then thirty minutes later it *did* happen again. The North Tower fell exactly the same way. So surreal to watch as the single most important historical event of my lifetime unfolded on live television.

Two days later I got a phone call from Kira. She was still in Prague. "It's so good to hear your voice." It was. Surprisingly good.

"Are you alright?"

"Me? Yeah, I was in LA, so..."

"What about Oliver and George?" She sounded pretty shaken up. Not like she'd been crying, but like she was at a funeral—real soft and thoughtful and kinda hushed.

"They're fine, thanks for asking." I was amazed she'd even remembered their names after only meeting them that one night. "Oliver & Alexis were out in Jersey and George & Helen were in Midtown. Although, it's crazy, George *did* have a meeting scheduled in one of the towers later that afternoon."

"Oh my God."

"I know, right? If the fuckers were flying on porn star time he might not have made it."

A little laugh, then a moment of silence before, "I was thinking about them... And you."

"I was thinking about you too. Musta been strange being in another country. Where were you when it happened?"

"In that bar on the edge of the square, you know the one where we went to wait for a cab." I knew exactly where she meant.

"Were you drinking a *pivo*?"

"*Pivo proceme*." For the first time I could hear her smile. *Beer please.* One of the few Czech phrases we'd picked up, and certainly the one we used the most. And now I could picture her clutching her draft Pilsner Urquell staring up at the television screen in disbelief. "Everyone in the bar kept saying how sorry they were. And how horrible it was and how badly they felt for us. And everyone on set has been so nice, too. I've never felt so loved as an American. It's amazing how much the whole world loves us right now."

"I know. Hopefully something good will come of it."

"I miss you."

"I miss you, too." And it was the truth. I did. "Maybe when you get back we can have some dinner?"

"I'd like that."

When we hung up, I realized I'd just asked her out for dinner. On a date. In Los Angeles. And I didn't care. I just wanted her. Here. Now. With me. When I woke up in the morning and when

I went to bed at night and all the time in between. I wanted her to come with me when I went to the bathroom. I wanted to go jogging with her. To go shopping with her. For groceries, for curtain rods, for clothes. For always. And I understood, I could finally hear what my body had been screaming at me for so long. I was in love with Kira Reed. *Fuck.*

I'd broken the second rule of affairs—right after *Don't Get Caught* is *Don't Fall in Love.* I almost wished the feeling would go away, but I knew it wouldn't. And I almost wished Kira wouldn't call me when she got back to town, but I knew she would. And when she did I was scared. But not scared enough to cancel our dinner.

She came over to my place first and her lips felt so good against mine. Like home. And her tongue belonged with my tongue, as if they were once joined together and were so happy to be reunited, so happy to say hello. We barely spoke except to purr, and when we ravaged each other it was phenomenal as always. Yet it wasn't as always. There was something extra.

Afterwards, I took her to my favorite closest restaurant—Vida on Hillhurst. We ordered their signature steak dish, which was strips of sirloin served over a bed of corn, mash, and Yorkshire pudding. It went down great with a double scotch on the rocks. "Thanks for thinking of me over there. Your call meant a lot."

"It was so good to hear your voice. I was worried. I tried calling you twice before but I could never get through."

"You know what's crazy?"

"What's crazy?"

"This is sort of our one year anniversary. The first time we met was last September."

"At the Argyle. I made you a Jack on the rocks."

"Yes you did."

"What a year..." She smiled. Then, in an overly formal voice that seemed to rein in the emotion of what she really wanted to say, "Well, Happy Anniversary." And we clinked glasses and drank. And then gazed. Until she broke the new silence in a similar tone. "It's been fun getting to know you."

But her eyes weren't formal. Not at all. And neither were mine. "Likewise." I felt a frightening momentum. And I tried to escape it by glancing down at my scotch—the ridged crystal, the ice cubes, the brownish liquid all dancing together in the candlelight like animated bacchanal revelers 'round the side of a black figure Greek vase. And this diversion wasn't worth a damn.

"What's wrong?"

Then I did a stupid thing. More than stupid. Irresponsible. Irrational. Even dangerous. "I'm not sure if I should say this..." And while it's true I was on my second double Johnnie Walker, I can't say that was the sole reason I reached across the table to take her hand. "In fact, I'm pretty sure I *shouldn't* say this, but... but I just gotta say this."

"Say what?"

"I... I *love* you." And I'd never been more sure of anything in my life.

She let it sit for a moment. A moment that sure seemed like one of those eternity moments, but in reality it was just a moment. And she deserved a moment. To think. To process. This hadda to be outta the blue for her. Or was it?

"I love you too. Ever since Indiana."

"I can't stop thinking about you."

"I know. Me too."

"So what do we do?"

"I don't know. Keep doing what we're doing?" I woulda

preferred to hear *I'm gonna leave my husband* but I guess this was better than *We gotta stop.*

After dinner we went back to my place for round two, and as I took her shirt off for the second time of the evening she said, "Play me the Jack of Hearts." At first I was confused. *The Jack of Hearts?* But then I loved her even more than I did before. She was actually requesting a Dylan song. And an offbeat one—"Lily, Rosemary and the Jack of Hearts" from *Blood on the Tracks.* Not one of the obvious fan favorites. In Vegas I'd given her copies of Bob's two best albums, that one and *Blonde on Blonde*, and evidently she'd been listening. So I put it on and we kissed and danced real slow, naked, pressed against each other, pressed never to be unpressed, while Dylan sang his ramblin' romantic epic about a bank heist in a western town. And when he got to the verse about Lily I knew why Kira liked the song so much—she was in the damn thing!

Lily was a princess, she was fair-skinned and precious as a child,
She did whatever she had to do, she had that certain flash every time she smiled.
She'd come away from a broken home, had lots of strange affairs
With men in every walk of life which took her everywhere.
But she'd never met anyone quite like the Jack of Hearts.

"You taste like scotch," she said.

"I'm sor—"

"No, I like it." She kissed me again before whispering, "You taste like *Ross.*" And c'mon, how could there ever be another girl for me.

XIX

When the Going Gets Weird, the Weird Turn Pro

From then on I was seeing Kira at least once a week, often twice, sometimes even thrice, and there was no denying it—we were having a full blown affair. Usually it was for dinner, but sometimes she'd drop by in the afternoon with fresh cut pineapple and I'd lick her pussy dead sober, and what a refreshing change it was to make love to her with sunshine filling the room along with Jerry Garcia's "Rueben and Cherise." And it was nice—the sex, the love, the warmth, the laughs, the inspiration.

But of course it was never enough. I always wanted more. I missed waking up with her. On the road we got to break eggs, but here in Los Angeles every hello had a farewell fast on its heels. And it was getting harder and harder to walk her out to her Mercedes SLK convertible and give her one last kiss through the open window as the hardtop packed itself into the trunk. We never talked about the pain, the longing, the frustration, but I knew what I felt, and I could certainly hear her tires screech as she pulled out and scream as she hurtled down Beachwood and back home. To Doug. It never bothered me before, but now that Kira & I were in love I despised her sleeping with Doug instead of me. Waking up with Doug instead of me. Eating eggs with Doug. Instead of me.

Come early November—after another one of those gut grinding, streetside goodbyes—I went back up to my apartment and beelined for the bar. I needed to get fucked up and fast. So I decided to play a little lonely game I liked to call *Cannonball Comin'*. The rules are simple. Take a pipe hit, then a shot of whiskey, a pipe hit, then a shot of whiskey, a pipe hit, then a shot of whiskey—one-two, one-two, one-two—keep running just like that until the game's over. *One-two, what the fuck am I gonna do...? Three-four, can't stand it anymore... Five-six, gotta be something I can fix...*

Of course, I knew what would make things right. But I also knew—better than most—that divorce was never easy. And this divorce was particularly difficult. Because Kira wasn't just married, she was MarriedCouple.com. Leaving her marriage would be hard enough, but leaving her livelihood was impossible. She'd spent over five years building her business. From scratch. Literally. She'd bought *Websites for Dummies* and designed the whole damn thing herself, loaded all her bi-weekly updates herself, handled all the customer support herself, managed all the crashed servers herself, everything, everything, everything—she'd carried it all on her back and had to sacrifice her body and soul to do it. Literally. And now that she'd finally amassed the members to make it the cash cow she'd always dreamed of, how could she possibly walk away?

Seven-eight, might be easier just to find another mate...

If only I could figure out a way for her to leave him without leaving the site. But how? It wasn't the kind of business you could run after a breakup. DivorcedCouple.com just didn't have the same ring to it.

Nine-ten, I need the help of wiser men...

Gonzo! I had it. Hunter S. Thompson's great battle cry, *"When the going gets weird, the weird turn pro."* Back at Wesleyan I had that stuck on my bathroom mirror. It'd been my mantra. And now it was my solution. Because if ever there were weird times, these were they. I had to turn pro. I had to do the site with her. I had to fuck online.

Eleven-twelve, ah, maybe this is something I should shelve...

But what exactly did that mean? What would I have to do? Take pictures of her nakee butts? Sure, no problem. Hold a video camera while she masturbates? Fine. Shoot her with other girls? Love to. Shoot her with other guys? No fucking way. But as far as me fucking her, how tough could it be? Just put the camera on a tripod, set the frame, and do my thing.

Thirteen-fourteen, idiot, you're talking about being seen...

Of course, I was well aware that the hard part wasn't the act itself. Plenty of folks were out there making their own private sex videos. The hard part was having an audience. And knowing that all my family and friends and coworkers and anyone else with a credit card and $19.95 to spare could see me and my Lil' Guy in action.

Fifteen-sixteen, c'mon, you can't handle a sex scene...

Well, how did everyone else in the biz handle it? From what I'd seen it wasn't something you were born with. It was something you eased into, a gradual progression thanks to a perfect storm of circumstances. Although just about everybody I'd met did seem to have a few things in common—a lot of body confidence, a love of sex, and some level of exhibitionism. Which really just meant they worked out a lot, they were kinda slutty, and they liked being the center of attention. Most of the women—and a lot of the men—seemed to get their start stripping because the pay and the hours were a helluva lot better than waiting tables. Also, they usually didn't have much to lose. Or many other options—it's not like they chose to become a porn star over going to law school. One fateful day they'd just answered an ad that had caught their eye...

Nude Models Wanted

$100 / Hour

And from that moment on they were chasing the money. For a few dollars more, tasteful soft focus nudity begot spread beaver shots, which begot dildo insertion, which begot girl-girl scenes, which begot boy-girl scenes, which begot anal scenes, which begot double penetration scenes, and by the time they'd begotten their breath back they were in Vegas standing onstage with four-teen guys winning an AVN Award for Best Bukkake Scene. So yeah, it was a well-lubricated slope.

Seventeen-eighteen, you almost make it sound clean...

For *them.* For me, things were a bit stickier. Of course, I didn't give a damn about the money. Although it couldn't hurt to add a zero, that's not what I was chasing. I was chasing Kira. But I did have my own "gradual progression"—my job. A year ago the idea never woulda crossed my mind, but now that I'd walked among them, fucking online actually seemed like a possibility for me.

Still, on the surface I didn't have much in common with the stereotypical hardcore performer. Body confidence? Well, I was definitely gonna have to join a gym. Exhibitionism? The thought of someone watching me fuck scared the shit outta me. Joy of sex? Big check there—making love to Kira was one of my favorite things to do in the entire world. Lack of other options? Nah, I had plenty. Nothing to lose? Negative again.

But so what? I had a helluva lot more to lose if I *didn't* fuck online. I'd lose Kira. The woman I loved. With all my heart. And wasn't sacrifice romantic? Edward VIII gave up the crown, the throne, and the sweetest of homes to be with the woman he loved. Wasn't this the stuff swoons were made of?

Nineteen-twenty, fuck, the bottle's empty...

I hadn't heard from Kira in almost two weeks—I'd even left a couple messages on her cell—but then, just a few days before Thanksgiving, I got a call. She told me she'd be picking me up around eight and to put on a suit because she was taking me out for dinner at a brand new steakhouse at the Grafton Hotel called Balboa. She arrived a little early, so she came up for a drink. But after her Jack & Coke and my Johnnie Walker, we went outside. And when I saw that she'd hired a stretch limo my heart just sank.

It was huge and white and I smiled on the outside, but inside I felt just like Abe Vigota in the *Godfather*. Because limos weren't for nothing. This was it. She was gonna break up with me for sure. I knew it. She'd crossed the line by falling in love, but now she'd had the chance to calculate the risk. To understand what was at stake. And she knew it was time to retreat. I was a dead man walking. *Fuck.* I never shoulda told her I loved her.

As we drove down Beachwood and sifted our way over to Sunset I'm sure we musta been talking about something, but there's no way I was listening. I was too busy wondering how she was gonna do it. Would she pretend to cry? Would she gimme the "It's not you, it's me" routine? Would she blame it on her husband, say he was getting suspicious and we had to stop? Or maybe she'd give me the icy cold Malkovich from *Dangerous Liaisons*, "It's beyond my control." If I got to pick, I think I'd opt for the Malkovich because I always liked that scene. But somehow I doubted it'd be up to me. Whatever she did, I just hoped I took it like a man. And I hoped I'd have another scotch going when she stuck me.

"I was thinking we'd stop for a drink first." She sure was cheery for what she was about to do. *Cold fucking bitch.* Hadn't seen this side of her. Not yet.

"Sounds good."

"How 'bout The Standard."

"Great." *Fuck.*

"You okay?"

"Yeah." I gave my eye a quick rub as if it was itching. "Just been a long week." *Kunt.*

The limo dropped us off and we walked out by the pool. The patio was nearly empty. And quiet. Too quiet. Was this gonna be it? She ordered shamps, and I asked for a double Johnnie Walker Red on the rocks.

"We only have Black or Blue." Classic Hollywood maneuver to up the ante on the bill. Nothing wrong with Red.

"Black's fine."

"No, bring him Blue."

"Baby, that's too—"

"Bring him Blue."

"A double?"

"No—"

"Yes. Yes. Bring him a double Blue," she said. But all I heard was, *It's all over now, Baby Blue.*

And, of course, it all made sense. This was where she was going to do it. Bet she hadn't even bothered to make dinner reservations. Shoot me down here, dump my body in a taxi, then ride off in the limo to go clubbing with Taimie. But I suppose if you were gonna get your heart broken there were worse ways to go than with a double Blue poolside on the Sunset Strip.

But we drank our drinks and nothing happened. We laughed a bit, and I waited. Nothing. Then the bill came and turned out I'd just had an $80 drink. But still she hadn't broken up with me.

And when we were seated at Balboa, still nothing. Maybe she felt the least she could do was treat me to a last meal. After all, wasn't that the protocol? Perhaps even one final fuck.

So I figured I might as well enjoy my filet. And it *was* amazing, easily one of the best I'd ever had in LA. Not quite as good as the cut at Prime, but still, damn good. And that lasted a while, but as I was filling up and easing into my third or fourth or fifth Johnnie Walker I just couldn't take it anymore. "Baby, are you breaking up with me?" And her face dropped. I'd caught her. I knew it. *Fuck.*

"No, I'm not breaking up with you." Then she actually had the balls to laugh. "Although technically I *am* still married, so I'm not sure how—"

"Why? Why are you doing this? Why now?"

"Baby, listen to me." She took my hand, "I'm *not* breaking up with you. I love you. I mean, look around. Does it look like I'm breaking up with you?"

"Yes."

"No, no. This is me taking you out for a nice night on the town."

"Why?"

"Whaddaya mean why? Because I love you. Because I think about you all the time. Because I wish we could be together *all the time.* Because—"

"So, you're *not* breaking up with me?"

"No."

"I'm gonna see you again?"

"Definitely."

"You sure?"

"Yes."

"Oh... cause I really thought—you know, when I saw the limo, and then the Blue Label, and the dinner..."

"Honey, I'm sorry."

"No, no, don't be sorry. What a wonderful night you planned. We should really do it again sometime." And then we both had to laugh, and after wiping back our welling eyes we leaned in for a kiss and, once again, all was right with the world.

"Wow..."

"Yeah," I echoed.

Then we laughed again and ordered another round and I swear my last bite of filet suddenly tasted better than my last bite at Prime, although in truth it's difficult to compare such things and really once you get into that kinda league it should stop being such a competition.

But looking over the dessert menu I got to wondering again. If she really did think about me all the time, if she really did wish we could be together *all the time*, then maybe she'd come to realize the only endgame that made any sense was us doing the site together. And maybe she felt she couldn't be the one to bring it up—she couldn't ask me to fuck online anymore than I could ask her to leave her husband. Both were decisions we had to make on our own, for ourselves.

"You know, I've been doing a lot of thinking lately... about your website."

"Oh yeah?"

"Yeah, and, well, if... if you ever... I just want you to know that... if you ever, for whatever reason, wanted me to do the site with you, I want you to know that I'd be willing to do it. With you."

"You wanna do MarriedCouple with me?"

"If you wanted me to."

"Have you even seen the site?"

"You just have sex, right?"

"Have you seen it?"

"No, not really. Just what you showed me."

"You should see it."

"I don't wanna see it."

"Why do you think you can you do it if you can't even see it?"

"Because if it was me doing it, and not Doug, then I could see it."

"Well, you'd have to, ah..."

"Do sit ups, I know."

But then she hardened. "I don't want you to do it. I don't want that for you. *You* don't want that for you."

"I want it for us."

"No. Trust me, you don't. Once it's out there, it's out there, and you can never get it back."

I thought about that for a moment. Perhaps a moment too long. "Maybe I could wear a mask."

Then she laughed. At me. And we never spoke of it again.

The following week Maggie finally got back from her long hiatus, and I couldn't wait to see her. And the dogs. But when I got over there she already had company. A new boyfriend—some guy she found in Jackson Hole and shanghaied back to LA. His name was Tom, and surprisingly he turned out to be a real sweetheart. A contractor by trade, they'd met at the Million Dollar Cowboy Bar where he'd been moonlighting as a bouncer.

After a while, Maggie and I left him behind and took the dogs for a hike. So good to see them. And Lucy looked great. She was even walking without her wheelchair. She still had a hitch in her get-along, but she was fine as long as we went slow and took plenty of breaks to let her rest. On our second or third such stop Maggie asked me what I thought of Tom. And I told her the truth, that I liked him. Because, unlike so many of her other temp boyfriends, there wasn't a single cloud hanging over him.

"Good, because," and a strange, faraway look came over her, "I married him."

Surely this was some kind of joke, so I joked back. "What? I'm sorry, I thought you said you *married* him."

"I did. I'm married."

"Bullshit."

"I'm not kidding."

"You just met him, right? How long have you even known him?"

"We got married five days after we met."

"Five days? C'mon."

"Look, we got matching tattoos." She pulled down the waistband of her sweatpants so I could just make out the top of Tom's name.

"After five days?" Then I grabbed her hand and held it up to my face and there it was—a wedding ring. "You're serious."

"Yep."

"Well, then..." I needed to be a good friend here. *What did good friends say?* Oh yeah. "Congratulations. That's great." *But was it?* "I'm so happy for you." *Was I?* Then I gave her a big hug. Yeah, I guess I was. Still, I couldn't resist, "You know, if you're trying to make me jealous I'm not so sure this is the best way to go about it." But I wasn't jealous. Instead I felt a strange calm, like a slow zen wave passing over me.

"Well *you* didn't want me."

"No, you're right." I loved her. I would always love her. And I would always want her to be happy. But there was no way *I* was ever gonna make her happy. Not like Tom would. Or not like I *hoped* Tom would. "We never woulda worked."

"I know."

"Besides, Lucy needs some stability in her life." *Stability.* Yeah right. Who among us had stability? Wasn't that just life? "Sorry Lucy. We tried."

Then we both crouched down and, together, we rubbed Lucy's belly. And she smiled real big and she sure was a happy dog.

XX

We Have This Schism

few days later Kira and I were finally doing another story together. This time out in the San Bernardino Mountains about 90 miles east of Los Angeles. The subject was an erotic artist named Sean Joyce who got his start with George Lucas at Industrial Light and Magic. Back then he'd use the leftover clay to make naughty little maquettes, but now he was on his own, working on a series of explicit bronze statues, which he'd somewhat ostentatiously dubbed *I Exalt Eroticism*.

Sean was ambitious, for sure, and perhaps even a tad eccentric, but his work actually looked pretty cool—athletic bodies depicted in acrobatic sexual poses, never in repose, always captured mid-act. I dug it. And him. I could tell his longwinded, far out explanations weren't just a big bullshit excuse for sculpting porn. Sean was deadly serious about all of it, especially what he called the *Divine Sensual Concert*. "We have this schism. Our spiritual aspirations are at odds with our sexual experiences. And as far as I'm concerned I see that as being maybe the greatest disease in our culture. The position I come from is seeing the erotic, not as the antagonist to the spiritual, but as the vehicle to it. I see my sculptures as being as holy as *The Pieta*. Holier, because what's more holy than the act of creation and the opportunity of two beings commingling in the ecstasy of love? To me, nothing is more sacred than this."

Shoulda been a fun story—the subject was intriguing, the location was inspiring, the host was irresistible—but the producer was fucking miserable. Because here I was, crammed into the back of Sean's dirty-bird Honda driving up and up this winding mountain road with Kira to my left pressed up against me. And I might have been reminded of how she'd been pressed up against me leaving the Ruzyne Airport if it had been Max sitting on the other side of her. But it wasn't Max. It was her husband. *Doug.*

Me, Kira, and *Doug* were all spot-welded together in the gawddamn back seat of this gawddamn tiny car while Sean drove and Henry, my brand new shooter, sat shotgun with the camera between his legs. We were on our way to a nearby trailhead that would lead us to an overlook where we were gonna film Sean taking pictures of Kira & Doug naked on the rocks—pictures he would later use as reference for his sculpture. Pictures that would soon test my threshold for pain.

Jealousy and guilt—the worst and most worthless of all human emotions—were raging through my blood, boiling my heart like a rabbit in a lobster pot. Leg to leg, arm in arm with her husband—and me, the other man, practically in their fucking lap like the muttiest mutt of a lapdog. Fucking pathetic. And I hated that Doug was always so damn nice to me. Because it made all my guilt even guiltier. The guiltiest. Fucking his wife in a hotel room or even in my apartment was like dropping bombs on a faceless population from miles overhead. But this was hand-to-hand, like sticking a knife into another man, another man who'd never done me no harm, whose only mistake was loving Kira before I did. This was close combat. And it was a fight I was beginning to lose my stomach for.

Worst of all I was partly to blame because, perversely, I'd actually been the one to write Doug into the script. For the story we needed to show Sean sculpting Kira, but my boss Bruce had felt that given the dynamic nature of the *I Exalt Eroticism* series a two shot would be more in keeping with the artist's *oeuvre*. And a helluva lot more entertaining for our audience. I wasn't so sure I agreed, but he'd insisted, so what could I do? I went ahead and added the line, *"My husband and I were so inspired by the beauty, passion, and power of Sean's work that we commissioned him to capture the spirit of our ongoing love affair."* My use of the word *affair* was no Freudian slip. It was fully intended as an inside joke. But still, *What the fuck was I thinking?*

I certainly wasn't thinking about sitting in the back of this shitty little Honda. Which finally, mercifully, came to a stop. As we unloaded ourselves I wondered what Kira had been feeling? I tried to catch her eye so I could guess, but when I did, she only smiled her actress smile. If I asked her later I was sure she'd say how terrible it was, but was that really true? Had it been, perhaps, a little thrilling?

As we walked the five minutes or so it took to locate a suitable spot I tried to focus my mind on the beautiful mountain views and the colored leaves and the cool, breathable air and all that was good about Lake Arrowhead. And I suppose it was nice, but I kept thinking it was just a poor man's Jackson Hole and I wished I was there now, in Teton Village staring up at the majestic Grand with a Snake River Pale Ale in my hand and a pair in my belly.

When Sean found the area of rocks he had in mind, Kira & Doug started pulling off their clothes. I could hear them smiling and giggling as I searched for a boulder off to the side without too many jagged edges and took a seat. And then I watched as Kira & Doug were directed through an endless variety of intertwining poses—each more sexual, more sensual, more loving, and more sickening than the last. And it was almost—no it actually was, in fact—too much to bear when Doug picked her up, cradled her in his arms, then held her aloft like Neon Deion high-stepping into the endzone—*Look what I got! Check out the spirit of our ongoing love affair, muthafucker!*

I saw the smile in his eyes and the gleam across his lips and I knew he didn't want to be any other place than right there at that very moment. He was actually enjoying himself. And that's when I understood. Finally. That I could never be Doug. I could never stand naked on these rocks balancing Kira high above my head while a stranger took pictures of my Balzac & Lil' Guy dangling in the breeze. I could never be a part of MarriedCouple.

And, as usual, Kira had known all along. She understood me better than I understood myself. She'd tried to tell me last week back at Balboa. And in a way she *had* broken up with me that night. *Casablanca* style—and I was Ilsa! Kira knew if I joined her online I'd regret it. *Maybe not today, maybe not tomorrow, but soon and for the rest of my life. Where she was going I couldn't follow, what she had to do I couldn't be a part of.* Noble or selfish I couldn't be sure, but either way, under the circumstances, she'd made the right play. At least we'd always have Prague. And Indiana. And even though I loved her and I honestly believed she loved me too, I knew from experience that love wasn't always enough. In fact, love was rarely enough.

When Sean had what he needed we all started back to the car. Kira lagged behind a bit, and so did I. "How you holding up?" she asked.

"You're never gonna leave him, are ya?"

"Never's a long time."

"But so is tomorrow."

Just then Doug called me over because he'd found a rock that looked vaguely like a human ass and he wanted me to take a picture with him crouching and smiling over it. So I did. And, as is so often the case, the drive back felt a lot shorter than the drive out.

Acknowledgments

Anyone who's ever bothered to read one of these back pages must have some idea how many people are actually involved with every single book that's lucky enough to get published. Without those mentioned below, *Embedded* would not exist.

However, it would be a tragic oversight if I did not recognize one person above all for having had an unparalleled influence on this work. For no good reason—no personal gain, no nuthin'—he gave so much of himself, despite living a life that was plenty busy on its own without all my overwritten pages showing up on his doorstep. Whatever this book is, it's better because of D. Besides being the surgical editor I so desperately needed, besides pushing me harder & farther & righter than I ever thought possible, besides talking me down when times got rough—besides all that, he's been a helluva friend for twenty years. Thanks, buddy!

Also, I wanna thank my agent, Lori, for refusing to quit until she found a buyer... My editor, Hillel, for taking a chance on a first-time author... Everyone at Sourcebooks for getting behind the project... K for so, so, so many things—but most of all for inspiring me like no other... My mother for always being there to listen to my latest lines—no matter how late or how obscene... J for always wanting to know just a little bit more... N for teaching me to put the seat down... L & L for all those smiles... S & G for being the best brothers a guy could have... G for wading through all my contracts and, more importantly, for being a friend... F for all our script meetings... And finally, everyone I ever met on the road for making it all worth writing about—you truly are "the mad ones."

About the Author

Ross Dale has been writing and producing television since 1998. He has worked for *The E! True Hollywood Story*, making documentary profiles of a wide variety of cultural icons, including Rod Serling, Marlon Brando, and Alfred Hitchcock. He's written and produced over a hundred stories for Playboy TV's *Sexcetera*, and was the co-creator of Playboy TV's *Naked Happy Girls*. He currently lives in Los Angeles. Check him out at www.RossDale.net and www.EmbeddedTheBook.com.